MARTIN MERE
LANCASHIRE'S LOST LAKE

The essence of the wetland landscape preserved at Mere Sands Wood in Rufford

Audrey Coney

MARTIN MERE
LANCASHIRE'S LOST LAKE

W. G. Hale and Audrey Coney

with contributions from Bill Pick and Alan Whittaker

W. G. Hale

LIVERPOOL UNIVERSITY PRESS

First published in 2005 by
LIVERPOOL UNIVERSITY PRESS
4 Cambridge Street
Liverpool L69 7ZU

British Library Cataloguing-in-Publication Data
A British Library CIP record is available.

ISBN 0-85323-749-2

Typeset in Minion with Chianti by
Northern Phototypesetting Co. Ltd, Bolton, Lancs.
Printed and bound in the European Union by
Bell and Bain Ltd, Glasgow

The publishers and authors are grateful to the Birkdale and Ainsdale Historical Research
Society for financial assistance towards the cost of publishing this book.

For
Amy, India, James, Lucy, Matthew, Oliver and Thomas
and
Benji, Danny, Fleur, Jade, Jenny, Jessica, Jonathan and Richard

Contents

Acknowledgements

First of all we thank members of the Birkdale and Ainsdale Historical Research Society for their constant interest and encouragement. We are especially grateful to Dr Sylvia Harrop for guidance and proofreading, to Pat Perrins for her assistance, and to Dr Harry Foster for providing photographs from the Society's archive. The Society's generous grant towards the cost of publication enabled us to include colour photographs in this volume.

We are also indebted to Pete Burrell, Dilys Firn, Ann Hallam, John Harrop, Dr Mary Higham, Charlie Liggett, Kim Neal, Enid Pimblett, Dominic Rigby, Pam Russell, Elizabeth Shorrock, Jim Sutton, Dr John Virgoe, Dr Mike Winstanley, Diana Winterbotham, and Joyce Yoxon for help and information; to Ron Cowell, Peter Isles, Dr Adrian Oliver and Ric Turner for information on archaeological sites and identification of artefacts; to Dr J. D. Drakeley, Dr G. H. Evans, Dr Silvia Gonzalez, Gordon Roberts and Philip Withersby for providing photographs; to Priscilla Barrett for allowing us to reproduce her drawing of an auroch; and to Professor F. A. Hibbert for advice on palynology. Our gratitude, too, to Ormskirk and Southport Libraries, the Lancashire Record Office, The National Archives, and the British Library. Plate 6.1 is reproduced from The Luttrell Psalter (Add. 42130 f.181) by permission of The British Library. Maps from the Scarisbrick muniments in the Lancashire Record Office (LRO, DDSc 143/23) are reproduced by permission of the Scarisbrick Estate Trusts, Buxton, Derbyshire.

Many local people helped us with our research and we particularly thank Hugh Caunce of Burscough; David Shingler and Donald Sephton of Scarisbrick; and John Hinchcliffe, Alice Yates, and Hubert and Mabel

Pilkington of Holmeswood. Robert Seddon who farmed at New Midge Hall deserves special mention because, without his help, Chapter 9 would never have been written.

Our greatest debt, however, is to Reg Coney and Marie Hale for their patience, encouragement and enduring support.

Abbreviations

BP	Before Present
LRO	Lancashire Record Office
NGR	National Grid Reference
OD	Ordnance Datum (referring to sea level)
TL	Thermoluminescence (referring to a method of ageing minerals)
TNA	The National Archives

List of Illustrations

Frontispiece. The essence of the wetland landscape preserved at Mere Sands Wood in Rufford.

Chapter 3

Chapter 4

Chapter 5

Chapter 6

Chapter 7

Chapter 8

Chapter 9

Chapter 10

Chapter 11

CHAPTER ONE

Introduction

W. G. Hale and Audrey Coney

If anyone now were to suggest draining the largest lake in England there would be a public outcry. There is, however, little to suggest that anyone other than a few fishermen, and possibly a thatcher or two, was concerned when, in the early 1690s, it was proposed that what was then the largest lake in England should be converted to dry land. Had that 'Ingenious Gentleman and Generous Undertaker, Thomas Fleetwood of the Bank, Esq.' (Leigh 1700: 17) known of the problems associated with draining Martin Mere he might perhaps have thought twice. When he died, in 1717, he was clearly under the impression that his efforts had been successful. His tombstone in North Meols Church proclaims that he 'wished his remains to be buried here because he had drained and made into dry land the immense Martinensian Marsh' (Brodrick 1902, translated from the Latin inscription).

Although Thomas Fleetwood believed that he had successfully drained the mere, the claim was far from true, since over the centuries following the first attempt to drain it, large areas have been flooded from time to time. Mitchell (1885) gives a relatively detailed map of the area flooded by water in the winter of 1848, which amounted to some 7.6 square miles (1968 hectares). This is considerably more than the area of Windermere at the present time (5.96 square miles, 1544 hectares). In its heyday Martin Mere must have been significantly greater in area than in the 1848 winter, as will be shown later, so that it was, at one time, much the largest lake in England. Leland described the mere in 1543 as 'four miles in length and three in breadth' (Toulmin Smith [ed.] 1964: 43), but Greenwood's map of 1818, drawn long after the initial drainage, shows it to be five miles from north-west to south-east. Obviously, it varied in size with the season, and the suggestion in some of the old literature that the mere had a circumference of some twenty miles may well be true. Maps associated with the 1714 court case show a westerly margin to the mere closely, if not exactly, following the line of the ring-ditch which may have been a pre-drainage feature. If this were the case attempts to contain the mere by means of a ring-ditch in the years immediately before its draining may well have confined it to a smaller area in summer. The area claimed to have been drained was significantly smaller than that apparently covered by the mere shown in the old maps (see Chapter 4).

Over the centuries many factors have contributed to the continued existence of the mere, ranging from the original depression in the glacial drift, through the formation of salt-marsh and sand dunes, to the blocking of water-courses and possibly the redirection of streams by natural causes. As time passed the mere became shallower, and now it is gone, swallowed up by its own processes of mud deposition and peat growth and, finally, by drainage.

Martin Mere was not the only lake in the area in former times, since to the south lay the much smaller Shorlicar's Mere, Renacres Mere, White Otter, Black Otter, Gettern Mere, Barton Mere and Church Lake. The Douglas was said to be in a region termed 'Linnuis' or Lake District (the name probably having Celtic origins) by Nennius (in Morris [ed.] 1980) and to some extent because of this more than one writer in the past has associated the mere with the Arthurian legend (see Chapter 5).

There are now signposts directing people to 'Martin Mere', but this is not the mere of the past; rather it is the Wildfowl and Wetland Trust Reserve (Underwood 2002) now established in a corner of what was the old mere. To those prepared to look there are, however, some echoes of the past still to be found. Signs pointing to such places as 'Mereside', 'Mere Brow', 'Mere Lane' and 'Mere Sands Wood' give some indication of where the mere lay. Records exist of the drainage and arguments relating to land ownership after the drainage, and some research has been carried out on the peats and geomorphological features of the old mere. As recently as the early 1950s, after periods of heavy rainfall, the mere reappeared. The establishment of a new pumping station at Crossens, however, has ensured that such flooding is unlikely to occur again. Now much of Martin Mere is good agricultural land formed from the peat which built up beneath its waters over a period of many years. It is no easy task cultivating this land; few furrows can be ploughed without turning up giant bog oaks, which may be six thousand years old, and pines which may be even older. Their presence suggests that the mere was not always covered by water, and that for periods of time when the water level dropped, trees flourished, the mere changing to forest and the forest to mere over much of its area on more than one occasion.

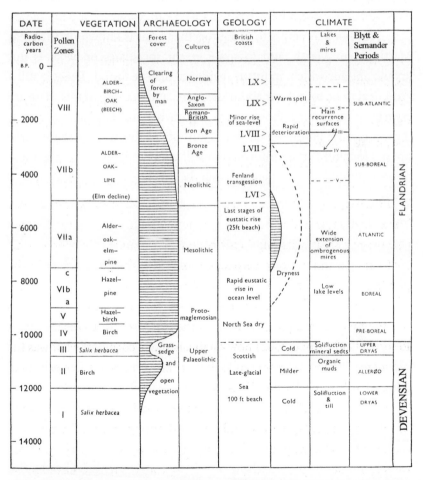

Fig. 1.1 *The main events of late Devensian and Flandrian time in terms of vegetation, archaeology, geology and climate. The last six Flandrian transgressions are shown. (After Godwin 1975, modified.)*

The mere is a product of the present interglacial period during which many events took place whose description, inevitably, requires a technical vocabulary. Fig. 1.1 outlines the main events of the late Devensian and Flandrian time and puts into context the various changes in vegetation, archaeology, geology and climate, together with the accepted nomenclature for these.

Until relatively recently, our interpretations of past events have been based on geomorphological phenomena and rough dating from botanical evidence (Hale 1985). Now palynological studies (pollen analysis) and radio-carbon dating, which enables items of biological origin to be dated relatively accurately, have changed our views of Martin Mere's past. This book attempts to bring together what is known of 'the great Martinensian Marsh' and to some extent speculates on what is not known and for which, in future, evidence may be found. There is still a great deal to be found out about the mere, and because of this there are aspects of its history about which arguments still take place; in fact, there are some points which we, as authors of this work, cannot agree upon. Hopefully, more information will come to light before the mere returns and hides the evidence, as surely it will.

CHAPTER TWO

Out of the Ice

W. G. Hale

Some twenty thousand years ago, as the last (Devensian) ice age was drawing to a close, the shoreline of the west coast of Britain lay far to the west of the present coastline, running from Anglesey to the Mull of Galloway, and including the Isle of Man in mainland Britain. In fact, at this time, Britain was part of the European continent and the English Channel was yet to be formed. As the ice retreated northwards it left behind it a massive plain of boulder clay, the product of the ice grinding away the rock surfaces, and on this plain immense blocks of ice remained on the surface, others embedded in the clay. This was a high arctic environment in which few organisms lived, but during the summer months, as the massive ice sheet which had covered most of Britain retreated, it was very wet and the newly formed valleys of the Dee, Ribble, Mersey and Lake District rivers probably formed a large delta in the Irish Sea, some 50 miles (80 km) westward of the present coastline. Precipitation over the areas drained by these rivers was probably greater than at present, so the volume of water carried would be larger and the rivers generally wider. The sea level 12,000 years BP was some 50 m (164 ft) below what it is at the present time (Fig. 2.1), so that the whole of the Lancashire plain and the land westward of it was a freshwater environment of streams and lakes, the latter formed in depressions in the till (boulder clay), and one of these, to the south of the Ribble, formed the embryonic Martin Mere. Behind what is now Blackpool another depression gave rise to Marton Mere, the names of both (Marton/Martin) having similar origins, meaning 'mere estate'. Lakes of this type were probably common in depressions over the new land surface and were fed by streams running into them formed from both precipitation and the

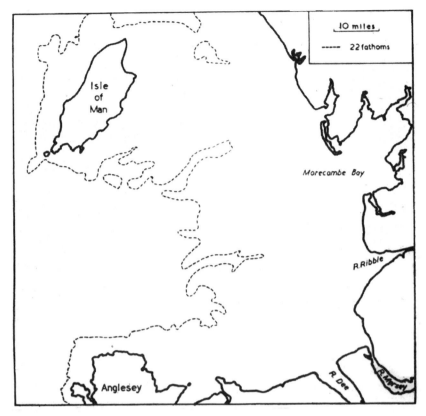

Fig. 2.1 *The coastline off north-west England 12,000 years ago, with the sea level some 50 m below that at present.*

melting ice. Such lakes varied in size from a few metres to several kilo-metres across. Where Martin Mere was to develop has been shown by borings to be a large saucer-shaped feature in the boulder clay. At the western end close to Banks village, boulder clay can be found within 60 cm (2 ft) of the surface, while at the lowest part on the mere it lies below peat, 750 cm (25 ft) from the surface.

Some ten thousand years ago, the Lancashire Plain was largely clear of ice and the lakes became established features of the landscape; glacial erratics (rocks carried from elsewhere by the ice) were common (see Plate 2.1) and many of these had their origins much further north, in the Mull of Galloway and in the Lake District. With the melt of the glaciers, the sea level was rising and the shoreline moved eastwards. This is

Plate 2.1 *A glacial erratic of Dumfriesshire granite dug out of the drift during the construction of the new Crossens Pumping Station in 1959.*

referred to as a eustatic rise in sea level, but a second factor is important in establishing the relation of land and sea levels. With the melting of the ice, its mass no longer depressed the land; the subsequent uplift is referred to as an isostatic rise in land level. The position of the shoreline, then, is a balance between eustatic changes in sea level and isostatic variations in the level of the land. Because the isostatic rise in land level was less than the increase in sea level, the shoreline continued to move eastward until, some ten thousand years ago (10,000 BP [Before the Present]), it coincided with what is now the 20 m contour, some 15 km (c.10 miles) off Formby Point.

Because of this isostatic rise the new shoreline did not encroach as far inland as would have been predicted on the basis of the quantity of water returned to the oceans. These are the facts on which early geomorphologists based their interpretation of post-glacial (Flandrian) events. Where isostatic rise in the land continued after the end of the eustatic rise in sea level, coastlines which had been formed were raised above the contemporary high-water mark in some places, to form raised beaches. Thus, it is not necessary to postulate a fall in sea level to account for such phenomena.

Isostatic land movements do not always raise the level of the land, and in East Anglia there is evidence for downwarping (the sinking of the land mass) to such an extent that the effective main eustatic rise in sea level continued for more than a thousand years longer than in the west. Godwin (1975) puts the date of 5500 BP on the completion of the main eustatic rise in the Somerset Levels as compared with 4000–4200 BP for East Anglia. Even now, north of a line between Holyhead and Dunbar the land continues to rise, and south of the line to fall, by a maximum of some 2–4 mm per year (Shennan 1989; Valentine 1953).

By 10,000 BP the Dee, Mersey and Ribble had their own outlets to the sea and the Ribble more or less maintained its pre-glacial bed, into which flowed the Douglas. The then Martin Mere probably had a channel through into the Douglas at its eastern end, through which the flow moved in different directions at different times, and was limited to the west by a bank of glacial drift and silt. To the west, streams draining higher land to the south-east of the mere ran across the plain into the sea, and no doubt at times of flood the mere overflowed into these westerly streams. Not until some seven thousand years ago (see Fig. 2.2) did the rising sea level affect the water table in the mere, and it was 3500 BP before the sea level approximated to the present-day level, referred to as Ordnance Datum (OD).

Until recently interpretations of post-glacial phenomena have been based on geomorphological evidence (largely the way things appeared to the eye), but with the advent of carbon dating it has been possible, using biostratigraphical evidence (plant remains in the soil layers), to map events more accurately. Borings made in north-west England by Professor M. J. Tooley have provided data which necessitate the reinterpretation of Flandrian events in the area, and particularly in the region of the Ribble Estuary. Prior to this work it was considered that the present sea level and post-glacial events could best be interpreted in terms of changes in the eustatic rise in sea level relative to the isostatic rise of the land.

With the climate becoming warmer the sea encroached over the boulder clay plain, which gradually supported a more temperate vegetation. North of the Ribble the boulder clay (Plate 2.2) lay in a deposit of greater thickness than to the south. The cliffs of the present northerly coastline

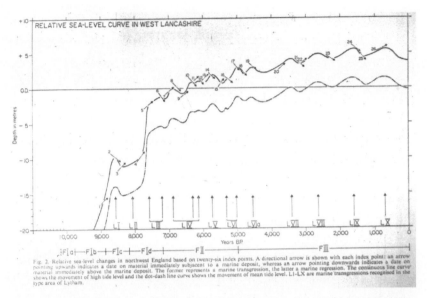

Fig. 2. Relative sea-level changes in northwest England based on twenty-six index points. A directional arrow is shown with each index point; an arrow pointing upwards indicates a date on material immediately subjacent to a marine deposit, whereas an arrow pointing downwards indicates a date on material immediately above the marine deposit. The former represents a marine transgression, the latter a marine regression. The continuous line curve shows the movement of high tide level and the dot-dash line curve shows the movement of mean tide level. L1-LX are marine transgressions recognised in the type area of Lytham.

Fig. 2.2 *Relative variations in sea level over the past 10,000 years in west Lancashire (after Tooley 1978).*

indicate that the eastern movement of the shoreline stopped short of the present coastline, which has been formed by subsequent erosion. From evidence such as this there can be little doubt that the eustatic rise in sea level produced a coastline close to the present one around the British Isles, so isolating them from the continent, between 8600 and 9000 BP, but subsequent events have been interpreted differently by different authors. According to Gresswell (1953), south of the Ribble the coastline encroached to approximately the 8 m contour line, and he suggests that this can still be seen in the form of a line of low cliffs referred to as the 'Hillhouse coastline'. This is only visible in certain places (Fig. 2.3), but it has been suggested that it corresponds to the 25 ft raised beach in Scotland. This is thought to date from about 7000 BP, which coincides with the 'Flandrian transgression' in other parts of the world. The 'Flandrian transgression' is one of some twelve transgressive overlaps (incursions by the sea) now recognised by Shennan et al. (1983). However, parts of the so-called 'Hillhouse coastline' are very much younger and others are older (shown by carbon dating), so it is probable that even south of the Ribble the coastline corresponding to the maximum eustatic rise in sea level was well to the west.

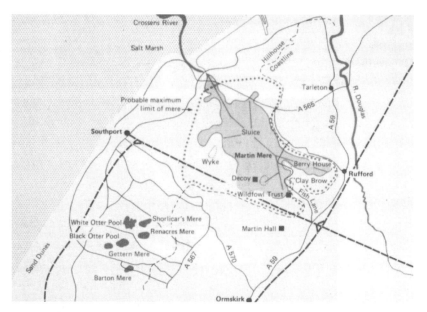

Fig. 2.3 *The southern coastline of the Ribble Estuary showing the position of the so-called 'Hill House coastline', Martin Mere and other freshwater lakes, now drained.*

Plate 2.2 *Glacial drift exposed beneath sand excavations in Mere Sands Wood.*

In the description of the post-glacial events following this transgression, Gresswell's argument is founded on the isostatic recovery of land level extending beyond 7000 BP, which supposedly caused the coastline to move westward again. There can be little doubt that such a westward movement (or several such movements) took place, but there is no evidence to suggest that this was caused by an isostatic rise. The coastline established by the end of the eustatic rise in sea level may well have reached parts of the 'Hillhouse coastline' to the south of Martin Mere, and it certainly lay, in the main, somewhere between Hillhouse and the present-day coastline.

Earlier interpretation of Flandrian events on the Lancashire coast assumed a static sea level. Binney and Talbot (1843) suggested that the features of the stratigraphy could be accounted for solely by the breaching of sand barriers and shoaling of inlets, whereas Reade (1871) suggested subsidence and uplift of the land (relative sea level change) to account for the stratigraphic successions.

Almost certainly, since the boulder clay was relatively soft, the encroaching sea would create, in places, a wave-cut platform which might rapidly disappear as resortment, erosion and redeposition took place. Along the new coastline a sandy beach was formed and it is likely that sandy beaches had been deposited on top of the boulder clay throughout the eastward movement of the sea. The sand forming the beaches and associated dune systems was of marine origin and early work on the Shirdley Hill sand, covering the area around Martin Mere, had suggested a similar origin. However, Godwin (1959) interpreted the Shirdley Hill sand as a cover sand of terrestrial origin and late glacial in age. It ranges in altitude from -16.7 m OD to +120 m OD on the Billinge–Parbold ridge, over a distance of some 20 km, and was first deposited when the sea level was some 50 m below its present level.

Gresswell associated the Shirdley Hill sand with the 'Flandrian transgression' and the 'Hillhouse coastline' and assumed a marine origin. Tooley (1977) supports the contention of Godwin (1959) that it is a cover sand of terrestrial origin recruited from the till and fluvio-glacial sands and gravels. Tooley further aged plant remains in the Shirdley Hill sand at Clieves Hill as late glacial, on the basis of the pollen spectrum, and this was confirmed as 10,455 ± 100 BP by radiocarbon assay. It seems likely that the sand was first deposited by meltwater streams as the glaciers receded and was then redistributed by wind over the boulder clay surfaces. It could not have been deposited by marine activity initially in the region of the 'Hillhouse coastline', since at the time of its deposition sea level was 50 m below that of the present day and the coastline must have been much further west. In addition it is spread over a much greater area and to a greater altitude than are coastal dunes. In places thin peat layers at the base of the accumulating sand indicate tundra conditions prevailing on the early post-glacial landscape. Near Mere Sands Wood the Shirdley Hill sand of late glacial origin overlies the so-called 'Hillhouse coastline', so that here, while it does not form a feature, it must be of greater age than 10,000 BP and clearly cannot have been a wave-cut platform resulting from the 'Flandrian transgression' 3000 years later. The 'Hillhouse coastline' thus has no reality. Again at Mere Sands Wood, the stratigraphic succession (Plate 2.3) shows strata ranging in age from 6000 to 9000 BP lying on top of the Shirdley Hill sand of Devensian age. However, above these strata lies more sand accumulated about 5000 BP and Tooley (1977) interprets this as the sand formation becoming active again, associated with changes in climate and the activities of the human population.

The deposition of sand, both on the beach areas to the west of the mere and on the mere area itself, increased the level of the land relative to the sea, and it is not necessary to postulate a continued isostatic rise in land level to account for the westward retreat of the coastline. Such a situation would exist in any area in which deposition was taking place, and sand movements affect the position of the high-water mark on many estuaries. The formation of dune barriers often prevents the encroachment of the sea, and dune formation certainly took place on the Ribble and in many other areas on the west coast of Britain. However, wherever this occurred there can be little doubt that, on occasions, such barriers were occasionally breached during periods of storm conditions. Despite the continuing eustatic rise in sea level, the deposition of approximately 1 m depth of Shirdley Hill sand in the mere area, and dunes over 6 m in height on the shore (together with minor fluctuations

Plate 2.3 *Peat horizons in a section of Shirdley Hill sand in Mere Sands Wood.*

in sea level), resulted in the retreat of the sea on both the north and south banks of the Ribble estuary. This must have been the case in many places, particularly those estuaries formed to the north of the southern-most extension of the Devensian ice.

Some 3 km to the west of Hillhouse, Downholland Silt was deposited on top of the Devensian Shirdley Hill sand, at least some of it clearly in brackish conditions, in lagoons on a rapidly emerging beach. Similar deposits occur on the north shore of the Ribble, and while they may reach a depth of 20 m, 8–10 m appears to be a more normal depth. Deposition of this type probably took place on many estuaries being formed at the same time.

There can be little doubt that when the deposition of Downholland Silt began the bed of the Ribble was considerably wider than it is at the present time. Deposition of Downholland Silt occurred between 6 and 7 km inland in some areas on the south side of the Ribble and slightly less than this on the north side, indicating a higher sea level than at the present time. By this time (c. 6900 BP) the topography of the boulder clay landscape had changed considerably and many of the undulations had been filled by blown Shirdley Hill sand. Tundra vegetation had given way to temperate vegetation, and peat formation took place in many suitable areas, particularly where freshwater lakes and pools existed in hollows in the underlying boulder clay. In the areas of Marton Mere in the north and Martin Mere in the south, large hollows in the drift were occupied by two large freshwater bodies. It is likely that several other such shallow lakes lay on the drift which extended towards the post-glacial shoreline, on both sides of the river.

The deposition of Downholland Silt, probably in lagoon/estuarine conditions, extended only slightly inland from Southport and not as far as Martin Mere, which was probably isolated from marine inundation by a ridge of boulder clay or possibly by a sand bar and dune formation. Tooley (1977) has demonstrated conclusively that there are no Flandrian marine deposits under Martin Mere, though there is evidence of a tidal and lagoonal area close to Churchtown; here the presence of roddons (silt banks on the edges of tidal gulleys subsequently filled with peat and now visible through erosion), which can be seen from the air (see Colour Plates 2.4 and 2.5 following p. 80), demonstrate the one-time presence of salt-marsh. Gresswell could not have been correct in interpreting the rise in ground alongside the mere as part of a coastline forming Martin Bay, and Hall and Folland (1967) incorrectly show the Downholland Silt as underlying Martin Mere. In the sections and bores recorded by Gresswell (1953) none of the mere samples is shown to contain Downholland Silt.

In pre-glacial times the Douglas (Asland), which flows into the Ribble from the south, flowed west across the area of Martin Mere north of Tarlescough. This post-glacial river bed has not been traced. The Yarrow, another tributary of the Douglas, found its way into the Ribble Estuary to the north. If there was no outlet from the mere to the sea in the region of Crossens, except in times of flood, the bed of the Douglas must have continued north to join the Yarrow (see Chapter 3), with only a branch into Martin Mere (Fig. 2.3). The discovery of an ancient river bed near Crossens (Reade 1871), pre-dating those of the Alt and Yarrow, is perhaps evidence for the Douglas following its pre-glacial course in post-glacial times until its mouth was eventually blocked and its course diverted. To the west of the outlet of the Douglas into the Ribble, Downholland Silt was deposited on the coastline and estuarine, brackish and freshwater Mollusca such as *Cerastoderma*, *Scrobicularia*, *Tellina*, *Natica* and *Cyclas* can be found in the silt. It is likely that in some parts the substratum built up in the way that present-day salt-marsh grows, with the outermost part of the marsh higher than the inland part, and this in itself probably went some way to prevent the incursions of the sea. It is also likely that salt-marsh vegetation was present on the Downholland Silt, and would assist its accumulation. Much of the silt was probably derived from the resorting of the boulder clay, but a large quantity of it must have been washed down-river and deposited at the river's mouth due to a reduced flow and tidal action.

In the region of Downholland Moss, south-west of Martin Mere, 12 m of Downholland Silt lies above 2.5 m of Shirdley Hill sand on boulder clay, and while this is greater than the normal depth of silt, clearly conditions for accretion were suitable for a considerable length of time. Present-day accretion rates in temperate conditions in Europe and

America are normally around 0.2–1.0 cm per year (Ranwell 1972), but may reach 10 cm per year on *Puccinellia* marsh (Jakobsen et al. 1955). This accretion, seaward of the old dune system, probably built up the ground level considerably, producing salt-marsh conditions immediately seaward of the dunes with mud-flats further out, similar to the situation at the present time. There can be little doubt that such accretion resulted in the westward movement of the coastline, a situation which has been experienced in the region of Southport during the past hundred years. It must be borne in mind, however, that the eustatic rise in sea level was still continuing, albeit more slowly than previously, and this did not cease until some 2000 BP. No doubt the rise in sea level was occasionally interrupted by the onset of minor cold periods, but it is highly unlikely that there were falls in sea level which could by themselves have accounted for the westward movement of the coastline; accretion must have played a large part, as it does in the development of many estuaries.

If it is assumed that the 'Flandrian transgression' reached approximately to Hillhouse itself (Fig. 2.2) then this required hardly any rise in sea level, compared with that of the present day. Gresswell (1953) estimated that a relative fall in sea level of 19 m compared with the present level was necessary to explain the events subsequent to the deposition of the Downholland Silt. In other words Gresswell suggested that there was an isostatic rise in the level of the land of approximatley 19 m plus the eustatic rise between 7000 BP and the end of deposition of Downholland Silt, say some 22 m. This rise was followed by an isostatic fall in land level of 18 m, which resulted in the present sea level being roughly equivalent to that at the time of the end of the 'Flandrian transgression'.

The relative fall in sea level suggested by Gresswell was postulated to explain the maintenance above sea level of much of the Downholland Silt upon which subsequently grew a forest of oak, birch and alder. This silt at the mouth of the Alt has been dated at 4000 BP by carbon 14 methods. However, there can be little doubt that during this period (7000–4000 BP) there was a real rise in sea level, though the rate was only around 10 cm per 100 years compared with the rate of 70 cm per 100 years in the period 9000–7000 BP which gave rise to the 'Flandrian transgression'. It follows, therefore, that between 7000 BP and the present day there must have been a rise in land level in the north-west of England of approximately 5 m, at least, to make the present-day sea level equal to the sea level at the height of the 'Flandrian transgression'.

The lack of evidence for a large isostatic rise in land level around 7000 BP does not mean that it did not occur, as there is evidence from other parts of the country, for example the Fens, of movements of this magnitude. In addition, Valentine (1953) estimated that at the present time the land north of a line joining Holyhead and Aberdeen is rising at a rate of up to 4 mm per year – four times the rate of eustatic rise in sea level during the last 5000 years of this rise. However, such a rise in land level followed by a subsequent fall, while it would fit Gresswell's explanation of post-glacial events, is not required to account for the sequence of events outlined by Tooley (1971), who puts forward cogent arguments for minor fluctuations in absolute sea level. The suggestion is made that during the series of Flandrian transgressive and regressive overlaps (encroachments by the sea followed by a retreat) the subsequent restoration of sea level was not brought about smoothly but by a series of oscillations which resulted in marine transgressions in some areas. Transgressions and regressions have been correlated in both subsiding and uplifting areas in the British Isles and in the Netherlands, so that it is apparent that real changes in absolute sea level can be demonstrated. By plotting both the transgressive and regressive overlaps Tooley (1985) has produced a figure showing relative sea level changes in north-west England (Fig. 2.2). From this it can clearly be seen that Gresswell's account of post-glacial happenings – a rise in sea level to the Hillhouse coastline, a regression to -13 m OD with the deposition of Downholland Silt, growth of forest on the silt with subsequent peat formation and, finally, inundation to the present sea level – is far too simplistic.

Long before any peat deposits occurred on the Downholland Silt, peats were laid down on other parts of the estuary. On the north side of the Ribble a peat deposit having a date of 12,320 ± 155 BP contained a layer of dense crowberry (*Empetrum*) stems, and birch (*Betula*) pollen, indicating a tundra origin. By 8000 BP reeds (*Phragmites*) were present where peat was being laid down in a freshwater environment. The peat deposition was interrupted by two transgressive overlaps, the second of which was the 'Flandrian transgression' of the Downholland Moss, recorded on the south side of the river. Underneath the earliest deposited organic materials in the region of Mere Sands Wood, at the most easterly extent of the mere, frost cracks and the disturbance and alteration of the soil by frost action (cryoturbated features) in the Shirdley Hill sand are evidence of the arctic temperatures of the Late Devensian Age, when Martin Mere experienced a periglacial climate. By thermoluminescence (TL) dating the quartz grains of the upper 20–30 cm of the Shirdley Hill sand have been dated as 11,730 ± 510 BP in the region of Mere Sands Wood (Bateman 1995).

In the early Flandrian, prior to 9000 BP, the first organic sediments were deposited on the basal materials of this part of the mere area (Tooley 1985), which consisted of dense clays or stony bleached white sands (tills, weathered tills or Shirdley Hill sand). Two further TL dates are available from sand associated with organic material at a higher level in the Mere Sands Wood section: firstly, 8740–2060 BP from coarse detritus mud in which *Betula*, *Pinus* and *Populus* pollen occurred; and, secondly, above this, 6940–1110 BP in similar mud and undifferentiated organic material in which *Quercus*, *Alnus* and *Ulmus* pollen was present. In this area of the mere organic sedimentation appears to have ceased following the *Alnus* rise, which is dated to about 7000 BP on the basis of similar events at Red Moss, near Horwich, Lancashire (Hibbert et al. 1971). Higher in this section are found what are termed the 'Mere Sands' (Wilson 1985), and these sands are considered to be of a different origin from the Shirdley Hill sand (Huddart and Glasser 2002). The most recent explanation of their origin (Wilson 1985) suggests a similarity to the beach and dune sands of the coast, differing significantly from the Shirdley Hill sand, while Tooley and Kear (in Tooley 1977) suggest that they are wind-blown reworked Shirdley Hill sand, and Crompton (1966) indicates a lacustrine origin from glacio-fluvial material and the Shirdley Hill sand deposits. The deposition of the Mere Sands may have prevented further biogenic sedimentation, but it is possible that material deposited later may have been eroded by water action and then the Mere Sands deposited on the eroded surface. Elsewhere in the mere no organic sedimentation has been recorded before about 7000 BP. Then, apparently in response to the rising water table, limnic sediments began to accumulate in the depressions which occurred in the undulations in the drift and evidence of the plant cover of that time can be found trapped in these sediments.

While numerous cores have been taken in different parts of the mere, few have been analysed for their pollen content and while good sequences occur for later deposits, information on late Devensian/early Flandrian deposits is rare. The fact that there is no record in the mere of sediments of Boreal and pre-Boreal times does not mean that we know nothing of this period. Biogenic sedimentation from elsewhere in the north-west has provided information which can be translated to the south Lancashire plain. Thus, we know that the pine maximum in north-west England occurred between 8000 and 7000 BP, on the basis of cores from Red Moss in Lancashire (Hibbert et al. 1971). The earliest pollen assemblages recorded in the region of Martin Mere are from Clieves Hill, to the south of the mere, and these are from some four thousand years earlier, when the area surrounding the mere was completely open and vegetation was only beginning to appear on the boulder clay and blown-sand-covered plain. The late Devensian age of $10,455 \pm 100$ BP was attributed to the sample (Tooley 1977) containing birch (*Betula*), herbaceous species including grasses and sedges, *Selaginella, Lycopodium, Filipendula, Taraxacum* and dwarf shrubs such as crowberry (*Empetrum*). This is a pollen spectrum typical of the arctic conditions of the Younger Dryas, where glaciers still occurred in the uplands. This stadial was, in fact, a significant hold-up in the general improvement of the climate, with a return to arctic conditions for more than a thousand years; it is referred to in Britain as Pollen Zone III (11,000–10,000 BP).

Around 1000 BP there was an improvement of the climate with the onset of the Boreal Period, and a section in Mere Sands Wood (SD44771568), close to the shore of the mere in its north-eastern extremity, gives a pollen diagram (Tooley 1985) that shows the early Flandrian dominance of birch (*Betula*) and pine (*Pinus*), together with that of light-demanding herbs and shrubs. Probably by this time wooded areas were extensive and the migration of plant species northwards, as the ice retreated, was continuing apace. Because of this, the plant species exterminated by the glacial conditions re-established themselves and formed communities of species which occurred together for only a short period of time before competition eliminated them. Britain was still part of the continent of Europe, so that there was no sea barrier to migration, and the new colonisers formed a unique and interesting vegetation (Pennington 1969).

Similarly, there was no barrier to the movement of animals and with the bed of the North Sea being dry land, as well as the area of the English Channel, many species moved into Britain as the climate improved. Most of the large animals which had roamed Britain between the Ice Ages had died out, but at the end of the Devensian it is likely that polar bears (*Thalarctos maritimus*) and Arctic foxes (*Alopex lagopus*) roamed what is now west Lancashire. The climate then was probably similar to that of the present-day coastal Greenland and Ellesmere Island, and in summer the vast population of insects, particularly crane flies and mosquitoes, supported wading bird populations similar to those of the high Arctic today. Terns and skuas probably nested and wildfowl were abundant. There is little fossil evidence from south-west Lancashire to cast light on animal populations around that time, but it is reasonable to surmise that the breeding birds in the area of Martin Mere were a mixture of those tundra-nesting species from North America which move into Europe during the autumn, such as knot (*Calidris canutus*), and the predecessors of the birds nesting in the European Arctic.

Then as now, Martin Mere was probably a haven for wildfowl and the ancestors of both species of Arctic swans, whooper (*Cygnus cygnus*) and Bewick's (*Cygnus bewickii*), probably nested in the area, though at different times. Several species of geese may have bred in the area and it is possible that at least the ancestors of four present species, pink-foot (*Anser brachyrhyncus*), white-fronted (*A. albifrons*), barnacle (*Branta leucopsis*) and brent (*B. bernicla*) were nesting birds. Long-tailed duck (*Clangula hyemalis*) would be among the first breeding birds as the ice retreated, to be followed, as the climate improved, by wigeon (*Anas penelope*), pintail (*A. acuta*), scaup (*Aythya marila*), and Barrow's goldeneye (*Bucephla islandia*). Phalaropes (*Phalaropus fulicarius* and

P. lobatus) would be found on the tundra and gyrfalcons (*Falco rustico-lus*) and snowy owls (*Nyctea scandiaca*) are likely to have hunted over the area. Lemmings (*Lemmus lemmus*) and other small rodents would provide their food supply and, as today in the Arctic, would occasionally reach plague proportions and attract increasing numbers of predators.

There can be little doubt that, at least during the summer months, human hunters encroached onto this harsh environment in search of food, and as the climate improved and trees began to grow on the retreating tundra it became possible for people to live there the whole year round, finding sufficient food in an increasingly hospitable environment. The sub-arctic climate of the Pre-Boreal (10,000–9500 BP) (Fig. 1.1) gave way to the warmer and drier Boreal Period (9500–7000 BP) and forest developed, initially surrounding the open mere with a developing tree-scape of birch, hazel, pine and a few oaks.

There is evidence to suggest that the level of the mere increased significantly around 10,000 BP, since in the region of Mere Sands Wood (the outflow to the Douglas) sheets of rounded, pea-sized gravel suggest the possibility of an increased discharge into the river.

At this time there was little or no biogenic sediment being deposited in the basin of the mere. It was open to the west, from which direction came the prevailing winds, and the resulting wave action may have cut the boulder-clay cliff on the north-eastern bank around this time – the 'Hillhouse coastline' of Gresswell. A possible alternative is that flood waters entering the mere from the Douglas cut the cliff, and may also have deposited the gravel as the volume of water entering the mere expanded, and the current slowed. It is also possible that at this time the River Douglas flowed through the mere as it did prior to the glaciation, and as the River Kent now flows through Kentmere, in Cumbria. This possibility is supported by the fact that during excavation of one of the sluices in the mid-1800s an old river bed was discovered at Crossens (Reade 1871). This was apparently cut lower than the beds of the Douglas or Alt, well into the glacial drift, so that it was clearly post-glacial. This old river bed had been blocked by marine silt and even if it was not the old bed of the Douglas, the stream originally flowing over it would have been prevented from continuing to do so. In these circumstances the flow from other streams entering the mere may have reversed the flow of the Douglas at the eastern end. If at that time the Douglas did not join the Yarrow north of where Rufford now is, then flowing into the Ribble, it may be that the reverse flow, or the prevention of the Douglas flowing into the mere, resulted in a new channel being cut through to the Yarrow.

Blown sand (Shirdley Hill sand) probably formed much of the bed of the mere around this time, and currents resorted and redeposited the sands continuously. Only around the very edge of the mere, and in very shallow areas, was there much marginal vegetation and there is no evidence to suggest that the late Devensian/early Flandrian rise in water level resulted in any significant peat development. Accumulations of up to 7.5 m (27.5 ft) of peat now occur in some areas of the mere, which, up to about 7000 BP, had been an open, shallow lake with very little peat formation. What vegetation existed around the mere at this time was supported by shallow soils on boulder clay, and pollen from zones I–VI (Fig. 1.1) is absent from the bed of the mere.

Marine transgressions affected the water table inland and in the region of Martin Mere the water level rose and the first organic sediments were deposited, beginning about 6800 BP. Only after the subsequent regressive overlap was peat laid down on Downholland Moss and with this came a lowering of the water level in Martin Mere. This resulted in a partial drying out of the peat and the establishment on it of oak woodland. Oaks with a carbon 14 date of 6400 BP (Hibbert pers. comm.) have been collected from peat on Martin Mere and oaks from Downholland Moss were probably growing at or shortly after this time. Elsewhere marine transgressions must have affected the water table immediately behind the contemporary coastline.

On Downholland Moss, Tooley (1977) has demonstrated three separate marine transgressive overlaps. In all these, rising sea level is demonstrated by salt-marsh facies, evident in cores, being succeeded by mud-flat characteristics, and falling sea level by the reverse. It is reasonable to assume that, as in earlier transgressions, rising sea level affected the water table on Martin Mere, and such a rise in water level may have resulted in the drowning and subsequent death of trees growing there

(Plate 2.6). In fact, such rises in the water table would have accounted for the majority of tree mortality. Rising water levels promoted peat formation and the preservation in the peat of fallen trees. Marine transgressive overlaps may well have affected the water tables further inland and also peat growth on the inland mosses.

From the presence of the first known oaks on Martin Mere, more than 2500 years elapsed before the first peat was deposited in the region of the present mouth of the Alt (4545 ± 90 BP), so that the so-called submarine forest of the inter-tidal zone in west Lancashire was relatively late in the post-glacial history of the estuary.

Like Martin Mere to the south of the Ribble, Marton Mere in the north appears to have been a freshwater lake, originating as a depression in the boulder clay. Here inundation by the sea appears to have been prevented by a boulder clay ridge to the south-east which rises to 7 m OD. The maximum transgression occurred just over 5000 BP and reached only a height of +3.03 m OD, so that Marton Mere has always been a freshwater mere. This is confirmed by the findings of Tooley of only freshwater deposits in the mere area.

Plate 2.6 *Pines killed by rising water levels fall in the direction of the prevailing westerly winds near to what was Renacres Mere. The majority of the bog oaks and pines lie in an east–west direction in the mere peats because of these prevailing winds.*

Tooley (1982) recognises twelve periods of transgressive and regressive overlap tendencies on the north coast of the Ribble and these are shown in Fig. 2.2. These can be correlated with overlap tendencies in other areas. Information derived from examination of soil cores and carbon 14 dating provides the evidence on which the events of the past ten thousand years on the Ribble can be reconstructed. One of the most interesting aspects of the post-glacial history of the estuary has been the expansion and contraction of the freshwater meres on either side of the river, the 'perimarine' zone of Hageman (1969). Similar meres were almost certainly features of many other estuaries. While the variation in these meres has resulted mainly from fluctuations in the water table caused by sea level changes, drying out of peat may well have lowered the level of the ground and seasonal rainfall clearly affected the size of Martin Mere until the middle of the nineteenth century (Fig. 2.4). There can also be little doubt that the size varied due to the development of floating *Sphagnum* and marginal reed swamp. While marine deposits are not found on the mere it is likely that on occasions the sea broke through the coastal dune system, and may have reached as far east as the Wyke, close to which roddons derived from an ancient salt-marsh can be seen (Colour Plate 2.4). The presence of salt-marsh at this site clearly points to higher salt-marsh seaward of it which may well have provided a barrier to the outlet of fresh water from the mere, thus extending its westward limit (see also Chapter 3). (The highest point of a salt-marsh is normally on its seaward side because of the pattern of deposition of silt, which is greatest as the incoming tide first contacts the marsh.)

Following the third Downholland transgressive overlap (5800 BP) peat was intermittently deposited in freshwater situations along the length of the margins of the estuary. The whole of this area was marshy and, apart from Martin Mere, other pools were present on these mosslands until relatively recently, though most, if not all, may well have had different origins unconnected with depressions in the underlying drift (Fig. 2.3). In the dune system west of Southport there are many pools (slacks) which have been formed by wind erosion, and from the air these look rather as the mere must have appeared after the first colonisation by sedges and before trees became established, even to the extent of islands being present (Plate 2.7).

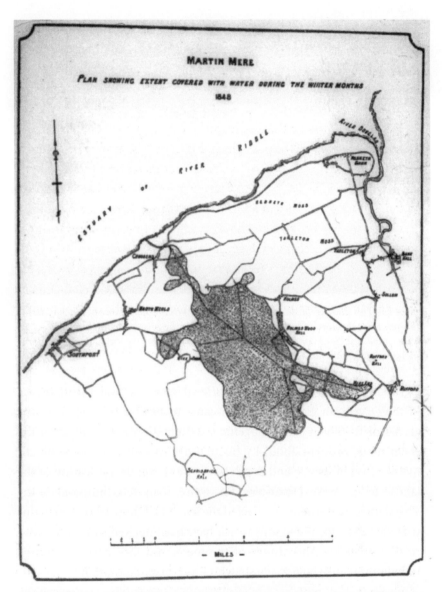

Fig. 2.4 *The area of Martin Mere covered by flood water during the winter of 1848 (after Mitchell 1885).*

Plate 2.7 *This slack in the dunes at Ainsdale has much the appearance of Martin Mere at the time when the surrounding area had been colonised by grasses and sedges but before trees were established. Slacks are generally much smaller than was the mere, but like the mere, many contain small islands.*

To sum up, Martin Mere had its origins in the meltwater from the ice of the Devensian glaciation which came to lie in a depression in the glacial drift. Blown sand, biogenic sedimentation and changes in the water table, brought about by fluctuating sea level and changing climates, affected its size and depth but it was a significant feature of the landscape of west Lancashire for more than ten thousand years. Throughout its existence it affected the lives of all those who lived in this part of the world, as the soils which have been derived from it do now. In those soils lies the history of the mere, and they have, from time immemorial, provided for those who lived on and around it.

CHAPTER THREE

The Changing Mere

W. G. Hale

Whereas the origin of the mere can be traced in the geology of the sur-rounding areas, its history lies in the basin of the mere itself. On top of the drift and sand, lake muds and biogenic sediments accumulated in its waters have preserved evidence of the changing habitats and climates. Pollen, particularly, gives an indication not only of the changing flora but also of the vicissitudes of the climate and the human activity in the area. Around 8500 ± 800 BP the sea was still distant from the mere and any changes in water content were most probably caused by periods of wet weather.

Biogenic sedimentation appears to have been initiated by a rise in the water table of the mere, coincident with a marine transgression recorded on Downholland Moss and dated 6980 ± 55 to 6760 ± 95 BP – the Lytham IV of Tooley (1985). Analysis of a core (MM1) taken from the south-western shore of the mere, near Greenings Farm (SD40171522), indicates that the basal sediments of stratum 2 (immediately above the drift) are no older than 7000 BP (Tooley 1977). Pollen (Plate 3.1) from these basal layers shows an increasing frequency of aquatic plants, such as the bulrush (*Typha latifolia*), lesser bulrush (*Typha angustifolia*), marsh pennywort (*Hydrocotyle vulgaris*), duckweed (*Lemna sp.*), white water lily (*Nymphaea alba*) and water milfoil (*Myriophyllum sp.*), which is consistent with an expansion of the area of the mere (Fig. 3.1).

We know that the mere as a whole, or areas of the mere, became dry land from time to time and then again reverted to wetland. Several explanations for such changes have been advanced in the past but recent work has shed more light on the reasons for such changes (Tooley 1985). The build-up of peat, which has resulted from dying vegetation, mainly

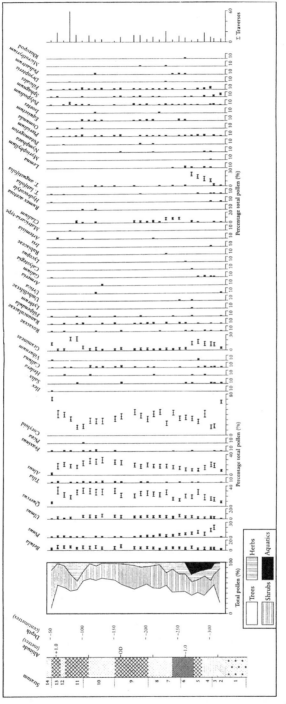

Fig. 3.1 *A percentage pollen diagram from a core taken near Greenings Farm (Tooley 1985; MM1) covering the period from c. 7000 BP to 5000 BP, from shortly after the alnus (alder) rise to about the time of the elm decline.*

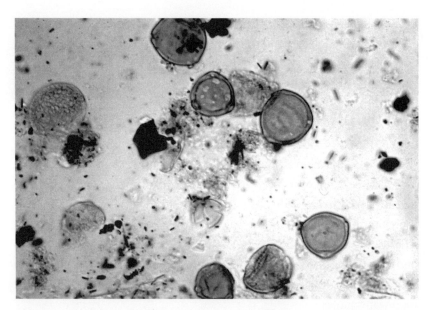

Plate 3.1 *Oak (thick-walled) and hazel (thin-walled) pollen grains, showing the character-istic differences between these species (photograph: G.H. Evans).*

reeds falling into the water, has itself raised the level of the mere (as much as 7.5 m (23.5 ft) in places); the water table has fluctuated as a result of variations in rainfall in different periods; and the fluctuating sea levels, the transgressions and regressions of Tooley, have also affected the level of the water table. As the table fell, so tree seedlings germinated on the margins of the mere, rooted and grew again, but as water levels rose, so the roots were drowned, the trees died and fell to the east, in the direction of the prevailing wind. Bog pines and bog oaks, together with other species, became buried in the peat as forest came and went, the different species reflecting the changes in environmental conditions. By the end of the Boreal, a period of warm and dry climate, some 7500 years ago, the sea had reached its highest level and Britain was now cut off from the continent of Europe, though relative sea levels continued to rise until Roman times due to the land mass sinking. The very fact of being an island had its effect on the climate of Britain.

Examination of the peat cores from the mere indicate that this period of biogenic sedimentation lasted for only some two thousand years, as the basal sediments are no older than 7000 BP and the surface sediments no younger than 5000 BP. This is shown by the presence of all the ther-mophilous tree species and the absence of a level which can be referred to the decline of the elm, which occurred about 5000 BP (Fig. 3.1).

After the rapid increase in aquatic plants, shown in the first six strata of core MM1 (Tooley 1985), wet and dry periods can be recognised between 7000 and 8000 BP through the changing ratio of oak (*Quercus*) pollen to that of alder (*Alnus*), a technique first used by Godwin as an indicator of water levels in the Fens (Godwin and Clifford 1938). Wet periods, indicated by an increase in alder and horsetails (*Equisetum*), do not always coincide with a rise in the water table indicated by a trans-gression; this possibly indicates increased precipitation during the wet Atlantic Period. Nor do dry periods always coincide with regressions and there are peaks of oak pollen during both Lytham IV and Lytham VI, indicating dry conditions on the mere during periods of probable high water tables.

No carbon dates are available for this core (MM1), which was assigned to Flandrian Chronozone II on the basis of its pollen content. Two other cores taken more recently from the *Carum* field (SD 4250142) at the Wildfowl Trust Reserve on Martin Mere (Molloy 1988) gave very similar results to those from core MM1. Again the cores were taken from the edge of the mere though below the area covered by water in the winter of 1848, 3 km west of MM1. The stratigraphic horizons show that layers of alder, sphagnum and *Phragmites* peats developed at different times but all were clearly associated with the mere edge over a 2000-year period. In many cases these peats show the accumulation of undegraded plant material, resulting from the absence of oxygen, which prevents decomposition (Plate 3.2).

Trunks of both pine and oak (Plate 3.3) are commonly found in the peat of Martin Mere and the pollen diagram (MM1) shows the decrease in pine pollen and the expansion of oak, which is typical of Pollen Zone VI (c. 7000 BP), at the base of the core. In pollen cores from northern England there is usually a pine phase in Zone VIc at the end of the Boreal Period. This period is thought to have had a more continental and less oceanic climate than at present and, whereas, in what is now southern England, hazel (*Corylus*) was the dominant under-storey, birch tended to remain in the more oceanic north-west. Hazel, however, was

Plate 3.2 *Undegraded plant material, mainly reeds and sedges, from peat in Mere Sands Wood.*

Plate 3.3 (a) *Bog oak and* (b) *pine root removed from deep in the peat during ploughing.*

common and may well have been the dominant vegetation in some areas around the mere; in fact, it only produces pollen in quantity when it is a canopy tree and unshaded. Moving into the Atlantic Period, which was wetter, deciduous trees replaced pines and this can be seen clearly from the pollen diagram.

The MM1 pollen core almost exactly covers the Atlantic Period, which is usually regarded as the climatic optimum, with the most northerly extension of lime (*Tilia*) in the British Isles. The core shows an increase in lime, which showed a late immigration from what is now the continent, since it was a warmth-loving (thermophilous) tree; its absence from Ireland, which was cut off from the rest of Britain about this time, supports this interpretation of the distribution of the species.

Cores taken by Tooley (1985) to the west of MM1 follow the mere edge and cross the Wyke, continuing on to Churchtown Moss. Tooley describes the cores crossing the Wyke (MM18–MM22) as being very different from the other cores taken in the mere. The Wyke cores contain grey clay, silts and sand with iron staining near the surface, marine shells at depth and only thin organic strata. These characteristics of the substrate imply water movement over the area, preventing continuous deposition of organic material, as water flowed out of the mere into the Old Pool, and/or as tidal waters came into the mere at times of high water level.

Tooley (1985) refers to freshwater deposits east of Mere Hall and brackish and lagoonal deposits west of it, a description which appears to have been taken by Chiverrell (2002), in Huddart and Glasser (2002), as indicating Mere Hall as a boundary between the two. Tooley's suggestion that marine incursions to the mere were prevented by a barrier of till and cover sand at the west end cannot refer to the Mere Hall area as this was the deepest part of the mere. Probably the position of the rise creating the barrier is shown by the westerly limitations of the mere at the time of draining. The mere shore ran along the line of the ring-ditch between Wyke Hey Farm (SD 382177) and Boundary Farm (SD 402192), that is, a south-west/north-east direction north of Wyke House, more than two kilometres north-west of Mere Hall.

Evidence of the existence of old salt-marsh lies to the west of the ring-ditch and this salt-marsh probably coincided with the maximum sea level in the area. At present the roddons are showing at about 3 m OD, close to the level of the flooding in the winter of 1848. These roddons are infilled by peat which could have been deposited in the mere if its surface exceeded this level. No dates are available for this peat, which could have formed outside the margin of the mere. However, the levels of the present salt-marsh, and the ground seaward of the roddons (over 1 m higher, and more in some places), suggest a date before the high sea level of Roman times, and possibly considerably before. It is quite likely that dune formation and sand barriers prevented the encroachment of the sea onto Churchtown Moss at the times of the highest sea level, but this remains as speculation until such times as the peat infill of the roddons is dated.

The mere thus contains two distinct sedimentary environments, the perimarine zone to the east of the Wyke and a tidal and lagoonal zone to the west, the grey clays of the Wyke effectively marking the limit of the tidal flat and lagoonal zone.

Whereas core MM1 (Tooley 1985) ends more or less at the time of the elm decline (5080–5010 BP at Red Moss; Hibbert et al. 1971), the core from Langleys Brook (McAllister et al. 2004) continues the sequence and includes charcoal remains and pollen indicative of Bronze Age communities (SD 417148). Another core (McAllister pers. comm.) taken during the same work on Tarlescough Moss (SD 439145) shows anomalies in the distribution of *Quercus* and *Alnus*, with both species showing peaks below dates of 8690–8620 BP and 9110–8940 BP, fifteen hundred years earlier than they would have occurred. A similar anomaly occurs in Mere Sands Wood, which Tooley (1985) explains in terms of sediment floating to the surface with rising lake levels and subsequently subsiding onto later deposits. Alternatively, redistributed pollen may have been washed below later deposits, as some old documents record movement of water both 'above and below the ground'.

With the rising sea level Britain was cut off from the continent, the 'native' flora were established, apart from a few species which were able to cross the sea barrier subsequently, and being surrounded by sea contributed significantly towards the increasing oceanicity of the climate. Increasing rainfall initiated peat formation at high altitudes in the Pennines and probably contributed to the development of the oligotrophic acid peats on the raised mosses surrounding the mere.

The increase in rainfall was coincident with what is termed the Flandrian transgression (Lytham VI) and in the pollen core this is indicated by an increase in alder. As a result of the higher water table and higher rainfall, the mere expanded and throughout the 2500 years of the Atlantic Period probably increased in size. Variation in sea level may have affected the water table, causing frequent changes in the overall size of the mere.

The relatively stable climate of the Atlantic Period resulted in the supposed climatic climax vegetation, the final stage of the succession being oak woodland in the north of England. Bog oaks in the mere peat are evidence of this and in places almost pure oak stands would have occurred; where the soils were base-rich, oak and elm would produce mixed oak forest. The pollen cores suggest that the latter was the case in the area of the mere and clearly alder and lime were present in addition to oak. The interpretation of pollen cores is not entirely straightforward since some plants produce more pollen than others: lime and ash produce much less than oak and birch, thus tending to be underestimated, while alder is overestimated because, being a wetland tree, it is common in more places where pollen is preserved.

The establishment of the mixed oak forest obviously reduced the areas available for plants requiring open habitats, though plantain (*Plantago*), sorrel (*Rumex*) and mugwort (*Artemesia*) are present in the mere cores, the latter two late in the development of the peat and possibly indicative of forest clearance.

In Britain there was no clear-cut change in climate or environment as the Atlantic Period ended, some 5000 BP, and the Sub-Boreal Period began. The mere was at about its maximum extension and the climate remained warm and gradually became drier and more continental. This was the time of the decline of the elm and there is a suggestion of this decline at the top of the core MM1, where elm pollen is less frequent than at any previous point. For a long time the elm decline was put down to Neolithic humans feeding its leaves and branches to livestock, but recently it has been attributed more to Dutch elm disease (Rackham 1986), which may in itself have been promoted by clearing the wildwood. What is not in doubt is that from the onset of the Sub-Boreal Period humans began to have a very significant effect on their environment. Towards the top of the pollen core MM1 there is an indication of the increase of the pollen of ash (*Fraxinus*) and elsewhere in the north and west of Britain this coincides with Neolithic temporary clearance of the wildwood. Ash is light-demanding and has difficulty in establishing itself under a full canopy, so that it is a good indication of clearance.

On the mere there are indications of this increased human activity in the section in Mere Sands Wood (Tooley 1985) where Shirdley Hill sands overlie the peat. This is interpreted as a reactivation of the early Flandrian deposits as a result of forest clearance by prehistoric peoples for pastoral and arable farming (Tooley 1977). Human presence in the area is shown by long series of footprints (including those of children) in lagoonal clays dating from 5750 ± 600 BP (10 cm below the prints) and 6650 ± 700 BP (20 cm below the prints) on the foreshore at Formby. These dates were obtained by an optically stimulated luminescence technique and the samples were taken below the prints to avoid contamination; there is, however, evidence of human footprints at this lower level (G. Roberts pers. comm.). The human footprints are associated with both red deer (*Cervus elaphus*) and roe deer (*C. capreolus*), domesticated cattle and aurochs (*Bos primigenius*). These traces of a past environment probably indicate humans hunting these animals in lagoonal conditions, where they came to drink (Roberts et al. 1996).

Despite these human activities, Martin Mere at this time was probably surrounded by woodland. Many of the trees, particularly the oaks, were very large and some in excess of 20 m (65.6 ft) high. This was the habitat of birds such as the honey buzzard (*Pernis apivorus*). The mere itself was for long periods surrounded by reed beds, which were likely to have sheltered breeding populations of bitterns (*Botaurus stellaris*), grebes (*Podiceps*) and several species of wildfowl. Molloy (1988) shows the presence of *Phragmites* and *Carum* in the field core and undegraded reeds are commonly found in samples of peat from the region of Mere Sands Wood. Marsh harriers (*Circus aeruginosus*), known to have nested in later years, were probably common breeders in the reed beds. Since the climate was considerably milder than at present, species such as pelican (*Pelecanus crispus*), which now nests much further south, and crane (*Grus grus*), whose footprints are commonly found in the lagoonal silts on Formby beach, may well have bred.

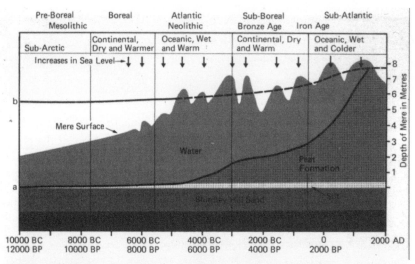

Fig. 3.2 *Hypothetical changes in the water level of Martin Mere during the past 12,000 years, (a) at the centre of the mere, and (b) in shallow water. Hypothesised increases in depth correspond in the main to the transgressions described by Tooley (1985).*

Because of the warm, dry climate Martin Mere was probably somewhat smaller than during the Atlantic Period, but continued fluctuations in sea level (four transgressions; see Fig. 3.2) probably affected the water table, thus continuing the frequent variations in surface area of the mere.

The indications of increasing human activity in the wildwood surrounding the mere may well suggest that there was an increasing use of the mere itself. Logboats (see Chapter 5) found on the mere are probably of a later date but it is likely that similar logboats were used on the mere much earlier in time; a logboat containing a stone axe was found in Loch Doon, Ayrshire in 1831 (Lyell 1832). The fact that the climate was much drier towards the end of the Sub-Boreal Period, with heather, pine and birch replacing the peat-forming communities on the bogs, probably made it easier for Bronze Age peoples to get around the mere area, and it is possible that with improving communications the human population of the area increased.

The onset of the Sub-Atlantic Period, some 2500 BP, coincided with the end of the Bronze Age and the beginning of the Iron Age. The climate deteriorated, becoming more oceanic, colder and wetter, and in

Plate 3.4 *Ron Cowell and David Huddart discuss the excavation the ancient trackway at Hightown.*

many areas peat formation increased significantly. In order to maintain communications, late Bronze Age peoples laid trackways on the peat. These are best known from the Somerset Levels, Cambridgeshire and Lincolnshire, but one from Pilling Moss dates from this period (c. 2500–3000 BP), and while none have yet come to light on the area of Martin Mere, possibly some were laid down, as there are other signs of human activity at this time. A trackway has been found at Hightown, some 15 km from the mere, running out of the present dunes into the Alt estuary (Gonzalez pers. comm.) (Plate 3.4).

As a result of the deteriorating climate peat formation on the south-west Lancashire mosses probably started again and there may have been some peat formation in the mere. Forest clearance continued and by Roman times the climate was better and similar to that of today, though it is possible that the mere continued to extend during the congenial climate of the Anglo-Saxon and Viking times when vineyards were common in the south of England. Fifteen hundred years ago a marine transgression (Lytham IX) recorded in various parts of the British Isles, together with high rainfall, may well have extended the mere so that its surface area was greater than ever previously, though with the peat and sand deposit it may well have been shallower than formerly.

At the western end of the mere are several locations whose names give an indication, not only of the maximum extent of the mere, but also of the time when this occurred. Wyke House is on a promontory which projected into the mere (Fig. 3.3) and to the south-west of this is Blowick. 'Wyke' and 'wick' are derived from the old Norse *vík*, a bay, and 'blavick' can be literally translated as 'dark bay' (Cheetham 1923). These names probably date from the tenth century, when the Vikings from Ireland settled various places in south-west Lancashire. Lower Blowick lies where Fine Jane's Brook joins the Old Pool, and the latter name, together with the adjacent Pool Hey, probably refers to a bay or inlet on the mere, the traces of which are clearly visible as a south-westerly extension of the winter mere of 1848 (Fig. 2.2). Originally this bay may have been formed by flood waters occupying the beds of Fine Jane's Brook and Sandy Brook, which flowed into the Old Pool, the mere waters then finding an exit to the sea at Crossens via the mouth of the Pool. However, since

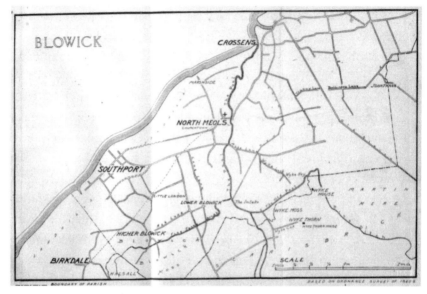

Fig. 3.3 *Map of Blowick (after Cheetham 1923) showing the Pool flowing out from the ring-ditch through the Wyke and entering the sea at Crossens.*

post-glacial deposits have a depth greater than 40 ft (12.2 m) at Blowick (the present site of Southport Gas Works; Reade 1871), it is likely that this area was under water from the times of the earliest formation of the mere, the deep depression in the till at Blowick being infilled by both peat and silt settling from the inflow over a long period of time. Some early reclamation may also have taken place, as is indicated on Cheetham's map by the 'Intak' to the west of Wyke House Farm (Fig. 3.3). There are many references in the literature to the Wyke in the 1500s and 1600s, by which time that area was surrounded by Blowyke Moss and the mere was a good deal smaller.

On its southern and western borders the limits of the mere were probably obscure, with the moss (raised bog) reaching to its shores and the mere overlapping onto the moss in periods of wet weather and/or high water table. If the Wyke or bay extended as far as Higher Blowick or even beyond Lower Blowick (a distinct possibility), this might well have left the promontory on which Wyke House stands as an island in the mere, or at least as an island surrounded by bog to the south and the mere to the north. In 1354 'The Wyke in Northmeles' is referred to as a 'certain parcel of Martin Mere' but by 1503 all that was apparently left of this embayment of the mere was the 'great moss ditch' which separated the parishes of North Meols and Ormskirk (Cheetham 1923). In 1440 a 'certain parcel of land', referred to as Otterhouseholme, was given by Gilbert Scarisbrick to two of his chaplains. By this time the term 'the Wyke' referred not only to the bay and the fishery, but to the area of land incorporating what was undoubtedly on occasions effectively an island, as the term 'holme' implies. It is possible that Otterhouseholme was the promontory, since 'the Otterpool' was probably an alternative name for the Old Pool.

When the Wyke was drained, the stream which joined the mere to Fine Jane's Brook retained the name 'Old Pool' and beyond this point was known as 'the Pool', which discharged into the sea at Crossens. It may well be that in the past Fine Jane's Brook discharged directly into the mere at times when it was high. The Old Pool forms a continuation of the man-made ring-ditch, and possibly had similar origins in early drainage to limit the mere.

There are other indications that the mere extended well beyond recorded limits to the west. Two logboats were found when the lake was dug out in the Botanic Gardens, Churchtown, at the end of the nineteenth century, and a third was found in cutting a drain in Meols Hall in 1890 (McGrail 1978). While these could have come from the original bed of the Old Pool, the fact that the remains of a wooden pier were also found may indicate a location on a much bigger area of water, and probably the shore of the mere. The two Churchtown boats have been lost and the Meols Hall boat was reburied, so that there is no possibility of a carbon date from them.

It is clear that over the centuries the mere has varied very much in size and from time to time varying water levels must have created and submerged islands, particularly where boulder clay came near to the surface. Most of the old maps show the presence of three islands (see Fig. 4.1), though it is possible that such detail was copied in most cases from the oldest original map. There can be little doubt, however, that such islands existed and several are named in the old literature.

In 1697, when the mere was drained (see Chapter 7), it was at a relatively low level and had been for some time, probably a hundred years

or more. This is clearly shown by Blakenase, a point some 800 m east of
Berry House, being shown as part of the shore of the mere (on maps
produced for the early-eighteenth-century court case relating to the
ownership of the mere bed: LRO, DDSc 143/23). While the name 'Blakenase' clearly means 'black headland' or 'black promontory' (which it
probably was when first named), records from the early fourteenth century indicate that it was then an island in the mere. The Burscough Cartulary records that on an island belonging to the priory and convent
'called Blakenase in their waters of Marton Mere', Thurstan de North-
leigh was granted a plot of land 90 ft long by 20 ft broad (probably only
part of the island). In granting the plot John, prior of Burscough, laid
down conditions governing the entry to the plot. Farrer (1903) considers these conditions to be a safeguard from the sporting propensities of
Thurstan's family and retainers. A later reference (early fifteenth century) in the Burscough Cartulary (see Webb 1970) refers to Blakenase as
'otherwyse callyd the Ilondys'.

The early-eighteenth-century sketch maps (LRO, DDSc 143/23)
which show Blakenase (see Colour Plate 3.5 following p. 80) merely as a

Plate 3.6 *The stone which marks the boundary between Scarisbrick and Burscough. This
stone was placed midway between the two Peels and is to be found in the hedge opposite the
entrance to the road off Fish Lane which leads to the windmill.*

promontory also clearly indicate the presence of three islands in the waters of the mere at the time of draining. One, Great Peel, is the mound of drift on which the present Berry House Farm is built. A second, Little Peel, lies some 200 m to the east, at the right-angled bend in Fish Lane. Midway between the two islands, in the hedge opposite the road leading to the windmill, lies the boundary stone between Scarisbrick and Burscough (Plate 3.6). The boundary here was originally set at a mid-point between the two islands. Plate 7.8 shows the reappearance of Little Peel during the floods in August 1956.

Some 1200 m due west of Little Peel, and just east of Crooked Wood (see Colour Plate 3.7 following p. 80), lies a peat-covered boulder-clay knoll which, on OS 6 ins, 1845, sheet 76, is called Wholesome Brow. In the 1714 case records it is usually referred to as Wet Holsome, though elsewhere it is written as Whetholsom, Wethalsome, Whettholson, Holsam, Housom or Whet Holsome.[1] It is very probable that the two Peels and Wet Holsome are the three islands shown on the old maps and that they were the only islands existing at the time of the drainage in 1697.

There is one other island mentioned in the old records. In 1580 Harrison, chaplain to Lord Cobham, in describing the course of the Douglas, wrote that 'it meeteth [...] with Martin Mere water, in which Mere is an island called "Netholm" beside others' (Procter 1908). Netholm farm lies to the east of Mere Brow and close to Holmes, which is on a rise in land between Holmes Moss and Holmeswood Moss. This rise in land is probably Netholm, which would effectively be an island at times of high water on the mere and when the mosses were also waterlogged.

It is possible that from time to time other islands were created, when there were particularly high or low water levels. When the water was high, Clay Brow may well have formed an island, though there are no records of this occurring. The fact that Fish Lane connects Clay Brow, Windmill Farm and Berry House suggests a crossing of the mere using

---

[1] There is a confusion in the literature between Whettholsom and Whassam (= Quassam). This arose through reading Whassam Heyes as Whassam Hyle, and the fact that there was a mill (Whawshaw Mill) at Whassam led to its translocation from its proper site, close to the present Scarisbrick pumping station, to the site of the windmill, built long after the draining of the mere, near Berry House.

high points which may have been islands (Windmill Farm = Little Peele and Berry House = Great Peele).

There has been a great deal of speculation in the past concerning the sites of the three islands, and a glance at some of the old maps (Fig. 4.1) suggests that the positions of the islands on the newer maps are based on those in the map of 1598. The maps of 1700 and 1745 must rely on previous maps for the position of the islands since they were drawn after the draining of the mere. Although the early maps were not accurate, it is possible that on the 1598 map the most easterly island is Clay Brow, while the most southerly island is in the position of the Wyke (i.e. Otterhouseholm) and the most northerly island possibly Netholm. Such an interpretation would certainly be appropriate were the mere considerably deeper, as it might well have been. However, the most likely explanation is that the islands are shown in the wrong places, and that they are in fact Great Peel, Little Peel and Wet Holsome.

There is the possibility that islands on the mere have in the past been used as crannogs and built up for habitation using timbers. There is no evidence of this on the mere, though the finding of several logboats has led to speculation that people may have lived here in this way, as they did in such situations in Scotland, Ireland and at Glastonbury in England (Blundell 1924).

So far little practical archaeological research has been carried out on the mere, and the sites of the islands of Great Peel, Little Peel and Wet Holsome would be obvious sites to investigate. The peat, too, contains much hidden evidence of the past of Martin Mere, and pollen analysis on parts of the mere so far not investigated may well divulge more of its history. For the most part the mere remains as a shadowy memory of times past in this part of Lancashire, but its sediments have much yet to reveal, and may eventually give an indication of the position of the mere shoreline at different times in its history and enable us to produce better maps than we now have.

CHAPTER FOUR

Mapping the Mere

W. G. Hale

At the time when Martin Mere was drained in 1697 no accurate maps of the mere existed and small-scale regional maps registered its presence with a roughly drawn outline (Fig. 4.1). Once drained, it was only on the north shore that an obvious shoreline was visible, in the form of a boulder-clay cliff. In periods of heavy rainfall the mere has been re-created and it is fortunate that someone took the trouble to map the flooded areas in the winter of 1848 (Mitchell 1885). This map (Fig. 2.3) shows the main drainage channels and the surrounding roads so that the outline of the mere can be traced relatively accurately onto the Ordnance Survey map (Fig. 4.2). Some of the features already discussed in previous chapters can now be seen clearly. For example, Berry House Island (Little and Great Peel) can be seen as such, and the Pool has formed south and west of Wyke House and approaches Blowick. Even so, the northern boundary of the water did not reach the boulder-clay cliff, so that clearly the water level in the winter of 1848 (between the 4 m and 5 m contours) was well below the maximum of the old mere.

The 1848 map provides the most accurate information we have for the areas of the mere at one time covered by water, but this is clearly a larger area than that drained in 1697. Prior to Mitchell's map, maps were constructed to illustrate points during litigation concerning ownership and, in this case, such litigation began in the second decade of the eighteenth century. Depositions made by witnesses in 1714 (LRO, DDSc 143/23) give accounts of features of the mere and of recollected boundaries and divisions, and our knowledge of the original mere immediately before and after drainage relies heavily on these depositions. The two maps shown in Figs. 4.3 and 4.4 have been drawn up on the basis of very

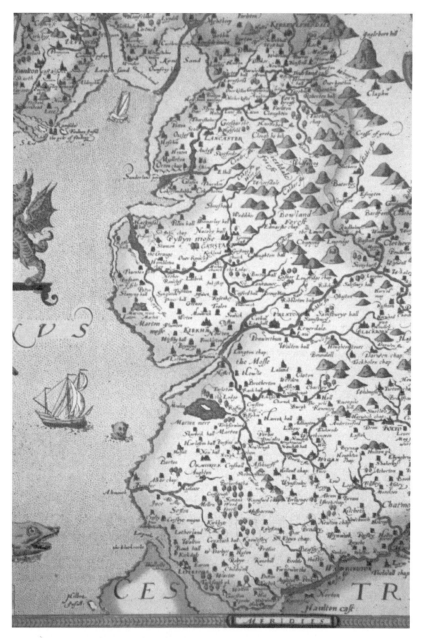

Fig. 4.1 Old maps of the area of Martin Mere (a) *Saxton's map of 1577*, reproduced by permission of the British Library, Maps C.3.bb.5.

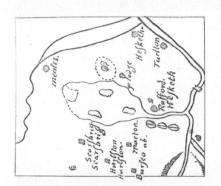

(b) *The Harleian manuscripts map of 1598*

(c) *Blaeu's map of 1662*

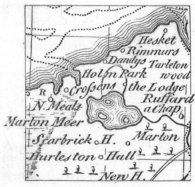

(d) *Leigh's map of 1700 (published after the draining of the mere)*

(e) *Bowen's map of around 1745*

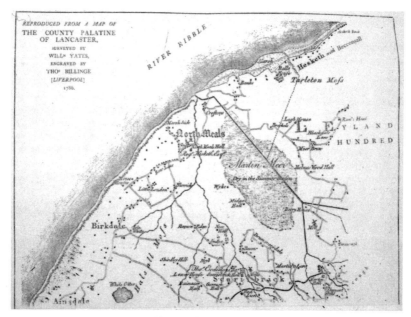

(f) *Yates's map of 1786*

(g) *Aikin's map of 1794*

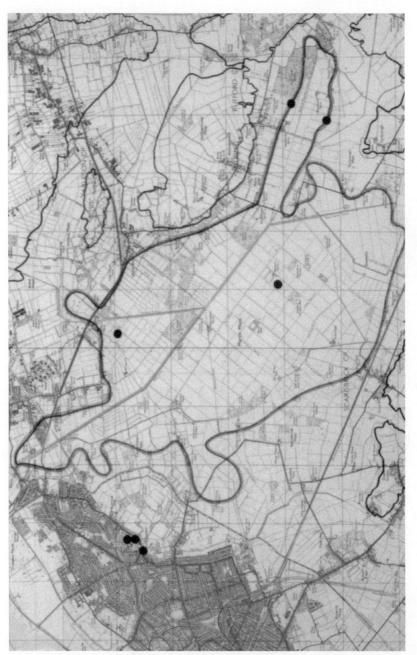

Fig. 4.2 *Mitchell's 1848 floodwater map superimposed on the Ordnance Survey map. The 8 m contour is highlighted. The dots mark the position of excavated logboats. Reproduced from Ordnance Survey mapping on behalf of Her Majesty's Stationery Office. © Crown Copyright 100043886 2005.*

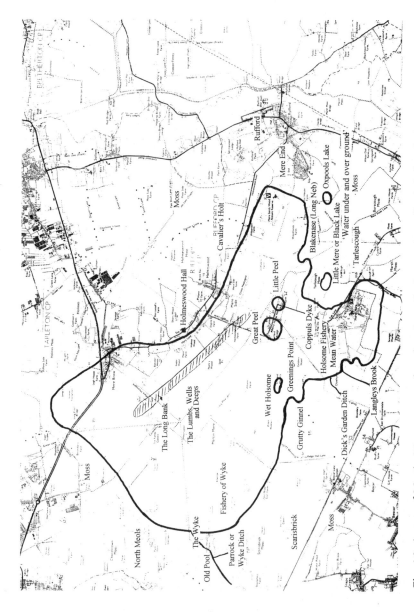

Fig. 4.3 A map of Martin Mere constructed to show its main features immediately before drainage, in 1697. Reproduced from Ordnance Survey mapping on behalf of Her Majesty's Stationery Office. © Crown Copyright 100043886 2005.

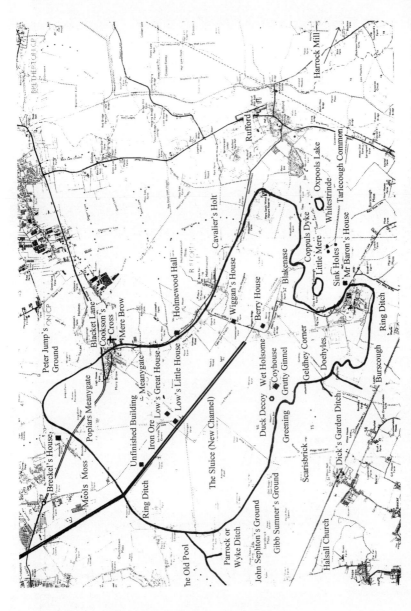

Fig. 4.4 A map of Martin Mere showing the main features after draining, about the time of the litigation in 1714. Reproduced from Ordnance Survey mapping on behalf of Her Majesty's Stationery Office. © Crown Copyright 100043886 2005.

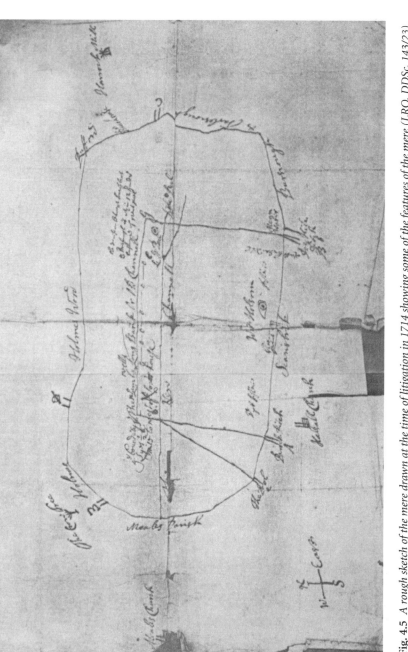

Fig. 4.5 *A rough sketch of the mere drawn at the time of litigation in 1714 showing some of the features of the mere (LRO, DDSc, 143/23).*

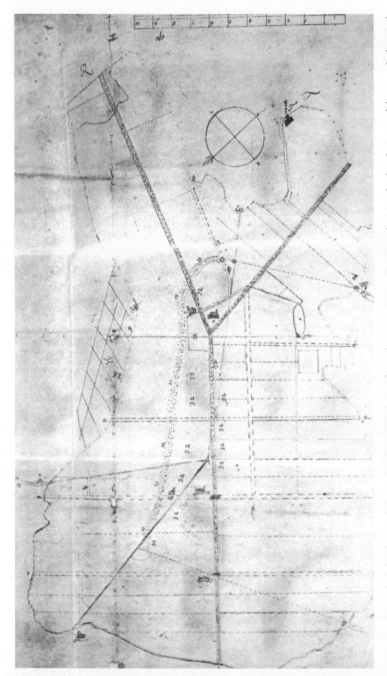

Fig. 4.6 (a) *Another sketch map (LRO, DDSc; 143/23) dating from the same time as Fig. 4.5, showing further features of the mere before and after drainage and giving a more accurate indication of the limits of the mere.*

Fig. 4.6 (b) *The key to the various markings on Fig. 4.6 (a).*

rough sketch maps (Figs. 4.5 and 4.6a) associated with the depositions of the litigation consequent upon the draining of the mere.

Apparently the mere in the 1690s covered an area of some 3632 statute acres, or 1717 acres of customary measure, which is approximately 5.68 square miles or 1470 hectares, this being the amount of land resulting from the drainage of 1695 (Anon. 1760). One Peter Rimmer, of North Meols, was about thirty years old at the time of the drainage and before that time he was employed on plumbing the depth of the mere. He was of the opinion that at the time of draining the mere was about 7 ft (2.14 m) at its deepest and that it was a similar depth where the Great Sluice was made. J. Sumner held that the mere was deepest in the region of the

Old Channel and that in places this exceeded 3 yards (2.74 m). Rimmer was subsequently employed in the draining of the mere and held that on the Burscough and Scarisbrick side, i.e. the south, it was much deeper than on the Rufford and Holmeswood side (the north), where it was very shallow. Another witness, Thomas Titterington, commented upon the size of the mere, which, he said, was five miles long and two miles wide, with a circumference of some 15 miles and an area of 3000 acres or thereabouts. The original document (LRO, DDSc 143/23) also refers to '3000 acres of the county measure', i.e. 2.12 times greater than the statute measure, but this is probably incorrect.

In many places the margins of the mere were very indistinct. Local people beating the seventeenth-century bounds between Burscough and Rufford had to traverse very wet and marshy areas before reaching the edge of the mere (LRO, DDHe 64/2, 64/11, 64/12). Furthermore, reeds grew in profusion in the shallow waters round the edge of the mere and these were collected for thatching and other purposes (see Chapter 6). Despite reeds occupying large areas around the rim of the mere, this large body of water must have been an impressive sight from Parbold Hill, stretching almost to the western horizon.

Down the deepest part of the middle of the lake, running roughly from east to west, lay the lumms (or lumbs), wells or deeps, which were reputed to be the best places to catch eels (also see Chapter 6). This area, known also as the Old Channel, was the line along which the New Sluice was laid and Thomas Ball, who was employed throughout the drainage of the mere while that work was in hand, also held that it was the deepest part of the mere and was its centre. This statement was corroborated by other witnesses at the 1714 enquiries, among them John Sumner, Peter Rimmer and Thomas Foreshaw. Along the Old Channel water flowed westward towards the Old Pool, probably as a result of influx from the Douglas and Langleys Brook. This water flow, together with currents generated by the prevailing winds, was influential in distributing the Shirdley Hill sand in the form of the Long Bank which formed a feature north of the Old Channel (see Colour Plate 4.1 following p. 80).

On the mere itself the only visible features, apart from the islands, were the bays and inlets and the mouths of the streams which ran into the mere. Descriptions of the islands were made in the 1714 depositions and James Worthington, aged 53, of Ormskirk, gentleman, described Wet Holsome as 'near half a mile from the shore' – a greater distance than is shown by any of the old maps.

The western and southern shores of the mere, in the 1690s, followed the line of the ring-ditch shown on the 1839 tithe map (LRO, DRL 171). Halfway along the south bank of the mere Greening Point formed a promontory pointing towards Wet Holsome. To the west of Greening Point lay the fishery of Wyke and to the east lay Holsome Fishery, both owned by the lords of Scarisbrick. Also west of Greening Point lay Grutty Ginnel, where the swans traditionally nested, and Dick's Garden Ditch on the boundary between Holsome Fishery and Burscough. Beyond this boundary, the fishing rights in the area called the Mean Water were held in common between the lords of Scarisbrick and the Earls of Derby.

Langleys Brook, in Burscough, is not mapped presumably because its position was not relevant for the purposes of litigation. To some extent, however, it would be responsible for the westerly flow of water along the 'lumbs, wells and deeps'. East of Dick's Garden Ditch was the most southerly part of the mere and this formed a bay nearly half a mile (800 m) across below Tarlescough, between what are now the sewage works and Clay Brow; the Wildfowl and Wetlands Trust Reserve now lies in this bay. North of this bay lay the two islands of Great and Little Peel and the inflow of Copples Dyke was also around half a mile (800 m) to the north before the shore swings eastwards towards Blakenase, also known as Long Neb (see Colour Plate 4.2 following p. 80). Inland, just to the south of Copples Dyke, lay the Little Mere, or Black Pool, and both dyke and lake were features denoting the boundary between Burscough and Rufford. According to the 1714 deposition of one J. Spencer, he had several times walked the boundaries between Burscough and Rufford which began at the Ox Pool Lake (otherwise known as Ox Pool Leach), and thence to places called Burkinshaw (Burchen shoa) and Whitestrynde, over a place called Sink or Cinque Fall, and then to Black Poole on the Little Mere and so to Copples (Coppie) Dyke or Ditch which ran into Martin Mere at the east end.

The Ox Pool Lake or Leach, lying to the east of the end of the mere, appears to have been a ditch or stream rather than a lake, and Burkinshaw was probably a birch thicket, since, in 1678, Edward Bridge records trees growing there within living memory (LRO, DDHe 64/12). Bridge also records (28 May 1672, DDHe 64/11) the presence of a 'whammy soggie pitt on the moss that hathe green leafes growing upon the watter' (*Lemna sp.*?) and a 'dry, black, heathy pitt', both close to Burkinshaw. The Sink Fall lay between Burkinshaw and the Black Pooles, and was made up of a series of pools, where the water appeared to run beneath the ground. Thus, to the east of the mere the ground was very wet and boggy and contained a series of pools.

At the eastern end of the mere, the maps show a very straight shore, suggesting some reclamation in the area prior to draining. In fact, this feature may well have been formed by a ditch, as such a ditch still exists along this line, forming the most easterly division of the Mere Sands Wood plantation.

To the south of Mere Sands Wood, a distance of some 150 m, runs Rufford Boundary Sluice, and this marks the centre of the most westerly arm of the original mere. Its continuation beyond the end of the wood marks the line of the inflow/outflow to the mere from the River Douglas. The road from Rufford to Ormskirk crosses this stream and on all existing maps the crossing is shown as a bridge, though there can be little doubt that the crossing was made originally by the ford from which Rufford was named (Plates 4.3 and 4.4).

On the northern bank of the mere, which is formed at this point by a boulder-clay cliff (Plate 4.5) immediately north of Little Peel, a small woodland, known as Cavalier's Holt, features on some of the court case maps. To the west, again atop the boulder-clay cliff, Holmeswood Hall was shown, on some maps amidst what appears to be enclosed parkland, captioned 'Holmeswood demesne'.

To the north-west of Holmeswood Hall the boulder-clay cliff forming the one-time edge of the mere disappears near what is now Mere Brow. South of the hamlet the limits of the mere must have been very indistinct and the area between Holmes and Holmeswood Moss must have been very subject to flooding. At Mere Brow a cross stood at the corner of

Plate 4.3 *Mere Sands Wood after the excavation of sand by the Rufford Sand Company and before planting of the reserve began. Evidence of the Shirdley Hill sand can be seen over all the fields. The closeness of the water table to the surface also shows well in this photograph.*

Plate 4.4 *An aerial view over the newly excavated Mere Sands Wood looking south-east towards the causeway. Rufford is to the top left and beyond it can be seen the River Douglas. In the left foreground an infilled stream bed can be seen.*

Plate 4.5 *The boulder-clay cliff on the north side of the mere near Mere Lane, Holmeswood. It is likely that the mere reached the base of this 'cliff', which was cut either by wave action from the mere or by water flow from an ancient river, possibly the Douglas following a different course.*

Tarleton Park, near Blacket Lane close to Howard's and Cookson's House, and a line taken through this cross from the Crow Tree on Meols Moss pointed directly at Halsall Church; Mere Brow watercourse now follows this line.

Following the line of the shore round what was its northernmost point at the time of draining, the only feature shown on the court case maps was Breckel's House in Meols Moss. From near this point (the present-day Boundary Farm) the Tarleton Runner (one of the main drains running into the Sluice) now extends almost directly south to the main sluice.

Maps of the north-western shore of the mere are featureless but this is hardly surprising since most of the area behind present-day Southport was clearly inundated by the mere, probably within the period of two or three hundred years of its being drained. Aerial photographs (Plate 2.4) clearly show the mere peats extending over this area and filling the old salt-marsh channels to form roddons. The inundation of this salt-marsh probably resulted from the development of a dune system seaward of the mere, resulting in the extension of the freshwater mere.

At the westernmost point of the mapped mere is shown the inflow of Parrock or Wyke Ditch, which is the Old Pool. On one of the deposition sketch maps these are shown to be separate, but this is a mistake. The Parrock Ditch drained the higher land around Ormskirk into the mere but also acted as an overflow to the sea at Crossens at times of high water levels on the mere, certainly in the later years of its existence.

While all the old maps (Figs. 4.5 and 4.6) clearly show features of the undrained mere, all were constructed around the time of the 1714 court case, well after the first drainage attempt in 1697, and were produced to show features of the drained mere area, particularly those associated with the boundaries of the various estates and parishes. The most obvious feature of the new mere were the drains, particularly the Great Sluice running down its centre to fork immediately north-west of Great Peel, forming branches constituting Boat House Sluice to the south and the Rufford Boundary Sluice to the east (Plate 4.1). In the fork, John Berry, a woollen draper of Croston, built Berry House on land leased from Thomas Fleetwood and close to it, just north of the Boundary Sluice, William Wiggins, a yeoman of Holmeswood, leased land for his house. Neither of these, however, was the earliest house to be built on the mere. This was constructed by Henry Lowe, a yeoman of Burscough, who leased land and built Lowe's Little House about halfway along the main sluice to its north. Subsequently he built Lowe's Great House closer to the sluice. Also on the northern side of the sluice, but some 800 m further west, is marked an unfinished building, and the existence of iron ore – presumably bog iron – on the mere bed. The first few buildings erected after the draining of the mere were built in the middle of the mere, where it would have been deepest. Running north-east/south-west across the mere was a series of tracks, called 'meanygates' or 'meanagates'. One called Poplar Meanygate ran from Peter Jump's to John Sephten's ground, a second from Cooksons at Mere Brow to Gibb Sumner's ground, a third from Holmeswood to Greenings and a fourth, called Coy Meanygate, from Holmeswood to Greenings by Wet Holsome and Grutty Ginnel.

Coy Meanygate was so-called since at its southern end it passed between a duck decoy built by the Scarisbricks and Coy House, built on the end of Wet Holsome for the decoy man. Quite when the decoy was built is unknown, but it is shown on one of the maps associated with the 1714 hearing, so that its construction took place some time between 1695 and 1714. It is shown on Greenwood's map of 1818 but does not appear on the tithe map of 1845, though this is no conclusive reason to assume its demise before that date.

The Martin Mere decoy appears to be the same size and design as the Hale decoy south of Liverpool. The latter may well have been copied from the Martin Mere decoy, and was functional in the eighteenth and nineteenth centuries. It was apparently owned, or partially owned, by the Scarisbrick family, on whose land the mere decoy was built. Possibly the mere decoy went out of use because its function was taken over by the Hale decoy. Possibly the Scarisbricks did not want or require two decoys, and possibly the Hale decoy was the more successful. While no records of catches exist from the mere, some records exist for the Hale decoy. A map in the Lancashire Record Office (DDSc 151/20, Fig. 4.7) showed the location of the mere decoy, and its exact size and shape were revealed by aerial photography, which also showed its longest side in line with Coy House. The decoy, like that at Hale, unusually had five pipes (Fig. 4.8), but no evidence remains of any tree planting around it, though the site of the decoy house is screened from the decoy itself by planting which still exists. Fields around the decoy on the mere were named after it, as was Decoy Lane, still in existence, and to this day the fields retain their original names such as Coy Crofts, Coy House Croft, Furtherest Coy Hey and Nearer Coy Hey.

There are, then, no accurate maps of the mere from the time when it was a feature of the west Lancashire landscape. However, from a study of the old documents, mainly the litigation papers (LRO, DDSc 143/23), it is possible to reconstruct maps which give an impression of the area before (Fig. 4.3) and after (Fig. 4.4) draining. These go some way towards showing what the mere looked like, but this can only be an impression. The real mere was an impressive waterscape, and no map can give a true impression of the grandeur of such a shining level.

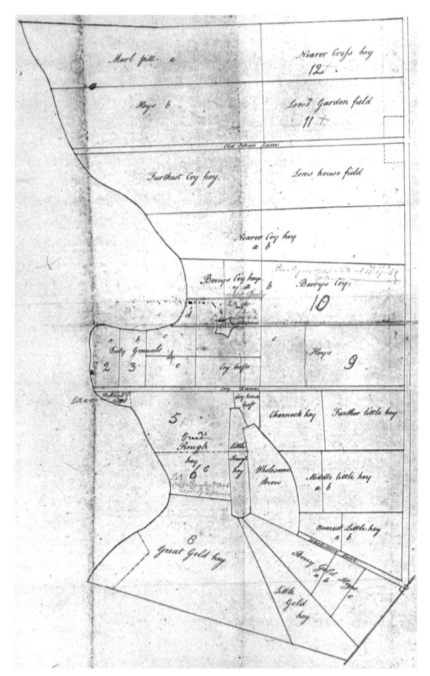

Fig. 4.7 *A map of the field system around Wet Holsome showing the location of the duck decoy (DDSc 151/20).*

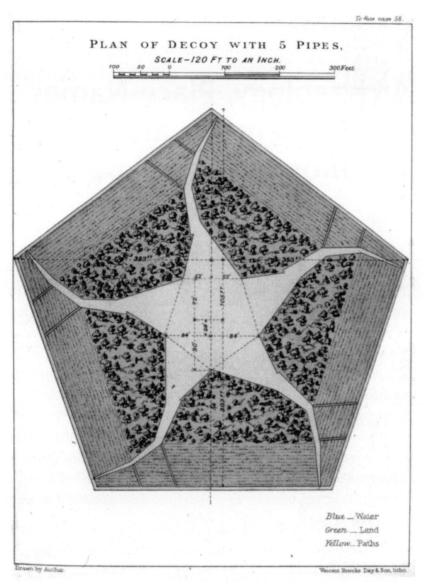

PLAN OF DECOY WITH 5 PIPES,

SCALE—120 FT TO AN INCH.

100   50   0   100   200   300 Feet

Blue — Water
Green — Land
Yellow — Paths

Drawn by Author

Vincent Brooks Day & Son, litho.

Fig. 4.8 *A plan of a duck decoy with five pipes which shows measurements very similar to, if not identical with, those of both the Martin Mere decoy and the Hale decoy (after Payne-Gallway 1886).*

CHAPTER FIVE

Archaeology, Place-Names and Settlement, and Traditions of the Mere

Audrey Coney with Alan Whittaker

'The past is a foreign country: they do things differently there.' The opening sentence of L. P. Hartley's 1953 novel *The Go-Between* prompts the realisation that present-day visitors to the Martin Mere area need to make considerable visual adjustment to perceive the landscape of the undrained mere. They must, in order to see beyond the legacy of three hundred years of drainage operations, mentally strip away the present rich farming terrain with its network of ditches, traversing roadways and tracks linking isolated farms. Behind this obliterative journey of over three hundred years lies a place dominated by water since prehistoric times.

Robert Neill captures this waterscape in his historical novel *Moon in Scorpio* (1952), and provides an atmospheric description of a remote, mysterious wetland:

> The spongy ground was flat, so flat that it was hard to tell where the water's edge was. It had, indeed, no edge; it was rather that as they approached it the ground became blacker and softer and wetter; there were pools here and there, and the pools became larger and closer; and then there was water, black and cool, rippling in the north-west wind. Yet there was no view of distance; the water was rippling in a forest of reeds, with tall bulrushes bending and swaying above them.

> There was the sigh of the wind in the reeds, and the soft lap and ripple of the water; and that was all. There was nothing, of sight or sound, to tell

of time or man […] Nothing stirred on the Mere; it was desolate, time-less, and forgotten. (1952: 157–58)

The mere, in fact, was not completely desolate, nor was it timeless and forgotten. It waxed and waned over thousands of years and the legacy of human activities includes artefacts as old as prehistoric and Roman times and place-names deriving from Viking, Anglo-Saxon or even ear-lier tongues. Several hamlets and villages, farms and fields that still lie at varying distances from the old lake fringe were part of the medieval landscape and some might have their origins far further back in time. Yet patches of woodland and great tracts of unenclosed pastures and heaths long remained. Even today there are parts of the old shoreline that are remote and difficult of access. In places such as these, where morning mists on wetland soils serve only to increase the aura of soli-tude and mystery, it is not difficult to understand why the area has spawned a host of myths and legends.

Archaeology

Martin Mere and its immediate environs form part of an arc of wetland soils stretching from the estuary of the Alt to the estuary of the Douglas. Humans probably reached this area soon after the ice retreated, their quarry doubtless including animals as large as the elk. When the ske-leton of such an animal was discovered at Poulton-le-Fylde in the 1970s, subsequent carbon 14 dating indicated that the animal met its death about 13,000–11,500 BP. This particular elk escaped its hunters but, some time before it collapsed into an icy pool, had been crippled by a barbed flint point embedded in its ankle (Hallam et al. 1973: 100–28).

There is no firm evidence for prehistoric hunters in the Martin Mere area at such an early date. Leigh, however, records the recovery of an 'exotic head apparently an elk', with horns spanning two yards across and lying four yards deep in marl in (North) Meols Moss (Leigh 1700: 63). Other large animals left their traces in these peaty soils. Dickson (1904) notes the finding of several red deer antlers and Hugh Caunce of Clay Brow Farm in Burscough recovered the bones and teeth of an auroch (a type of wild cattle) on his land (*Ormskirk Advertiser*, 20

February 1969). It seems likely, too, that the Neolithic/Bronze Age people who hunted these and other animal species along what is now the Formby coastline were equally well aware of the fenland resources of Martin Mere (Plate 5.1; Gonzalez et al. 1997: 271–81; see also Chapter 3). The draining of Martin Mere at the end of the seventeenth century brought to light eight logboats, one with 'plates of iron on it'. Leigh's illustration of one of the 'Indian Canoos' found in the slutch shows a simple and slender construction, with two small opposing semi-circles cut into the top of the sides beyond the mid-point. Presumably these were for oars. Leigh also records and illustrates a stone artefact, which he describes as 'like a whetstone' (but which was probably an axe-hammer) and a 'copper' (bronze?) palstave. These were found in a moss 'not very remote from the canoo' (Leigh 1700: 17, 181 and facing page). Over the following three centuries other artefacts, among them seven more canoes, were discovered. Archaeologists must also be grateful for the generations of observant farmers who picked up chance finds as they worked their land. Farmers often noticed these finds in newly ploughed earth as they followed the horse and the plough. Unfortunately, the advent of the tractor now means that such discoveries occur less often: tractor drivers sit several feet above the soil.

On the other hand, systematic fieldwalking can still pay dividends. Such a programme was initiated by the West Lancashire Archaeological Society in the late 1970s and early 1980s in response to plans, currently in abeyance, to re-align the A59 trunk road. Part of the projected route skirted built-up areas of Burscough and Rufford to cross former moss-land near the old lake basin and the eastern extremity of the mere. The results of fieldwalking demonstrated the hazards and benefits of the exercise. Overwhelming quantities of broken eighteenth- and nine-teenth-century pottery were recovered, most of which had been trans-ported to the area in manures from Liverpool (Coney 1995). While interesting in itself, this pottery was no help in understanding the early archaeology of this wetland area. By contrast, finds of flints and earlier pottery were few, such objects being less conspicuous on the ground, and correspondingly harder to detect. Yet these were the artefacts that indicated a human presence in prehistoric, Romano-British, medieval

Plate 5.1 *Prehistoric human and red deer footprints on Formby Beach (photograph by S. Gonzalez).*

and Tudor times. Their recovery demonstrates how fieldwalking even a small area of mossland can produce useful results. While these artefacts might not provide actual evidence for archaeological sites, they do suggest a human presence in the wetland. In fact, the recovery of this lithic and ceramic material is remarkable: palaeobotanical research undertaken by Margaret McAllister showed that, in the Tarlescough Moss area at least, most peat deposits later than mesolithic times have long been stripped away. McAllister's research ran concurrently with this programme of fieldwalking and produced some evidence for burning and woodland clearance around 8500 BC. There may be a natural origin for this but human intervention is also feasible. Her core from the Langleys Brook area of Burscough is unusual in that it extended the pollen record through the Neolithic and into the Bronze Age. In addition to evidence for charcoal and a rise in pollen from dryland weeds, the appearance of cereal grains, consistent at about 3610 ± 110 BP, points to increasing cultivation (McAllister pers. comm; McAllister et al. 2004).

Lithic material recovered from mereside fieldwalking in Burscough and Rufford included a number of small brown flint nodules derived from glacial gravels, and a few pieces of flint and chert, dating perhaps from Bronze Age times, which showed evidence of flaking and retouch. Among them were (a) a translucent thin waste flake of black flint, brought perhaps from the Yorkshire wolds, with light grey impurities, a chalky cortex and a small striking platform; (b) a large irregular flake in the same material, not struck from a prepared core but showing utilisation along the long concave side; (c) an opaque light grey flint, possibly a waste flake from a prepared core; and (d) an irregular flake from a piece of coarse black chert, struck from within the original cobble, and with a line of steep retouch along the side and possible utilisation along the platform. The use of such coarse material indicates the poverty of resources and perhaps the expense of importing good quality flint and chert (Ric Turner pers. comm.). In the same vein Middleton has suggested that, because of the scarcity of natural flint, the cores, blade blanks and finished implements used by prehistoric people in the wetlands of what is now south Lancashire were, perhaps, carried from site to site until they could no longer be re-sharpened or re-worked. Be that as it may, a mesolithic site at Banks near Southport produced over 700 worked flints, while the chipping floor on former heathland at Mawdesley, within 10 km (6.2 miles) of Martin Mere, produced about 500 pieces of flint and chert (Middleton 1997; Ron Cowell pers. comm.). Furthermore, find-spots listed in the Lancashire Sites and Monuments Record strongly suggest that the locality between the southern edge of Martin Mere and Derby Farm in Burscough would repay further investigation. Artefacts recovered from this area include a flint knife and other flint material, a stone axe and a stone axe hammer (Lancashire Sites and Monuments Record).

Chance finds from Martin Mere include several bronzes. The palstave illustrated by Leigh dates from the period 1500–1100 BC. Another example of the same type of implement is unusual in that the fitting groove for the handle was on the side rather than on the flat edge. The discovery of at least three spearheads is also on record, two of which were found together in 1899 (Farrer and Brownbill [eds.] 1906: I, 231; Brodrick 1902; Davey and Forster 1975, nos. 43, 108; Leigh 1700: facing p. 181). Palstaves would have had numerous uses including felling and shaping wood; spearheads were doubtless effective implements for catching fish or hunting animals. The iron arrowhead found embedded in a bog oak on land at Clay Brow Farm, however, is clear evidence that one disappointed hunter in the wildwood missed his quarry (*Ormskirk Advertiser*, 20 February 1969).

Bob Middleton (1997) has suggested that some of the stone axes from Pilling Moss may have been deliberately deposited. In the Fens, a Bronze Age socketed axe was found near a male skeleton (Turner and Briggs 1986: 144–49). Is it possible, therefore, that some ritualistic significance might also be attached to bronzes from Martin Mere? In this context, Leigh's oft-quoted remarks of 1700 are worth repeating. In discussing mosslands generally, he records, almost as an afterthought, that 'sometimes in Mosses are found human Bodies entire and uncorrupted, as in a Moss near the Meales in Lancashire' (Leigh 1700: 63). While this appears to be one of the first documented instances of bog bodies, such findings are not now unusual: by 1986 over 85 individuals had been recovered from peat deposits in 50 sites in England and Wales (Turner and Briggs 1986). We will never know whether the unfortunate individuals found in lowland Lancashire mosslands met their deaths by natural causes, accident, murder or ritual killing. When the remains of a young adult male were excavated from Lindow Moss in Cheshire in the 1980s, though, subsequent inspection revealed a gruesome story. Lindow Man, as he came to be known, was probably rendered unconscious after blows to the head caused depressed fractures of his skull. Yet he did not die immediately from this injury, as there was evidence for swelling around the wound. The actual moment of death came when his neck was broken by a garrotted ligature. A slit to the throat severed the jugular vein. Naked apart from a fox fur band around his arm, he was then dropped face downwards into a pool of water in boggy ground. After Lindow Man was excavated, analysis of pollen from body tissues and the surrounding organic soils provided conflicting dating. The most convincing argument is that he met his death about 300 BC. This date, coupled with the nature of his injuries and deposition in a pool of water, strongly suggests that he suffered the 'triple death' of pagan Celtic ritual (Ross 1986; Stead 1986; West 1986).

The largest artefacts ever recovered from Martin Mere were logboats – dugout canoes that would have been used on the lake and local rivers for fishing and transport. The true total may be rather more than the fifteen so far recorded: some logboats were perhaps not recognised for what they were; others may not have been reported because farmers were loath to disclose the fact of their discovery so as to avoid the ensuing fuss (Brodrick 1902). Fig. 4.2 shows the positions of those that can be positioned with any accuracy. Logboats were crafted from hollowed-out tree trunks and probably plied the waterways of the British Isles over an immense span of time. In Ireland they have been found in association with crannogs (lake dwellings) and were still in use in that country in the late seventeenth century and perhaps into the eighteenth century as well (McGrail 1978: 12).

Martin Mere's logboats are often described in the literature as canoes. Of the fifteen for which records exist, almost all have rotted away and the whereabouts of only one example is known with certainty. That example is in the Botanic Gardens Museum in Churchtown in Southport

(Plate 5.2). Carbon 14 dating of this logboat gave a conventional radio-carbon age of 1560 ± 70 BP. When calibrated, this result indicates a 95 per cent probability that the parent log was felled within the date range AD 380–645 and a 68 per cent probability that the event occurred between AD 425 and AD 600 (carbon 14 reference, Southport No. 07.06; W. G. Hale pers. comm.). This particular boat was discovered in 1899 in the North Meols part of the mere during ploughing. It lay about 3 feet (91 cm) deep in peaty earth above a deposit of beech or hazel leaves and branches (Brodrick 1902). Brodrick suggests that this find-spot lay near the centre of the old lake but McGrail's grid reference (NGR SD 40271897) locates it near the final shoreline. The logboat was in good condition when Brodrick examined it soon after discovery, the only damage being at the bow where it had been struck by the plough. Its length was 16 ft 6 ins (5.03 m) and the greatest width was 4 ft (1.22 m). Three ribs, about 3 ins (7.5 cm) square, were fastened to the sides of the boat with wooden pegs and two holes towards the bow contained thole pins 6 ins (15 cm) in length. A flat board, which Brodrick suggested was part of a seat, lay near the centre of the vessel. There was evidence for adze marks, and cracks in the stem and stern had been repaired with lead patches (Brodrick 1902). When McGrail re-examined the boat in 1974, he classified it as a first-rate all-round logboat of canoe form. It weighed 500 kg and had been fashioned from half an oak log split longitudinally, with 78.8 per cent of the parent log worked away. The girth of the original tree was 4.46 m. (14 ft 8 ins). Its diameter measured 1.42 m (4 ft 8 ins) at 1.5 m from the butt end and 1.20 m (3 ft 11 ins) at 14 m. This butt end formed the bluntly rounded stern. The prow was more pointed and the base of the logboat was generally flat, with only slight evidence for a keel. A recess at the stern contained three vertical holes, one of which accommodated a treenail. Adze marks, ribs, pins and patches noted by Brodrick had disappeared. Neither was there evidence for the 'seat'. Other measurements provided by McGrail include: external height 0.61 m (2 ft); side thickness 50 mm (2 ins); bottom thickness 90 mm (3.5 ins). He assessed the boat's manoeuvrability as moderate, but reckoned that the vessel could have been propelled by oars at good speeds. It would carry a crew of one man standing and seven kneeling and, at standard freeboard, transport one man standing and up to 920 kg of turf (McGrail 1978: 153–56).

In 1861 a large canoe was discovered to the west of Mere Sands Wood in Rufford (NGR SD 4415), a position that suggests a location towards the edge of the lake as it narrowed towards Mere End. This logboat was exhibited at the London Exhibition but when returned to Rufford was allowed to rot away. In January 1869 another logboat was found on the opposite edge of this stretch of water at Brickfield Farm in Rufford (NGR c. SD 4396 1536). Robert Ashcroft, whose plough struck the logboat, was convinced that it had been left on the lake shore for it rested on an incline and on a bed of gravelly ripple-marked sand. When found, it lay 5 ft (1.52 m) below the surface in peaty soil and in almost perfect condition. Hollowed from a single log, it measured 13 ft long (3.96 m), 2 ft 10 ins (86 cm) wide and 1 ft 8 ins (46 cm) deep; it had four seats and the semi-circular bow contained round perforations. This boat was extremely heavy, requiring the strength of several men to lift it, and was secured by iron hoops. But it was left exposed to the mercy of the elements and, by the time that the find was reported in the *Preston Guardian* in April 1869, had 'shrivelled up into a mere ghastly caricature

Plate 5.2 *Longboat from Martin Mere on display in the Botanic Gardens museum, Churchtown, Southport.*

of its former self'. Its eventual fate is unclear. This may be the logboat once housed at Rufford Old Hall, although in 1958 the hall's curator could only describe the Brickfield Farm boat as 'formerly' there. McGrail tentatively identified a wooden construction in an outhouse at the hall as the Brickfield Farm boat, but clearly had reservations over its authenticity. Yet there was still a logboat on display in Rufford Old Hall in the late 1970s. Iron plates were fastened to its side (Smith 1870: 272–73; McGrail 1978: 165; W. G. Hale pers. comm.).

The Rufford boats and the one now in the Botanic Gardens Museum were apparently found in locations on or very close to the final shoreline of Martin Mere. It might be argued that they also mark a much more ancient fringe. If so, then the branches that underlay the boat now in the Botanic Gardens Museum at the time of its discovery might be stabilisation for a soggy landing place. Records exist for an additional four logboats. A small canoe was discovered in 1897 towards the middle of the mere, near the junction of Warings Ditch with the Sluice. It was left to decay. Of the remainder, one was found about 1890 near Meols Hall (NGR c. SD 3655 1853), and the others came to light during construction of the lake in the Botanic Gardens. The Meols Hall boat was never dug out and is presumably still *in situ*. The fate of the other two is uncertain (Brodrick 1902). As mentioned in Chapter 3, these three boats were found at some distance from the final shoreline of the mere and their locations may mark its earlier limits. On the other hand, they were found on the edge of the watercourse that once linked Martin Mere with the coast. In historic times this passed near to Meols Hall and seemingly flowed across the site later occupied by the Botanic Gardens lake in Churchtown.

Martin Mere's mosslands have been exploited for millennia and some of the flints from near the old lake edge in Burscough and Rufford have already been described. In addition, the West Lancashire Archaeological Society's fieldwalking programme recovered ceramics dating from Roman, medieval, Tudor and later times. Among several fragments of Roman pottery recovered were rims from a large thick-walled vessel (Plate 5.3) and a much thinner piece of hollow-ware. This pottery complements other evidence for Roman coins from the Martin Mere area.

Brodrick, for instance, notes the discovery in 1899 of a coin of Vespasian near to where two of the Bronze Age swords were found. Other currency was found nearby, but the finders kept the location secret (Brodrick 1902). This might suggest a yet-to-be-recovered coin hoard, similar to those already found within 10 km (6.2 miles) of Martin Mere in Scarisbrick and Lathom (Lancashire Sites and Monuments Record). The fieldwalking programme also produced several sherds of coarse medieval pottery. Among other ceramics recovered was a piece of northern reduced greenware, embellished with an incised decoration, and dating from late medieval to Tudor times (Plate 5.3); and the base of a small Cistercian-ware vessel, probably a tyg. A few seventeenth-century clay pipes were also found. There were, however, certain finds from fieldwalking that proved undateable or defied classification. They include a sherd of coarse unglazed grey pottery that seems to be neither prehistoric, Roman nor medieval. A piece of worked stone from a field on the sandy edge of the mere in Rufford is another enigma. This semicircular object bore evidence of pecking around the curved edge and what was possibly a failed attempt at perforation along the straight edge. The intention was perhaps to make a perforated disc – possibly a round hammer or net sinker – but the object was apparently discarded after it broke in half.

Fieldwalking also furnished unexpected evidence for metalworking (Plate 5.4). Parts of two copper crucibles were especially difficult to date, as the form of this type of vessel remained constant over several centuries. Quantities of slag were recovered and, while most fields produced

Plate 5.3 *Sherds of pottery from fieldwalking.*

Plate 5.4 *Evidence for copper-working from fieldwalking.*

at least a small scatter, this material was most extensive in a field bordering a track on the fringe of Rufford Park. This position might suggest a relatively recent arrival as hardcore, but expert opinion was divided as to date and nature. On the other hand, pieces of bog iron – a brittle, porous variety of brown haematite found in bogs – were also recovered. Their presence near the edge of the old lake indicates that raw material for smelting iron was available locally. In fact, mereside people were well able to recognise iron-bearing deposits when they saw them: maps of the newly drained mere showed an 'unfinished building at Iron Ore' (LRO, DDSc 143/23), and a sheet of iron pan was still visible when the writer visited the area.

The archaeology of Martin Mere indicates a human presence in the area over several millennia and holds out the tantalising prospect of settlement sites as yet unknown. Indeed, evidence from air photography from the Langley's Brook and Martin Hall areas of Burscough indicates places where an older landscape of trackways and small enclosures sometimes underlies present-day fields (Lancashire Sites and Monuments Record). There is also a growing body of evidence to suggest that the local Romano-British population was largely aceramic and that, for this period at least, more attention should be paid to a few sherds of pottery as indicators of nearby settlement than would normally be the case. For example, excavations at the multi-period site at Duttons Farm in Lathom produced little in the way of artefacts, yet these helped to date the remains of hut circles and trackways to Iron Age, Romano-British and medieval times. It seems that in the lowlands of what is now Lancashire the use of pottery began to die out in the fourth century AD and that in its stead came eight centuries of aceramic culture (Ron Cowell pers. comm.). It is for this reason that Martin Mere's archaeology during Anglo-Saxon, Viking and early Norman times remains obscure. Some logboats, though, might derive from this time. This dearth of artefacts from the centuries before the Norman Conquest contrasts strongly with the place-name evidence which provides abundant evidence for Anglo-Saxon and Scandinavian tongues. Some of this is now considered.

Place-names and early settlement

The fenland landscape is seen reflected in several major and minor place-names around Martin Mere (Fig. 5.1). This countryside may be inherently damp but it has long been exploited. Many field-names found on nineteenth-century tithe maps were passed down through earlier centuries and are frequently traceable to similar names in medieval and early-modern documents. They were given by the men and women who lived by this land. There is space here to explore only a little of the place-name legacy they left us.

Martin Mere takes its name from the pre-Conquest vill of Martin which, in a sort of circular linguistic journey, is itself named from the mere. The vill of Martin was divided by 1066, as Domesday Book describes the place as 'half of *Merretun*'. The name means 'the *tūn* (or estate) by a lake' (Morgan [ed.] 1978: 169c, d; Ekwall 1960: 317; Higham 2003). Fenland products were especially important in the economy of places such as this, with surplus fish, fowl, rushes and reeds no doubt traded with communities where such commodities were less abundant. In fact, the undivided vill of Martin is perceived as a component of a pre-

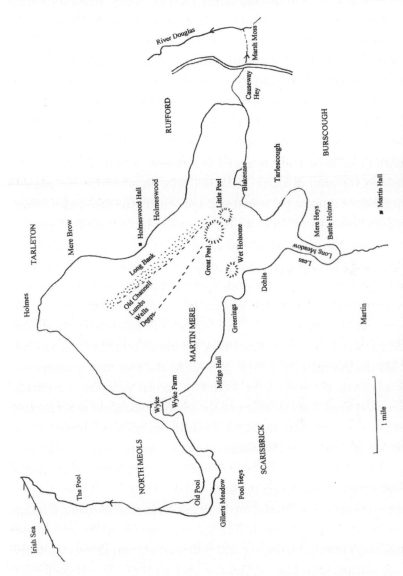

Fig. 5.1 *Map showing locations for some of the place-names mentioned in this chapter.*

Conquest multiple estate, an ancient administrative and economic unit that almost certainly pre-dates Anglo-Saxon times. Dues from component vills of a multiple estate were paid to a central place and, in a time when these were paid in kind rather than in money, fenland produce probably formed some or all of the render from Martin. In 1066 the capital demesne centre for Martin lay within the royal estate of West Derby (Morgan [ed.] 1978: 269c, d). An earlier, smaller administrative area was centred perhaps on Lathom (Coney et al., in progress).

Remnants of early multiple-estate organisation can often be perceived in the layout of later administrative areas. The medieval and early-modern division between the hundreds of West Derby and Leyland passed through Martin Mere, and this allowed fenland products to be available for both districts. In West Derby Hundred lay the lakeside townships of Burscough, Scarisbrick and North Meols; in Leyland Hundred lay Rufford and Tarleton. The name of Martin is absent from this list because the place was divided before the Conquest and absorbed into two neighbouring places. The undivided Martin probably stretched along the shores of the mere from Rufford in the east to North Meols in the north-west. Tracing the process of partition is complicated, but Domesday Book states that Uhtred (a powerful Anglo-Saxon thegn who held numerous estates in West Derby Hundred) held Hurlston and half of Martin (Morgan [ed.] 1978: 269c–269c, d). This moiety comprised the northern portion of the township known today as Scarisbrick. Domesday Book does not mention the whereabouts of the other portion but this was apparently absorbed into Lathom, another Uhtred vill and a strong contender for that thegn's demesne centre. In the twelfth century this half of Martin was granted to Burscough priory and eventually became part of Burscough township (Webb 1970: 19). There was perhaps a counterpart to Martin on the opposite shore of the mere. It is suggested that a place known as Holmes, and containing the present-day hamlets of Holmes, Mere Brow and Holmeswood, was absorbed into the neighbouring townships of Tarleton and Rufford (Ann Hallam pers. comm.). The name 'Holmes' derives from Scandinavian *holmr* and indicates patches of relatively higher, drier ground in a marshy area (Ekwall 1960: 246; Fellows-Jensen 1985: 135–36). The fields of the present-day

Holmes hamlet lie on poorly drained Salop series till, with those at Holmeswood occupying imperfectly drained Astley Hall and free-draining Crannymoor sands (Soil Survey, sheet 75). The hamlets of Holmes and Mere Brow have long been part of Tarleton township, but are separated by erstwhile mossland from the principal settlement at Tarleton on the banks of the Douglas. By contrast, the hamlet of Holmeswood backs onto Holmeswood Moss and lies in Rufford.

The place-names of both Martin and Holmes well describe their wet-land landscape. Furthermore, the place-name Rufford (Old English *rūh*, rough, and ford; Ekwall 1960: 396) encapsulates the bumpy and uneven crossing point over the eastern outlet of Martin Mere to the Douglas. By contrast, the names of other lakeside townships contain elements relating to landscape features lying further away from Martin Mere. That of North Meols, for example, focuses on the coast rather than on the lake. Termed *Otegrimele* in Domesday Book, it perhaps contains the Scandinavian personal name *Oddgrimr* together with Scandinavian *melr*, sandbank. Similarly, Scarisbrick's place-name derives from Scandinavian *skǫr*, opening, hole, depression, and *brekka*, hill or slope, and is likely to describe features within Scarisbrick Park, where rising land beside the Eas Brook provides a sense of elevation that is relatively rare in this township. Burscough's place-name contains Old English *burh*, stronghold, and Scandinavian *skógr*, wood, and reflects pre-Conquest woodland by, or belonging to, a defensive site (Fellows-Jensen 1985: 78, 150–51, 158, 221, 375). The *burh* may have lain about two miles away from Martin Mere: it probably underlay the priory (Webb 1970: 7). As regards Tarleton's place-name, Fellows-Jensen followed Ekwall in suggesting that the first element is *Þóraldr*, a Scandinavian personal name in the assimilated form *Taraldr*. She noted, though, that the *Taraldr* form only appears in Norwegian sources in the fourteenth century (Ekwall 1960: 460; Fellows-Jensen 1985: 190). This led Insley to look for alternatives and to propose that the first element of Tarleton is *Tar-la*, a pre-Celtic Indo-European name for the Douglas, itself a Celtic river name. He suggests that the name *Tar-la* 'survived the coming of Celtic speech, though possibly only as a local name of a stretch of the river'. Then at some stage it was transferred to the settlement and taken over by

English settlers. Insley also suggests that Tarlescough, an area of former woodland near the mere in Burscough, contains the same element
(Insley 1999).

Insley's examination of the Tarleton place-name opens up the
intriguing possibility of great continuity of settlement in townships near
to Martin Mere. The actual fringe of the lake, however, was generally
eschewed by those seeking a dry place to live. Farmsteads here were few
and far between. Yates's map of 1786 reveals that, almost a century after
the initial drainage, not many people chose to live virtually on the edge
of the lake (Yates 1786: 32). Where the land lay below the 8 m (25 ft)
contour, and sometimes only 2–3 m above sea level, there was just the
hamlet of Mere Brow in Tarleton and a handful of farmsteads. Where
there were better opportunities for agriculture on relatively drier soils
above the 8 m contour, though, hamlets such as Holmes, Holmeswood
and Tarlescough (see Colour Plate 5.5 following p. 80) and the larger
settlement at Rufford are found. The place that was almost certainly the
principal settlement for the undivided vill of Martin also lay above the
critical 8 m contour, and is represented today by a cluster of farmsteads
in Martin Lane in Burscough. Of farmsteads perching just yards from
the undrained mere, Wyke and Midge Hall in Scarisbrick are of some
interest, as in all probability the earliest inhabitants of these damp and
remote places were more concerned with fishing and wildfowling than
with agriculture. Wyke Farm lies on a small low promontory between
the old bed of Martin Mere and the former outlet into the Wyke. While
Scandinavian incomers would have called the outlet *vík*, creek or bay,
the suggestion has been made in Chapter 3 that the promontory was
known as Otterhouseholme in the medieval period. Neighbouring
Midge Hall occupies an almost imperceptible rise, only 2 m above sea
level – a narrow slip of earth once sandwiched between mossland and
mere (OS 6 ins, 1845, sheet 75). An earlier name for Midge Hall might
have been *Miggehalgh*. The *Miggehalgh* on the edge of Leyland Moss
evolved into Midge Hall and there is a similar name, *Midghalgh*, near
Barton Brook in the parish of Lancaster. A place called *Miggehalch* with
common rights in Martin is mentioned in the Burscough Priory cartulary (Ekwall 1960: 133, 148; Webb 1970: 236–37). The name derives

Plate 2.4 *Roddons exposed by erosion of the peat at Bankfield Farm, near the Three Pools Waterway, Churchtown – evidence of an ancient salt-marsh.*

Plate 2.5 *A gutter on the salt-marsh at Banks, showing the formation of levees which result from the deposition of silt as the incoming tide spills over. These levees, which give rise to the roddons after the peat which has subsequently covered them is eroded, are often used by waders (in this case bar-tailed godwit and knot) for roosting during high tides.*

Plate 3.5 *Aerial view along the length of the mere from Blakenase (bottom right) to the gas holder at Blowick (top centre). Little Peel was sited in the area of the farm in the centre of the picture, and Great Peel was behind it, beyond the windmill.*

Plate 3.7 *Wet Holsome (Wholesome Brow), the third island in the mere, seen from the air. The island lay behind the V-shaped piece of woodland (just below right of centre) known now as Crooked Nursery. Very slightly to the right of the centre of the picture, and cutting the field boundary, can be seen the five-sided outline marking the position of the old duck decoy.*

Plate 4.1 *Aerial view down the length of the Great Sluice which followed the line of the Long Bank. The right bend in the Great Sluice marks the limit of the mere at the time of drainage (1697); the Sluice was dug out by hand from this point to the coast at Crossens. Clay Brow is in the left foreground.*

Plate 4.2 *Looking east from Little Peel towards Blakenase and the point where the Brickfield Farm boat was found in 1869.*

Plate 5.5 *Part of the hamlet of Tarlescough in winter.*

Plate 5.8 *The old fringe of the mere near Martin Mere Wildfowl and Wetlands Centre.*

Plate 5.10 *Windmill on the mere.*

Plate 6.1 *Medieval fish-traps in a mill leat.* (The Luttrell Psalter, *1989, p. 31).*

Plate 6.3 *Aerial photograph looking west over Holmeswood. The curve of woodland fringes the late-seventeenth century shoreline of Martin Mere. The white building immediately to right of centre of the woodland is Holmeswood Hall.*

Plate 6.4 *The mute swan and cygnets were targets for Martin Mere's wildfowlers.*

Plate 6.5 *Reeds edging a lake at Mere Sands Wood.*

Plate 6.7 *Horses grazing on the former island of Little Peel.*

Plate 8.1 *The Dalmation pelican* (Pelicanus crispus) *probably inhabited Martin Mere in warmer periods in the past (after Keulemans, in Dresser 1871–96).*

Plate 8.7 *The marsh harrier* (Cyrcus aeruginosus) *nested on the mere until into the twentieth century but is now an infrequent visitor (in Meyer 1842–50).*

Plate 8.8 *The bittern (Botaurus stellaris) probably bred on the mere until the time of drainage in 1697, and possibly later; the creation of new reed beds by the Wildlife and Wetlands Trust may result in the species returning to breed (in Meyer 1842–50).*

Plate 8.9 *The ruff (Philomachus pugnax) was last recorded breeding on the mere area in 1910, the next recorded breeding in Lancashire being in 1976. However, it has probably bred on the mere area, and certainly on the marshes, without being recorded. Outside the breeding season it is a common visitor (in Meyer 1842–50).*

from two Old English elements: *mycg,* midge, and *halh,* and means slightly raised ground in a marsh, or low-lying land liable to flooding. In fact, Gelling has tentatively suggested that some instances of *halh* may have been used for the lowest eminence on which settlement was possible. This would certainly fit the site of Scarisbrick's Midge Hall. It is not difficult to imagine this place on the edge of Martin Mere as a midge-infested locality; nor is it surprising that Leigh in 1700 should describe the fenny and maritime parts of Lancashire as frequented by malignant and intermitting fevers, rheumatism and other diseases (Leigh 1700: 6; Fellows-Jensen 1985: 178–89; Gelling and Cole 2000: 125; Stiles 1997).

It was argued in Chapter 3 that the Wyke embayment once extended westwards as far as Blowick. On OS 6 ins, 1845, sheet 75, the Wyke left its traces as a creek-like feature feeding into a small stream, the Pool, which then flowed north towards the Ribble estuary. The Wyke had long been improved by the time these maps were compiled, yet the water-course that drained its area was called the Old Pool. This might suggest that 'pool' was another name for this westerly outlet of Martin Mere. In fact, it may be presumed from matching fifteenth-century Scarisbrick field-names, such as Polehey and Gyliot Meadow, with several fields on the nineteenth-century tithe map called Pool Heys and Gillerts Meadow, that the original Polehey was a large enclosure separated from the edge of the Wyke only by a strip of meadow land (OS, 6 ins, 1845, sheet 75; LRO, DRL 1/71; Powell 1898: 206). It seems that Old English *pōl* was used to describe flowing water such as creeks and small streams. Old English *mere* was more descriptive of a body of standing water, either great or small, but not part of a larger feature (Gelling and Cole 2000: 21–26, 28). The distinction between the two elements is well illustrated by Old Pool alias Wyke and Martin Mere.

On the other side of the lake, beyond Mere End in Rufford, water flowing towards the Douglas seems not to have had a distinguishing name. There are, however, several fields in Rufford called Causeway Hey and Marsh Moss at the point where this outfall was crossed by the Ormskirk–Preston road (LRO, DRB 1/170). They indicate that this marshy area was wide enough to require a causeway on both sides of the bridge. In a time when there was neither bridge nor causeway over this difficult area, it was in all probability the rough ford that gave its name to Rufford (see above).

The principal feeder stream of Martin Mere was perhaps Langleys Brook, which flowed into the lake from the Burscough shore. Seasonally flooded areas along its banks went by the name of Long Meadow, which suggests that the name 'Langleys' derives from Old English *lang*, long, and *læs*, meadow. There was still a field called Leas here in the nineteenth century (LRO, DRL/13). This area was probably an inlet of the mere when waters were high, with the rather drier Battle Holme (modern Batloom) lying west of its upper reaches. It seems more likely that this place-name describes a fertile pasture than a combat site: Old English *battel* can mean rich, fertile or productive, and sixteenth-century *Battleholme* was part of the demesnes of Burscough Priory (*Oxford English Dictionary*, I, 1989: 430; OS, 6 ins, 1845, sheet 84; TNA, DL 29 158/33). Other fields near the fringe of the mere were sometimes called Greening, a name that apparently includes the Scandinavian element *eng*, meadow (LRO, DRL 1/71).

Within the old mere basin nineteenth-century field-names such as Mere, Mere Heys and Martin Mere are extremely common and are a useful guide to defining areas once covered by water. Some Mere Heys, those in Burscough adjoining Langleys Brook, for example, lay to the landward edge of the final shoreline. The Merehey in Burscough is mentioned in the dissolution records of the priory, and it may be argued that a single large enclosure was later subdivided (LRO, DRL 1/13; DRL 1/71; DRB 1/170; TNA, DL 2198).

The islands of Wet Holsome, Great Peel and Little Peel, of course, were pre-drainage features. If seventeenth-century names such as Wet Holsome, Wett Holsom, Whetholsom, Wetholsom and Wethalsome (LRO, DDSc 143/23) mean 'at the wet hollows', this would be an apt description for the damp peaty island. Great Peel and Little Peel islands were on firmer land. Part of Great Peel island was boulder clay. Little Peel island lay on sand (Soil Survey, sheet 75).

The term 'peel' has various meanings. Definitions given in the *OED* (XI, 1989: 430) are: a stake; a palisade or fence formed of stakes; a stockade or palisaded enclosure; a small castle or tower. Any one of these could be appropriate for a feature on an island in Martin Mere. On the other hand, Cheetham's hand-written notes of questions to be asked of plaintiffs in the court case of 1714 include the words: 'Where there any and what Islands, or Piells of land encompased and surrounded with water, in the Mere'. He gives the definitions of the term *piel* in the *English Dialect Dictionary* as: a border stronghold; a dialect form of 'pool'; the least particle of grass. He also notes that in Shetland and Orkney a piece of ground having very scant pasture is described as not having a peel of grass upon it (Cheetham papers, Southport Reference Library). We differ as authors in our explanation of why the term 'peel' was attached to these two islands. The writer of this chapter supports the view that it refers to tower houses. W. G. Hale favours the explanation of peel as a scanty pasture. He takes the view that the two small symbols for Great and Little Peel on some maps compiled for the eighteenth-century court case (LRO, DDSc 143/23; Fig. 4.6) define the general locations of these islands rather than the sites of tower houses. He queries why, when these maps depict post-drainage buildings as actual houses, they should depict pre-drainage buildings by symbols. For what purpose and for what reason would building materials be transported to islands in the mere? Why, if buildings were present, were they not used as landmarks for defining post-drainage ownership or pre-drainage navigation?

This present writer believes that, when Cheetham examined the court case records, he read 'piell' instead of 'parcell'. In the briefs and other documents relating to this litigation the phrase appears as 'Islands or *parcells* [my italics] surrounded with water'. Sometimes the first element of 'parcell' is abbreviated by a line through the letter 'p' and the resulting word looks very similar to 'piell' (LRO, DDSc 143/23). In lowland Lancashire the name 'peel' is invariably found in association with a tower house and/or a moated site. Among local examples are Peel Flat (beside the moated site in Longshaw Wood in Rufford) and Peel Yard (associated with the former tower house at Aughton Old Hall). In the countryside overlooking Martin Mere, the tower house at Holmeswood Hall is still extant although the tower house at Martin Hall has been demolished (see Plates 5.6 and 5.7 and Chapter 6). Within Martin Mere itself the name 'peel' first appears in the fifteenth century, when the

Burscough/Rufford boundary was set by arbitration and the *pelus* and the
Black Nase were awarded to the prior of Burscough (Webb 1970: 225).
Although boundary disputes continued into the sixteenth and seventeenth centuries, the 'peel' remained a marker on the township divide
(for example, LRO, DDHe 64/2, DDHe 64/12). In 1672 the final stretch
towards Martin Mere was said to have led from the 'nebb called the
Black neese shooting straight towards the Litle peelle in the meere'
(LRO, DDHe 64/11). About 1678 the Burscough jury said that when
walking this division they aligned themselves on the windmill on Har-
rock Hill, the 'peele in the meere' and (North) Meols Church (LRO,
DDHe 64/12). While documents like this are never specific as to whether
the term 'peel' refers to a building or to an island, the final marker on a
map of about the same date depicts a small single-storey building, lying
within the lake, and bearing the caption 'The peel on Martin Mere' (Fig.
6.2; LRO, DDHe 122/1). This map is certainly not depicting a tower
house but, if its name is any guide, this small building might have
replaced such a feature.

For both political and economic reasons a tower house would be an
excellent place from which to observe the mere. In that time when the

Plate 5.6 *Holmeswood Hall.*

Plate 5.7 *Martin Hall (photograph by Philip Withersby).*

mere was covered with water, Great Peel and Little Peel islands were in different fisheries and held by different landholders. Furthermore, the hundredal boundary over Martin Mere lay nearby. Court case depositions provide a very specific reference point for Great Peel: 16 roods (a rood being a local measurement equivalent to 8 yards) from the lacustrine boundary between Scarisbrick and Burscough fisheries. This suggests the site of a building rather than an island. If this is true, some eighteenth-century litigation maps perhaps recorded Great and Little Peel by small but carefully placed symbols because it was necessary to show such precise points. In fact, there is still a well near to where Little Peel tower house is presumed to have stood. Perhaps Wet Holsome island was depicted merely by a general island outline because it had less importance as a boundary marker (see Fig. 4.6a, b; LRO, DDSc 143/23). Berry House Farm is today the principal building on the former Great Peel Island and is apparently the third farmhouse to carry the name. But these houses were post-drainage features and none occupies the position of Great Peel as defined by litigation maps. It must be admitted, though, that if there ever was a tower house on Great Peel island it lost its status as the eighteenth century progressed: in a deed belonging to manorial lord William Scarisbrick, there is mention of just a 'messuage or cottage called the Peel' in his drained lands of Martin Mere (LRO, DDSc 135/1).

The channel between Great and Little Peel islands flowed into the deepest part of the lake, a long linear feature that was remembered by a variety of names on eighteenth-century court case maps: Old Channell, Lumbs, Wells and Deeps. The word *lumm* means a pool, and it rather looks as though water movement within this deepest part of Martin Mere scoured out a series of hollows within the channel. Beyond, on the Holmeswood/Rufford side, the name of the submerged sandbank known as the Long Bank indicates much shallower water (LRO, DDSc 143/23).

Around the mere, great tracts of unimproved wetland soils left a legacy of mossland names, including Holmes Moss and Sollom Moss in Tarleton; Blowick Moss and Churchtown Moss in North Meols; Wood Moss and Drummersdale Moss in Scarisbrick; Tarlescough Moss and Burscough Moss in Burscough; and Holmeswood Moss in Rufford (OS, 6 ins, 1845, sheets 75, 76, 84). Most of this land was enclosed by the mid-nineteenth century but the field-name 'moss' remained ubiquitous. The medieval name of Blakenase, 'black ness', also indicates a dark, wet and peaty area projecting into Martin Mere. In addition to numerous Moss Heys, there are many other field-names that describe the past appearance of the land. For example, Turf Moss and Turfroom in Burscough define old peat extraction areas; Gorsey Brow in Scarisbrick and Heath in Rufford call to mind places yellow with springtime gorse and purple with summer heather (LRO, DRL 1/12; DRL 1/70; DRL 1/71). Today, fields such as these are part of an intensive arable landscape, but this was definitely not arable land at the time these names were acquired.

Names indicating old woodland areas are less frequent. Mere Sands Wood in Rufford lies within the lake basin and began life as a planted game covert, so really cannot be considered here, but Holmeswood Wood is still in part ancient woodland and survives beside the old mere edge. There are other woodland names in places where no trees now grow. For instance, the name of medieval *Byrchynshaw* on the Burscough/Rufford boundary indicates a strip of birch trees, for it includes the Old English element *sceaga*. This element was often applied to a narrow tract of woodland and, as here, is frequently found on the township verge. Tarlescough's place-name contains Old Norse *skógr*, wood. Its trees were felled in the sixteenth century (see Chapter 6; also Webb 1970: 19, 225). Nearby, and hard by the old shoreline of Martin Mere, the nineteenth-century field-name Warth Wood derives perhaps from Old English *waroð*, streamside land (Field 1972: 247). Another aptly named field near the Burscough shoreline is Car, from Scandinavian *kjarr*, damp woodland. The Car lay near the Dohile on the Burscough/Scarisbrick boundary. Seventeenth-century 'Dohile' evolved into nineteenth-century 'Doehyles', a name retained today (LRO, DRL 1/13; OS, *Explorer* series, 285), and Pam Russell suggests that this was acquired through popular etymology. She proposes that the first element has nothing to do with female rabbits and that 'dole', share, is more likely (pers. comm.). The fact that the seventeenth-century Dohile was a stinted pasture held in common between the Scarisbricks and the Earls of Derby supports this (LRO, DRL 1/13; DDSc 143/23; see Chapter 6). Unfortunately, all too often there are insufficiently early forms for place-names around Martin Mere. Nevertheless, even field-names from the nineteenth century can sometimes provide useful information for vanished buildings. One example is the Boathouse Hey near the former edge of the mere in Tarlescough (LRO, DRL 1/13). This name proved particularly useful since it indicates where the Earl of Derby's fishermen kept their boat several centuries before. Colour Plate 5.8 (following p. 80) shows how the old edge of Martin Mere remains visible near the Wildfowl and Wetland Centre. The Boathouse Hey lay just beyond the line of trees on the opposite side of the road.

Myths and legends

Martin Mere and its surrounding district spawned so many myths and legends that no overall picture of the area can be complete without some discussion of the subject. The following account is not intended to be comprehensive and some conclusions are speculative and even contentious. Of the several traditions linking the area with Arthur, the most intriguing was recorded by Camden in the seventeenth century and has perhaps been told and re-told for centuries. In referring to Lathom, Camden states that the 'Duglesse, a riveret; creepeth and steeleth along quietly this place, nere unto which our Noble Arthur, as Ninnius writeth, put Saxons to flight in a memorable battaile'. He then describes how Martin Mere emptied itself into the Douglas (Camden 1971: 749). According to Nennius, or Ninnius, four of Arthur's twelve battles – the second, third, fourth and fifth – were fought on a 'flumen, quod dicitur Dubglas, et est in regione Linnuis' ('a river, called the Douglas, which is in the region of *Linnuis*'). Nennius, a Welsh monk, wrote his *Historia Brittonum* about AD 829, a date that postdates the events he described by several centuries. But Nennius apparently had recourse to earlier material: he himself stated in the *Historia Brittonum* that he compiled his history by making 'a heap' of all the documents he could find (Morris [ed.] 1980: 1; Barber 1973: 15). Furthermore, his account of Arthur's battles has the appearance of being a prose summary, in Latin, of a lost Welsh poem (Morris 1973: 37, 111). Nennius's original manuscript is also missing but several copies are extant and one, Harleian MS 3859, is in the British Library (Alcock 1971: 56–57).

Camden was not alone in linking Arthur's battle campaigns with the Lancashire Douglas. Whitaker, the eighteenth-century Lancashire historian, was of the same opinion. On the basis of local tradition and archaeological finds of human and animal bones and horse-shoes, however, he places the sites of three of these battles in the Wigan area. Baines quotes extensively from Whitaker's *History of Manchester* (1795, vol. I): he equates 'Linnuis' with Martin Mere; repeats the local legend that, following Arthur's battle near Blackrod, the Douglas was crimsoned with blood as far as Wigan; and makes the unlikely suggestion that Wigan's place-name derives from Anglo-Saxon *wig*, fight, plural *wigen* (Baines 1836: 31–32). More convincing is Ekwall's suggestion that Wigan derives from *tref Wigan*, a British name meaning 'Wigan's homestead' (1960: 517). Breeze agrees that this a British place-name but believes 'little settlement' to be the appropriate meaning (2000: 232–33).

Arthurian traditions also abound in the local folklore of Martin Mere itself. It was supposedly into this lake that the nymph Vivian, mistress of

Merlin, disappeared with the abducted infant Lancelot, and here that, in subterranean caverns beneath its waters, the child was educated. As Lancelot du Lac, so Roby supposes, he later resided in the area; ruled over the whole or the greater part of Lancashire; and even gave his name to the county itself (Roby 1928: 17). Of course, Lancashire was never 'Lancelot's shire'. Its name incorporates that of the county town, Lancaster, which means 'Roman fort on the River Lune' (Ekwall 1960: 285). The Holmeswood bank of Martin Mere is particularly well endowed with Arthurian legend and stories of supernatural events. A pit near the old lake shore and close to Holmeswood Hall was known as King Arthur's Pit (Plate 5.9) and at least one early-twentieth-century tenant of the hall farm reported seeing boggarts and ghosts in its vicinity. This pit may be identical with that known to local children half a century later as the place where Arthur's sword was deposited. Another local tradition asserts that Arthur's sword once rested in Holmeswood Hall. There are other traditions of shadowy night-time figures passing marl-pits near the old mere edge and of a horse at the hall needing to be brushed only on one side, as by next morning both sides had been groomed. There may be ulterior motives behind some of these traditions. Procter surmised that stories of ghosts near King Arthur's Pit were fostered by local gamekeepers since this pit lay near a pheasant breeding area (Procter 1908: 98–118; Enid Pimblett and Marion Yates pers. comm.).

From the opposite side of Martin Mere in Burscough comes a further tradition connecting the Battle Holme area with Arthurian combat (see, for example, Jesson 1982: 14). Price, however, believes this to be the site of a long-forgotten battle held by local legend to have taken place between Dane and Saxon on the banks of the River Douglas (Price 1901: 181–219). Price paid little heed to either veracity or context: Battle Holme lies about a mile distant from the Douglas and, as stated in the place-name section of this chapter, the name seems more likely to refer to a fertile pasture.

There is no doubt, though, that Arthurian battles on a River Douglas have been the subject of much academic debate. It is equally true that there is still no consensus among historians as to the true locations for

Plate 5.9 *King Arthur's Pit, Holmeswood.*

either *Dubglas* or *Linnuis* or even as to whether Arthur existed at all. *Dubglas*, a British name meaning blue, black or dark river, gave rise to several river and settlement names such as Dalch, Dawlish, Divelish, Dulais, Devil's Brook and Douglas (Ekwall 1960: 138, 140, 143). Indeed, the frequency of the name *Dubglas* led Alcock to suggest that the phrase 'in regione Linnuis' was added to the *Historia Brittonum* as a gloss to aid identification (Alcock 1971: 65). Yet locating *Linnuis* is no easy task. The name is Old Welsh (Jackson 1953: 543) and in all probability its first element is *llyn*, lake. The second element is *wys*, a Welsh suffix for tribal and district names (Jackson 1953: 543). Thus, *Linnuis* means the people, or the district, of the lake.

The British name for Martin Mere is unknown but *Linnuis* would be an apt choice for the lost tribal or district name for at least part of the surrounding area. It might even be argued that support for Arthur would have been strong in this locality. After all, a system of tenure that arguably pre-dates Anglo-Saxon settlement was still in evidence in 1066 (see above). Moreover, on the basis of place-name evidence, Gelling envisages Welsh being spoken in Lancashire until at least the end of the eighth century (Gelling 1991: 5–12). A north-western context for

Arthur's second, third, fourth and fifth battles is also feasible, given that Alcock regarded the Southern Uplands as the most likely site for the seventh battle in the Caledonian forest and that Chester-on-Dee (earlier *Cair Leon*) rivals Caerleon-on-Usk as a contender for the ninth battle in *urbe Legionis* (Morris [ed.] 1980: 76; Alcock 1971: 61, 63).

Yet twentieth-century academic historians ignored Martin Mere and the Lancashire Douglas in their discussions of the whereabouts of *Dubglas in regione Linnuis* (see, for example, Barber 1973; Alcock 1971; Morris 1973). Alcock followed Jackson in proposing that ninth-century *Linnuis* derived from a British-Latin word such as *Lindenses.* While he notes that neither this nor another suggested loan-word, *Lindensia,* is on record, he considers that both could have existed as derivatives of the known word *Lindum.* He favours Lincoln or Lindsey, the name for the northern part of Lincolnshire, as the most obvious candidate for *Lindum,* but admits that there is no evidence for a Douglas river near those places. Other alternatives include the Loch Lomond area, where a Glen Douglas runs into the lake, and Ilchester, usually identified with an earlier *Lindinis,* and in the area of which there are two rivers named Douglas (Jackson 1953: 332, 543; Alcock 1971: 65–66).

Twentieth-century academic historians were, however, careful to separate the historic Arthur, as recorded in pre-Conquest documents such as the *Historia Brittonum* and the *Cambrian Annals,* from the chivalrous and mythical King Arthur, as described by writers such as Geoffrey of Monmouth in the twelfth century and Malory in the fifteenth century. While the familiar guise of King Arthur and his knights is plainly fictitious, Morris believed the historic Arthur to be 'as real as Alfred the Great or William the Conqueror; and his impact upon future ages mattered as much, or more so. Enough evidence survives from the hundred years after his death to show that reality was remembered for three generations, before legend engulfed his memory' (Morris 1973: xiii). Writing only two years earlier, Alcock viewed Arthur as the 'leader of the combined forces of the small kingdoms into which sub-Roman Britain had dissolved' and deemed his victories to be real, widespread and celebrated (Alcock 1971: 359, 363). Barber conceded that 'Arthur won a reputation in his lifetime that gave him a special place in the memory of the

British people' (Barber 1973: 24). Morris noted that while some of Arthur's knights may have had their origins in real people, their connection with the historic Arthur was unfounded (Morris 1973: 118).

But *was* Arthur a real person? While several academic historians in the 1970s believed in an authentic Arthur, their ideas did not go unchallenged. By the 1980s and 1990s the tendency was for scholars to prefer a totally mythological, unhistorical Arthur. The cut and thrust of the argument has recently been charted by Higham. In his view, writers from the fifth and sixth centuries to the end of the twentieth century primarily dealt with Arthur's historicity according to their prevailing political and cultural position. Higham himself distrusts Nennius's account of Arthur's campaigns and doubts that the list is truly historical. Given that there is only hypothetical evidence for a pre-existing document, he even argues that the list could be Nennius's own work. Higham views this list as complementing the vision of Arthur as a pan-British war leader and giving out a powerful message as to divine protection of the people and their role within God's plans for their island home (Higham 2002: 10–34, 146, 148, 271).

While arguments for or against a real Arthur will doubtless continue, there is no denying that Martin Mere and its surrounding wetlands became a focus for many of his legends. Why? One answer may be that this evocative, mysterious and extensive tract of water would inevitably attract Arthurian tradition. A second, more speculative answer is that some of these myths contain shadows of even older beliefs. Those concerning Arthur's sword, and the nymph Vivian disappearing into the lake with the infant Lancelot, might conveniently mask earlier folk memories of gifts to a heathen fertility goddess or even human sacrifice. After all, some of the bog bodies of North Meols moss and other places near Martin Mere could suggest pagan practices. Pagan customs clung on for a long time in Lancashire. In the nineteenth century Beltain fires were still lit on All Hallows' Eve (31 October) and on the Fylde, just across the Ribble from North Meols, farmers burned wisps of straw on a fork and encircled their fields to protect their crops from weeds. In the mosses of Marton near Blackpool and other places, fires were kindled for the purpose of succouring departed friends whose souls were supposedly detained in Purgatory (Hardwick 1973: 31; Harland and Wilkinson [eds.] 1972: 49; Thornber 1985: 99). This last custom mixes both pagan and Christian beliefs. It demonstrates that, despite strong local Christian legends, such as those linking medieval churches dedicated to St Cuthbert at Lytham, North Meols and Halsall with the wandering remains of St Cuthbert, Bishop of Lindisfarne, older religious beliefs were not completely eliminated even in the nineteenth century.

In discussing Lindow Man in the context of oral traditions and dialect names for boggarts and boganes, Turner attempted to show that 'evil forces, associated with peat bogs and watery places, underlie a whole body of English and Celtic folklore and dialect' (Turner 1986: 176). He notes that 'poems of the medieval period, Beowulf and Sir Gawain and the Green Knight, share imagery with what has independently been surmised as forming part of the ritual of bog burial' (Turner 1986: 176). 'Boggart' is a common term in northern England for a class of fairy that comes under the broad heading of 'bogies'. Etymology associates them with bogs and peat mosses and they range from the mysterious to the downright dangerous. They can turn milk sour and haunt houses but in some instances their behaviour is much more sinister: the terrifying bogane of St Trinian's in the Isle of Man, for example, is an anti-Christ figure. With the spread of Christianity many oral traditions became diffused and lost some of their power. As a result the boggarts of Northern England must have retreated to occupy the role of ghosts and minor devils (Turner 1986: 170–72, 176). The boggarts of Lancashire were often viewed as malevolent figures. There are nineteenth-century tales of them perched astride a gate or fence and sometimes leaping onto the shoulders of a terrified passerby (Harland and Wilkinson [eds.] 1972: 49).

Tales of the supernatural abound in the Martin Mere area. Besides the boggarts and ghosts of Holmeswood already mentioned, a white horse is said to gallop across the Holmeswood part of the old mere basin. Many manor houses had their resident apparition. In addition to the grey lady of Martin Hall in Burscough, there are stories from Scarisbrick of the green lady said to haunt Gibb's Garden and Gibb's Garden Plantation, and of a noise like a coach crossing over an old log road

(Cheetham 1912; Robert Seddon pers. comm.). A log road is perhaps not as fanciful as it sounds: Eccleston's improvements in the 1780s included surfacing roads over the softest parts of the mere with sand and faggots (Aikin 1968: 325). Most sinister of all, however, and entirely relevant to any discussion of folklore associated with peat bogs and bog bodies, is the tradition that evil spirits dwelling on the island of Wet Holsome were 'moved on' by one of the priors of Burscough (Donald Sephton pers. comm.). In fact, at least one head of this religious house was not averse to resorting to black magic if it suited his purpose. In 1454 the prior, Robert Woodward, and two of his canons were accused of divination, sacrilege and practising black magic in order to find hidden treasure (Haigh 1969: 5). The most recent of all the mere's ghostly tales revolves around the mill at Windmill Farm on the former island of Little Peel (see Colour Plate 5.10 following p. 80). About 1830 the miller's two sons were rebuilding the mill when, as one brother worked on the roof, a beam slipped and killed the other. Construction ceased after the accident but the ghost of the unfortunate victim was said to haunt the derelict shell at night. A steam engine was eventually housed in an adjacent building and provided power for a time (*Southport Visiter*, 27 October 1973).

A melodramatic tale of another type of supernatural being – a mermaid – and child abduction can be found in Roby's 'Mermaid of Martin Meer' (1930: 208–27). The story concerns a baby taken from its natural father by a vengeful 'meer-woman', who always announces her arrival by a murmuring sound and departs by gliding swiftly away over the surface of the lake. She leaves the baby with a local fisherman and the infant is later fostered by a Captain Harrington. Some years later the child is abducted from Harrington, who is himself captured and taken to a ship to be confronted by the captain, the child's real father. He believes that his child died in infancy, blames Harrington for her death and threatens to shoot him. As he pulls the trigger, the 'meer-woman' appears and tries to intervene but is accidentally shot instead. The extent to which Roby embroidered an older and otherwise unrecorded legend of a mermaid and a stolen child is unclear. But if he did, these characters may be masking more sinister traditions of a water deity and child sacrifice.

While Roby was obviously acquainted with the landscapes in which his legends were set, he was given to gross elaboration and even complete distortion. One reader of his books remarked that 'for invention he scarcely knew his equal' (see the Introduction to Roby 1928: xiii). Another was even more forthright. He regarded Roby's use of the word 'traditions' as a misnomer and considered that when presented as such in the accepted sense of the word, his work was worse than useless and calculated only to mislead (Hardwick 1973: 128). Roby's unsavoury tale of the prior of Burscough's incarceration and violation of Margery de la Beche in a building near his monastic mill is a case in point. The abduction of Margery de la Beche is a historical fact but the ringleader when she was snatched away from her Wiltshire manor on that Good Friday morning in 1347 was John de Dalton, who eventually married her. Two people were killed in the outrage and many were injured but John and his party fled north to Lancashire, where they apparently took refuge in the lands of several local landholders without their knowledge. Among those later accused of being accomplices were the priors of the monasteries at Upholland and Burscough. There is, though, no evidence to support Roby's 'tradition' of the imprisonment of Margery de la Beche by the prior of Burscough, Thomas de Litherland. De Litherland was certainly indicted for his part in the affair but was allowed bail on the bond of several Lancashire gentry who declared his innocence. He was later pardoned and remained as prior until his resignation in 1385 (*Calendar of Patent Rolls, 21 Edward III*, VIII, 1905: 269–71, 460; 498; Farrer and Brownbill [eds.] 1906–14: II [1908], 150).

Roby did not distort the fourteenth-century legend of the eagle and child to the same extent, although he certainly expanded it. What is arguably the oldest version appears in a poem written about 1562 by Thomas Stanley, bishop of Sodor and Man (Halliwell 1850: 216–20). Bishop Stanley's version is set in Tarlescough Wood near the Burscough shore of Martin Mere and is discussed here because of this location. The poem, once described as 'some uncouth rhymes', is quoted by Halliwell in his *Palatine Anthology*. After describing the unfulfilled desire of octogenarians Lord and Lady Lathom to have a child, it includes the lines

...And in Tarlesco wood an egle had a nest,
With her three farye byrdes that were even ready fligge,
She brought to them a goodly boy, yonge and bigge,
Swadled and cladde in a mantle of Scarclette.
Lord Lathum this hearing, for none age did lette,
But to his wood of Tarlesco he rod apace,
And fownd the babe preserved by Gods greate grace,
Nort withstanding uncovered was his face,
Yeat not devoured nor hurte in any place.
The lord made the fayre babe downe to be fetched,
From daunger of the egles hyt dispatched,
Brought him to hys lady at Lathum Hall,
Tooke it as theire owne, and thanked God of all
It was unchristened it seemed out of doubte,
For saulte was bownd at his necke in a linnen cloute,
They christened hit and named it Oskell,
And made yt theire heyre after them to dwell... (Halliwell 1850: 216–18)

Other accounts of the story place the action in a park rather than in Tarlescough Wood and tell a more elaborate story. Sir Thomas Lathum was desperate for a son and heir after twelve years of marriage produced only a daughter. When his mistress gave birth to a boy, Oskatell, he devised a scheme whereby his wife might willingly adopt the boy and yet remain ignorant of the circumstances surrounding his birth. Sir Thomas arranged for the baby to be laid early one morning at the foot of a tall tree in the park. Then, as he and his wife neared the tree, Sir Thomas heard a cry and 'discovered' the baby. His wife consented to adopt Oskatell and the eagle and child later became part of the family crest (Seacombe 1793: 49–57; Roby 1928: 89–117; Draper 1864: 17). There is, however, an even more fanciful version of this story. It relates how, during English/Irish wars, the Irish queen fled into the wilderness where she gave birth to a son and a daughter. Both twins were abducted: the girl was kept in Ireland with the fairies but the son was taken by an eagle which flew away to England to Lathom Park. Here, Lord Lathom heard its cry, instructed the servants to bring the child to him and later adopted the infant (Harland and Wilkinson [eds.] 1973: 259–60).

The Lathom legend is not unique: other landed families can recite traditions akin to those recited above and there is even an example that supposedly dates from the time of King Alfred (Draper 1864: 18–19; Harland and Wilkinson [eds.] 1973: 259–60). Discovering a baby in this way was an accepted means of explaining the succession of a bastard son, for it allowed a family's estates to remain intact. Bagley wondered, though, whether Sir Thomas Lathom had need of this device unless all three sons mentioned in his will were illegitimate (Bagley 1985: 3).

In complete contrast to most of the myths and legends of Martin Mere, the traditions of lights shining out across Martin Mere from Martin Hall, Holmeswood Hall and Berry House Farm are almost certainly factual. These lights were concerned with the need to guide fishermen and others out on the mere at night to a dry landfall and are discussed in Chapter 6.

CHAPTER SIX

Managing the Fen

Audrey Coney

This chapter examines the fenland economy of Martin Mere from medieval times until about 1697, when the lake was drained. In addition, it deals briefly with the way the land was used in the eighteenth century. That exploitation of the fenland products of Martin Mere has its roots in prehistoric times is evident from the spearheads, axes and other artefacts recovered from the lake basin and its surrounding area (see Chapter 5). More precise evidence for how the lake's resources were managed, however, survives mainly in documents dating from the mid-fourteenth century to the early eighteenth century. Most of these sources owe their origin to disagreement among local manorial lords over their lacustrine bounds. They provide a wealth of information on how the mere was divided into fisheries and the way its economy was organised. In fact, it is probably true to say that, had there been no discord, our knowledge of Martin Mere from the fourteenth century to the drainage operations of the 1690s would be extremely limited. It seems ironic, though, that the best evidence for fenland management derives, not from the time when the lake was in being, but from the immediate post-drainage era. The need to delineate township boundaries across the newly drained land led to discord among local manorial lords, who failed to agree on where these divisions should lie. The result was litigation, and reference has already been made in Chapter 4 to the proceedings of a case heard in the Palatine Court of Lancaster in the early eighteenth century. This action was brought by Robert Scarisbrick and the Earl of Derby against the other landowners who, like them, had held portions of the lake shore. It produced a corpus of documentary material that is invaluable for understanding life in these wetlands. Of special importance are the statements of witnesses taken at the Wheat Sheaf Hotel in Ormskirk on 19 May 1714 and the ensuing solicitors' briefs (LRO, DDSc 143/23). Although these witnesses could portray in detail only the final administration of this wetland, they were people with first-hand knowledge of the resources of the undrained mere. Their way of life was born of several centuries of experience and, in its fundamental characteristics, surely reflects much older practices.

Boundaries in the mere

In the early fourteenth century the mere and its outlet into the Wyke were fished in common, which meant that fishermen could work in any part of the lake. The situation is clarified by a case heard at Preston in 1353 when Richard Aughton, manorial lord of North Meols, brought two Rufford fishermen before the Justices of Pleas. Aughton claimed that the fishermen had been catching bream in the Wyke, an area he regarded as his property. The defendants, on the other hand, pleaded that the Wyke was part of the mere and consequently should be fished as undivided territory. They were acquitted after their plea was upheld (TNA, DL 37/3). Manorial lords were in the habit of leasing their fishing to local people, but their rights and those of their fishermen to fish in any part of the mere ceased with the appearance of separate fisheries. Even in the first half of the fourteenth century, the prior and convent of Burscough may have viewed waters lapping part of the Burscough shore as belonging to them: in their lease of the island of Blakenase, the area is described as lying in *their* water of Martin Mere (Webb 1970: 72–73). As noted in Chapter 3, Blakenase was an island in the early fifteenth century, but by the time that the lake was drained, it lay on the brink of the mere (LRO, DDSc 143/23). Apportionment of the lake was perhaps a gradual process but may have been complete by the end of medieval times. Separate fisheries had long been the norm by the time that the lake was drained in the 1690s. In effect, the fisheries were extensions of township boundaries across the waters of the lake: segments of the mere to which portions of shoreline were attached. The right to a particular stretch of water was vested in the lord who held its land boundary. By contrast, in Windermere, the ownership of the shoreline had no bearing at all on adjacent fishing rights (Kipling 1972: 174–75).

The Scarisbricks of Scarisbrick were particularly fortunate in their share of the lake. Not only did their township incorporate by far the longest length of lakeside, but its waters also provided a particularly good habitat for fish. When Robert Scarisbrick drew the sketch map of Martin Mere reproduced in Fig. 6.1, he outlined his total fishing area, and in addition provided several locations for places that will be mentioned in the text below (see also Figs. 4.5, 4.6a, b, and 5.1). Fishing conditions were also good in the smaller Burscough fishery possessed initially by Burscough Priory and later by the Earls of Derby. Scarisbrick and Burscough waters occupied the southern portion of the lake, an area described in the eighteenth century as 'the deeper side and stocked with reeds and more Comodious for Fishing' (LRO, DDSc 143/23). Scarisbrick waters included Great Peel and Wet Holsome islands, while Burscough's territory contained Little Peel island and, until it became attached to the mainland, Blakenase. Waters lapping the shores of North Meols, Tarleton and Rufford were less favourable. There were no islands in these waters to provide extra resources. The shores of Rufford and the Holmeswood part of Tarleton were perhaps the least favourable of all. This was the shallowest part of the lake and 'having no Cover for fish' had little value (LRO, DDSc 143/23).

Because the right to an individual fishery was the prerogative of whoever held its shoreline, it was rare to find any part of the water in multiple possession. One exception was the short stretch of water that once separated Blakenase island from the edge of the lake. Another was the Mean Water against the Dohile pasture in Burscough. The first of these anomalies resulted from early-fifteenth-century disagreement between the prior of Burscough and Nicholas Hesketh of Rufford over boundaries across the mere and adjacent mosses. The ensuing award set the mossland divide between *Byrchynschaw* and the highway. Although it also decreed that the *pelus* (Little Peel island) and the island of Blakenase should be priory property, the water between Blakenase and *Byrchynschaw* was to be fished in common by both parties (Webb 1970: 225). Medieval dispute also lay behind the dual occupancy of the Mean

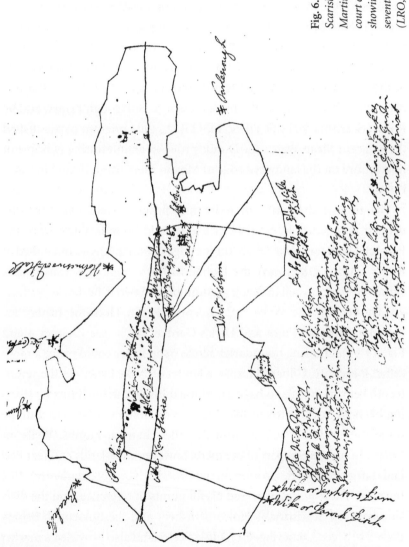

Fig. 6.1 Robert
Scarisbrick's sketch map of
Martin Mere, drawn for the
court case of 1714 and
showing the total area of his
seventeenth-century fishery
(LRO, DDSc 143/23).

Water. In this instance the parties involved were Burscough Priory and the Scarisbricks of Scarisbrick. During early medieval times a long tract of intercommoned pasture lay between the townships of Burscough and Scarisbrick. By the time that township boundaries through this pasture were set by arbitration in 1395, however, almost all this land had been enclosed. The exception was an area of moor, meadow and pasture lying between *Blakelach* and Martin Mere, which was to remain in common for pasturing by the priory and its successors and by the lords of Scarisbrick and their successors (Webb 1970: 64–65, 108–10). This seems to be the area known in the seventeenth century as the Dohile. It was intercommoned by the Earl of Derby, successor to Burscough Priory, and by Robert Scarisbrick (LRO, DDSc 143/23). As the same two parties fished the adjacent Mean Water, the Dohile provides an interesting example of how tenure on the landward edge of Martin Mere was reflected in water rights.

The terrestrial bounds of individual fisheries were normally well defined. For example, Scarisbrick's long land boundary ran from the Parrock Ditch, or Wyke Ditch, on the edge of North Meols and ended at Dick's Garden Ditch near the Dohile in Burscough. But Scarisbrick's shoreline was unusual in that it accommodated two fisheries. Wyke fishery lay betwixt the Wyke and Greening Point. Holsome fishery lay between Greening Point and Dick's Garden Ditch (see Chapter 4 and Fig. 6.1). Delineating boundaries across open water could prove a more difficult exercise. Gilbert Sumner, a tenant of Wyke fishery in the seventeenth century, seems to have ascertained his lacustrine limits by steering his boat northwards in the direction of Holmeswood Hall until he came to the deeper water known as the Channel, Lumbs, Wells, or Deeps. In the eastern part of the mere, however, the islands of Great Peel and Little Peel were prominent landmarks lying conveniently close together. These places provided useful points of reference, and the division between Scarisbrick's Holsome fishery and the Burscough fishery passed between them (Fig. 6.1). Little Peel island also provided a marker for the boundary between Burscough and Rufford, which followed a line of sight from Blakenase to Little Peel (Fig. 4.6). One tenant who leased the Burscough fishery used the distant steeple of North Meols church as an additional alignment. In the northern portion of the mere a more complicated procedure defined the watery division between Burscough and Scarisbrick and between Rufford and Holmeswood. This boundary was located by looking south towards the steeple of Halsall church from Cookson's house, on the division between Holmes in Tarleton and Holmeswood in Rufford, and by sailing into the mere until the old mill at Rufford in the east aligned with Copples Dyke (LRO, DDSc 143/23).

Violation, or perceived violation, of water territory could have serious consequences. This fact is well illustrated by legal action brought against Sir Thomas Hesketh of Rufford by Henry Bannister, manorial lord of Holmes, and his tenant, John Hunter (TNA, DL3/74). The plaintiffs declared that fishermen from Holmes were fishing peaceably in their own waters on 15 March 1558, when they were attacked by a gang of four men sent by Sir Thomas Hesketh. It seems that these four men accused Bannister's men of fishing in waters lapping Hesketh's estates, and their subsequent assault left the Holmes fishermen so 'stryken' that they were unable to carry their net home. The following day, after Henry Bannister sent Hunter and others to fetch this net, they were involved in a further assault involving a different band of Hesketh's men. Walking staffs were apparently the principal weaponry and Hunter and some of his opponents were injured. Bannister's fishermen later denied that they had fished in waters adjoining Sir Thomas Hesketh's lands, while Sir Thomas himself denied any personal involvement at all. He admitted only to hearing that the alleged attackers were fishing in waters near his demesne. Litigation usually generates conflicting evidence and this example is no exception. The case does, however, provide a further demonstration of how individual lacustrine territories were well known to local people and how their position was governed by the shoreline. One witness remembered how old men had several times pointed out the part of the mere that belonged to Henry Bannister. Another stated that Sir Thomas's part of the mere lay against his (Sir Thomas's) lands.

Animosity between Bannister and Hesketh portrays the violent face of Martin Mere. The same two people were locked in dispute over possession of a close of land near the mere in Holmes. Bannister was apparently staking his claim there when he was set upon by seven of Hesketh's men. In fear of his life, he jumped into a boat on the mere and rowed away. His attackers allowed him to land again only after he undertook to provide them with a net worth 10s. 0d. (Farrer 1903: 117).

Waters belonging to Henry Bannister and Thomas Hesketh were again a source of contention in 1561. It was eventually agreed that Bannister should fish to the north-west of the 'Lum', one of the alternative names for the Old Channel, and that Hesketh should fish to the east. The 'Lum' was defined as that part of the water where the

> windy mill of Rufforth shall seeme and appear to such as shall be upon the water to stand opose it directly amend and treat upon head against the East poynt of a hill called Wrightington Hill att a certain House called dwery House in the East part of the said water, and in like manner directly opose it and straight a gainst a certain other place called the faren Lee in the west part, and that the steeple of the Parish of Halsale in the south part of the said water shall be likewise seen and appear at the same place to be and stand directly opposit and head upon head and against a certain Cross situated and standing att the north end of the pale of the park within Tarlton called the holmes Park and so butting directly upon the tree or saplin standing in the East part of a Certain yard or Garden now in the holdinge of Abraham in the north holmes. (LRO, DDSc 19/10)

The Heskeths continued to assert their authority over trespass in their waters into the seventeenth century. When Gilbert Sumner strayed into waters below their Holmeswood demesne, Hesketh's servants immediately confiscated his fishing tackle. So why did members of this family claim in the eighteenth-century court case (LRO, DDSc 143/23) that their ancestors, and others by their leave, usually fished upon any part of the mere without disturbance and that other proprietors had the same liberty? The reasons are not hard to find. First, waters in the Holmeswood–Rufford sectors of the lake were the least profitable for fishing. Second, after the lake was drained, sandy soils in this part of the lake basin would be regarded as less fertile for agriculture than organic muds further to the south.

The produce of the fen

The rhythm of fenland seasons revolved around fishing, fowling, egg-collecting, gathering rushes, reeds and wood, cutting turf, and grazing animals. The daily life of those who exploited the resources of Martin Mere was very similar to that followed in the fens of East Anglia and in the Somerset Levels (Darby 1940; Ravensdale 1981; Williams 1970).

Martin Mere's most important resource was its abundance of fresh-water fish. This was the view of those who held the fishing rights at the time that the mere was drained. The mere, they said, was profitable only as a fishery (LRO, DDSc 143/23). Tight control of fishing was necessary to conserve the mere's stocks of pike, perch, roach, bream and eels. There were basically two sorts of fisherman on Martin Mere: the professional who used specialised equipment; and the casual angler with his rod, line and little hand-nets, who was regarded as fishing for pleasure. The wide-ranging forays by the Heskeths of Rufford and their tenants seem mostly, though not totally, to fall into the latter classification. Angling was transient and posed little threat to fish stocks. It was normally tolerated provided permission was first obtained. Professional fishing tackle was in a different category. This equipment had larger capacity, lay out all night and caught far greater quantities of fish. The stand taken against unlicensed professional fishing on Martin Mere has a parallel in the considerably smaller White Otter Mere in nearby Halsall. One seventeenth-century tenant of this fishery, a man named Jump, was said to deny 'scarce anybody liberty of fishing with rod and line for pleasure and diversion', but would not allow anyone to lay in night nets and the like because of the damage to fish stocks that might occur (LRO, DDSc 143/23). Edward Scarisbrick's late-sixteenth-century inventory itemises equipment used by his lessee fishermen (LRO, WCW Edward Scarisbrick, 1599):

xvij bowe nettes for the meyre [mere] in Thomas Yates kepeinge	vjs
The same Thomas xij pyke nettes other	vjs
ij boats with a sayle in his kepeinge also	xxiijs iiijd
John Sumner hath xxiiij bow nettes and xij pyke nettes	xiiijs
He hath also ij boates with one sayle & ij heare teythers [hair tethers]	lxiiijs iiijd
a greate nett for the meyre	xxs

The inclusion of boats and tackle among Edward Scarisbrick's moveable goods demonstrates that these articles were viewed as his property. Scarisbrick township was unusual in that there were two fishermen with four boats between them, but this was because there were two fisheries in these waters. Elsewhere, one boat was usually the norm. A fisherman's boat was obviously a vital part of his equipment, and the tenant of the Earl of Derby's Burscough fishery would have been devastated when in April 1693 the boat was stolen from its boathouse. John Sumner was paid 4s. 0d. by the Burscough bailiff 'for a Boate and for himselfe and four others to assist in seekinge the Earles Boat at Martin Meer, the Boat house being broke upen and the said Earles boat taken away' (LRO, DDK 1553/1). This boathouse gave its name to the main drainage channel for the Burscough portion of Martin Mere and may have stood for some time after the mere was drained. The building continued in local memory into the nineteenth century: only the width of a lane then separated the field called Boat House Hey from the former lake shore (LRO, DRL 1/7; see Chapter 5).

Martin Mere's fishing equipment also included long lines, 'pyches' and 'engines for catching fish' (LRO, DDSc 143/23). The 'pyches' were doubtless akin to the 'putts' and 'putchers' in use on the River Severn. These were wicker fish-traps which tapered from a wide mouth to a narrow tail. Similar traps, measuring six to seven feet at their greatest extent, were used on the bed of the River Dee in Cheshire where they were joined together in rows (*Notes and Queries*, vol. 164, Jan.–July 1933: 154, 191, 213, 267, 303; *Country Life*, 1 October 1904: 473–75). Those in use in Martin Mere may have been more similar to the medieval fish-traps shown in Colour Plate 6.1 (following p. 80). Fish-traps were also widely used across Europe. The 60 putchers still used to catch salmon at a fishery on the Severn in the 1990s were made from willow and bamboo and placed in two ranks near a handmade weir of hazel rods (*Weekend Telegraph*, 9 August 1995). Willow has long been used in fish-trap construction. It survives immersion in water for a considerable length of time (Bond 1988: 84). Some of the fishing tackle used on Martin Mere occasionally caught mammals as well as fish, and one witness in the eighteenth-century court case remembered the time that he found a great quantity of fish and a strangled otter in his nets around Great Peel. These nets were probably seine nets strung out into shallow waters surrounding the island. Nets were also used in the Old Channel, the deepest part of the mere (up to three yards deep in places), and situated near to where the Sluice now flows (Plate 6.2). Fishermen ascertained the position of this channel by testing for depth with their oars. 'Long lines' were also in use in this part of the mere. They were cast according to wind direction, but were usually laid east to west and aligned on North Meols mill. Made of hemp, these lines measured up to 60 yards in length and were kept on the surface by 'corks' made from bulrushes, which also served as markers. Hooked 'short lines' were attached at intervals and dangled down to the bottom of the lake. This equipment stayed in position overnight and was used for catching eels. The Old Channel was regarded as the best place for eel fishing in the whole of Martin Mere (LRO, DDSc 143/23).

Differing fishing conditions within the lake resulted in a variety of rents and practices. For example, Robert Hesketh, seventeenth-century manorial lord of North Meols, adopted a rather lethargic attitude to the lake's resources. The fact that greater quantities of saltwater fish were

Plate 6.2 *The Sluice.*

readily available to him on the opposite side of North Meols was perhaps a contributory factor. Nevertheless, Hesketh often went out on the lake himself and gave part of the catch to whoever assisted him. Occasionally, one of his servants went fishing instead. There was a time, however, when John Sumner paid a rent of 8s. 0d. for the right to fish in North Meols waters. He also paid 5s. 0d. for the fishery of Holmes. This was another fishery for which a money rent was not always demanded. One fisherman, a man named Breckell, initially paid rent to his manorial lord. But the fishing was poor and it was eventually agreed that, when pike or other valuable fish were caught, Breckell would present them to his landlord. The Bannisters of Holmes did not extend such largesse to every tenant fisherman. When Gilbert Sumner fell into arrears with his rent, Bannister ordered his steward to seize both boat and tackle.

Render in kind was extremely unusual in seventeenth-century Lancashire, but was a feature of certain fisheries in Martin Mere. For example, in 1669, Thomas Abraham, or Abram, paid an annual rent of 35s. 0d., and renders of thirty pike or 2s. 6d. for each fish not provided, and 30 pounds weight of eels. He received in return a messuage, Scarisbrick's profitable Holsome fishery, and the island of 'Weete houlsome' (Wet Holsome). Abram also agreed to keep and maintain a fishing boat, and to bring the pike 'quicke and alive' to Scarisbrick Hall at or before the feast of St Martin the Bishop in winter (11 November). Landlord James Scarisbrick was clearly keen to ensure that his pike arrived in a fresh condition. They would require careful handling, for these fish have a well-deserved reputation for ferocity and part of Holsome fishery was noted for their presence: its offshore bounds began at the Pike Lake (LRO, DDSc 143/23). The choice of Martinmas as the date for this pike render is intriguing: this feast marks the centre point of the annual slaughter of animals that could not be fed through the winter. Martinmas became an occasion for feasting because this was the last occasion when unsalted meat would be eaten until spring (Hutton 1997: 386). Perhaps pike were consumed as part of the festivities at Scarisbrick. Perhaps it was merely convenient that they should be salted down at the same time as other meat. Perhaps it was a way of conserving fish stocks. The pike render for

Holsome fishery remained the same when John Sumner was tenant. He, however, rendered only six pounds' weight of eels.

Rent in kind was also a feature of the seventeenth-century Burscough fishery leased by James Barton. Barton paid the ancient yearly rent of eight pike or 2s. 6d. in lieu, and an additional 30s. 0d. for a messuage and tenement in Tarlescough near the lake shore (LRO, DDSc 143/23). In fact, the bailiff's account for 1693–94 confirms that his eight fish were sent to Knowsley and Lathom for the Earl of Derby's consumption (LRO, DDK 1553/1). When the earl's sixteenth-century predecessors, Burscough Priory, possessed this fishery salted fish were kept in a fish-house (TNA, DL4 11/36). Although neither this building's location nor its appearance is known, the fishhouse belonging to the Abbot of Glastonbury at Meare provides a comparison (Coles and Coles 1986: Plate 6 following p. 88). This stone building lay close to the water's edge and stood two storeys high; fish were salted and stored on the ground floor (Bond 1988: 82). Martin Mere's fish renders were considerably less than those from tenant fishermen in the Somerset Levels and in the Fens: the Abbot of Glastonbury received 7,000 eels annually from both Clewer and Martinsey; two Wisbech fishermen of the Abbot of Ely rendered 14,000 eels annually (Darby 1940: 19; Williams 1970: 26; Bond 1988: 81).

The men who made a living from Martin Mere frequently worked more than one fishery: for example, fisherman Breckell leased the rights to both Holmes and North Meols waters; Edward Hesketh was tenant of Scarisbrick and Burscough fisheries for a time; and John Sumner ten-anted virtually every fishery. What is difficult to ascertain, though, is to what extent men such as Sumner held different fisheries concurrently. Fishing could also be a family affair. For instance, Gilbert and John Sumner were apparently father and son. Both took leases of the Scaris-brick fisheries and may even have fished these waters together for a time. They were probably descended from the John Sumner who was fisher-man for Edward Scarisbrick at the end of the sixteenth century (LRO, DDSc 143/23; WCW Edward Scarisbrick, 1599). Setting out and retriev-ing fishing tackle could be demanding tasks and fishermen sometimes sought assistance from family and friends. Edward Hesketh and his wife worked together as a team in casting nets, laying lines and examining and reclaiming equipment. James Worthington, the Scarisbrick steward, often accompanied James Barton in Burscough waters and Thomas Abram enlisted extra help whenever he required an additional pair of hands. One of Abram's helpers, William Hulme, went out on the mere 'sometimes for hire and sometimes for pleasure'. He held the fishing boat steady while the long lines used for catching eels were 'shot' in the channel, and helped to cast the nets and other tackle used for catching pike and other fish. On occasions, he even delivered the pike render to Scarisbrick Hall. After Abram's death, his widow continued to lease the fishery and sometimes employed Hulme to set out equipment. When Abram's eventual successor also died, Hulme helped his widow 'fish the year out'. There is also some evidence for tenants selling their interests in a lease or sub-letting their fisheries. For example, Edward Hesketh transferred his interest in the Burscough fishery to James Barton. When Barton later farmed out his rights in these waters to John Sumner for 40s. 0d. annually, Sumner provided the pike render for the Earl of Derby (LRO, DDSc 143/23).

Casting nets and laying lines at night could be a hazardous exercise, and any fisherman out on Martin Mere in fading light would welcome illumination to guide him home. There are, in fact, local traditions of lights shining out across the lake's waters from Holmeswood Hall (Plate 5.6), Martin Hall (Plate 5.7) and Great Peel island. While these traditions often state that the lights' purpose was to guide recusants to Mass in these secluded places, lonely fisherman out on the dark mere would find their beams equally welcome. Lights shining over the wetland have a parallel in Freiston near Boston in Lincolnshire, where the Marine Hotel burned an oil lamp in its landing window to guide wildfowlers back from the marshes (Janet Withersby pers. comm.). It is a feature of the traditions of Martin Mere that its guiding lights are associated with tall or conspicuous buildings. Holmeswood Hall occupies an elevated position on the bank of the mere in Holmeswood and overlooks a curve of woodland below a steep wave-cut cliff (see Colour Plate 6.3 following p. 80). This crenellated tower house (Plate 5.6) measures 25 ft × 23 ft (7.6 m × 6.9 m) externally and was formerly a lodge of the Heskeths of Rufford. A stone set in the east wall displays the initials of Thomas

Hesketh and the date 1568, and may derive from an earlier construction: a century ago Farrer regarded the present building as relatively modern (Farrer and Brownbill [eds.] 1906–14: VI [1911], 116–17). Dating Holmeswood Hall, however, is not an easy task. The brick walls are rendered, but they are two feet thick and reported to be infilled with brick rubble. They perhaps provide a local example of the early use of brick at a time when the properties of this material were not fully understood.

Today, Berry House Farm is the principal house on the former Great Peel island and the tradition of a guiding light shining out across the mere was associated with its barn. But this is a post-drainage feature, so perhaps the tradition was transferred from a much earlier building. The case for and against a tower house on Great Peel island was set out in the previous chapter.

A particularly bright light would be needed to reach the mere from Martin Hall in Burscough (Plate 5.7). This place lay half a mile from the lake shore. There is no doubt, though, that the building itself would be visible from the water, as it was sited at about 22 m OD whereas the edge of the old lake barely touched 2 m. The present Martin Hall was built in the 1960s. Its predecessor was a brick building with three distinct phases of construction. The oldest part was built of brick, contained mullion windows, stone copings and quoins, and was three storeys high. Cheetham's measurements for this part of the building indicate that the height of the end gables was 38 ft (11.5 m), the width of the walls was 2 ft (61 cm) and external dimensions were 26 ft × 24 ft (7.9 m × 6.3 m). Martin Hall was, therefore, just slightly larger than Holmeswood's tower house and, like that construction, almost square in plan. Cheetham dated the oldest part of Martin Hall to the late sixteenth century. He also recorded the tradition that its topmost room served as both chapel and lighthouse, 'a lamp being kept burning in one of the windows on the north side'. In support of this tradition, Cheetham noted the presence of windows on the north elevation facing the lake and their absence from the south wall (Cheetham 1912). The predecessor to this late-Tudor Martin Hall was a moated and timber-framed grange of Burscough Priory (LRO, DRL 1/7; TNA, DL29 158/30).

Apart from the fisheries, the most valuable asset of Martin Mere was the substantial wildfowl population. Wildfowling and egg-collecting were closely regulated and officially restricted to landlord and tenant. Yet poaching was a constant problem. In the eighteenth-century court case John Sumner and Henry Halsall both recalled how they used to go to Great Peel on Sundays and holidays to help in keeping poachers at bay, and so prevent nesting birds being disturbed. The main culprits were people coming by boat from Tarlescough in Burscough. Lessee fishermen had the right to take birds and eggs in their own territory, and Mary Hesketh recalled how her husband took all the wildfowl that he could catch and then disposed of it to his own use (LRO, DDSc 132/23). Some wildfowl from the mere were despatched to the Earl of Derby's household. In July 1693 the bailiff paid Edward Lawson 6s. 8d. for nine wild ducks and a hen, and for carrying them from Burscough to Knowsley. A year later John Sumner received 5s. 0d. for four live young wild geese and for the carriage of them from Scarisbrick to Knowsley (LRO, DDK 1553/1). Eighteenth-century court case records mention only geese, ducks and swans, but many other types of bird would have nested on the islands and around the mere's fringe (see Chapter 8). Wildfowl on Martin Mere were often caught in 'grins' – snares with running nooses – but one poignant account describes a method of catching nesting swans. As the wildfowlers approached, the adult swans swam away with their young either tucked under their wings or carried on their backs. The swans grew tired after being chased for some time, dropped their cygnets and became easy prey for their pursuers. The mute swan (see Colour Plate 6.4 following p. 80) had a favourite nesting place at Grutty Ginnell near Greening Point in Scarisbrick (LRO, DDSc 143/23).

The reeds that grew in the shallows of the mere (see Colour Plate 6.5 following p. 80) provided cover for fish, sanctuary for wildfowl and a supplementary income for tenants. Mary Hesketh described how she could earn 10s. 0d. a day by harvesting five bunches of reeds at 2s. 0d. per bunch or 3d. per hundred (LRO, DDSc 143/23). This suggests that there were 800 reed stems in every bunch. That being so, a day's work in cold, wet and windy reedbeds involved cutting 3000 stems and Plate 6.6 illustrates just how unpleasant this task could be. Water-reeds were abundant along the Scarisbrick shore and also around Little Peel island in Burscough waters. The latter even had the alternative name of Reedy Peel. The right to its reeds is mentioned in James Barton's lease of 23 March 1685 (LRO, DDSc 143/23). Because reeds were used as a thatching material, local thatchers doubtless watched the drainage of Martin Mere and adjacent wetlands with concern. Reed thatch is extremely durable, and can last for 75 years compared to 25 years for wheat straw. In the sixteenth century North Meols reed was supplied to John Aughton of Ormskirk to 'thacke his berne' and the name 'Le Thak' occurs in connection with a rood of marshland in Burscough (Farrer 1903: 35–36; TNA, DL 43/4/6A; DL 43/4/6B; DL 29/158/11).

In order to maintain his premises, fisherman Thomas Abram had the right to cut rushes and to dig stubs, roots, bushes, shrubs and underwood on Wet Holsome. Abram doubtless found the pliable stems of the moisture-loving willow useful for baskets and fish-traps. Damp island soils provided ideal conditions for willow and alder and also supplied an underground source of dead timber. Great quantities of the latter were dug on Great Peel. The men who made a living from exploiting this fen

Plate 6.6 *Harvesting the reeds in the Fens (photograph by Philip Withersby).*

referred to these buried roots, trunks and branches as 'stooks' or 'moss-wood' (LRO, DDSc 143/23). These ancient trees grew in the prehistoric wildwood. Their wood is hard, burns with a clear, bright flame and was formerly used for both torch and firewood (Camden 1971: 747). In his travels through eighteenth-century Lancashire, Defoe was intrigued by the 'antient Fir Trees' found within the mosses. He believed that 'Nature [...] has been guided to produce Trees here under Ground, as she does in other Places above Ground'. He also records that they were 'very full of Turpentine' (Defoe 1927: 669–700).

Those tenants with islands in their fisheries had the additional bene-fit of grazing and Colour Plate 6.7 (following p. 80), taken a few years ago, shows horses on the former island of Little Peel. John Sumner often cut grass for his horses on Great Peel and there are several references to graz-ing on Wet Holsome. Animals were either ferried across to the latter place or driven through the half-mile stretch of water that separated this island from the Scarisbrick shore. The Scarisbricks and their lessee ten-ants frequently pastured colts and calves on Wet Holsome and, provided that permission was obtained, tenants could sub-let their grazing to other pastoral farmers. Consequently, Mary Hesketh recalled how she and her husband received 30s. 0d. for 'score' of cattle on this island (LRO, DDSc 143/23). The word 'score' was often used of an area of stinted pasture, i.e. a pasture where the number of animals was strictly limited (Wright [ed.] 1898–1905: V [1904], 259). On Wet Holsome, three weaning calves were equal to one beastgate and one beastgate was worth 10s. 0d. In all probability the cattle that grazed these lush island pastures were black Lancashire longhorns – large beasts with wide-spreading horns. They fattened rapidly, produced excellent cheese and made good draught animals (Camden 1971: 787; Kerridge 1967: 316).

The islands of Martin Mere could, however, support only a limited amount of pasture. Far more extensive were lakeside mosslands provid-ing grazing and turbary, and meadows supplying hay for winter fodder. The improvement of these places was a long and gradual affair. On the other hand, certain closes abutting Martin Mere were several centuries old by the time that the lake was drained. For example, the enclosed Holmeswood demesne on the northern shore is deemed to be a medieval landscape feature, and fifteenth-century Polehey and Gyliot Meadow in Scarisbrick, together with sixteenth-century Merehey in Burscough, have already been mentioned in Chapter 5. The dates when these places were first enclosed is not known. The priory's enclosure of the Merehey, though, probably followed hard on the heels of the agreement of 1303, whereby the prior and Gilbert de Scarisbrick could each reclaim forty acres or more on either side of their intercommoned mossland (Webb 1970: 64).

When improvement affected areas of intercommoning or ill-determined township bounds, however, territorial dispute was rarely far behind. The Burscough/Scarisbrick boundary was a continuing source of disagreement in the thirteenth and fourteenth centuries (Webb 1970: 63–65; 221–24). Furthermore, the line of Burscough's boundary with Rufford was still being disputed in the eighteenth century. The early-fifteenth-century award that set the lacustrine limits of the prior of Burscough and Nicholas Hesketh of Rufford had also defined the township boundary over adjoining mossland. This new division led from the mere to a marker in the middle of *Byrchynshaw* and thence to another marker on the highway between *Bewdissherd* (in Lathom) and Rufford (Webb 1970: 225). When this mossland divide was again subject to dispute in the seventeenth century (see for example LRO, DDK 128/3; DDHe 62/2, 64/12) the line claimed by Rufford ran slightly west of the medieval division. It is clear from a map drawn up at about the time of this dispute that enclosed lands of both townships were creeping towards the boundary, that much still remained to be improved, and that parts of the boundary area were particularly wet. Between 'Berkinshaw' (earlier *Byrchynshaw*) and Martin Mere, the line passed the White Strinds; the Sinkfall; the place where the 'watter' went under and over the ground; the Little Mere or Black Pools; and Copple Ditch, 'Emptying itself into the Mear' (Fig. 6.2; LRO, DDHe 122/1). The Burscough/Rufford township divide underwent further slight adjustment about 1720 (LRO, DDO 5/2).

Burscough Moss and Tarlescough Moss were still only partly improved in the 1750s. The turf of Tarlescough Moss was deemed to be superior to that of Burscough Moss, but only the three farms of Tarle-

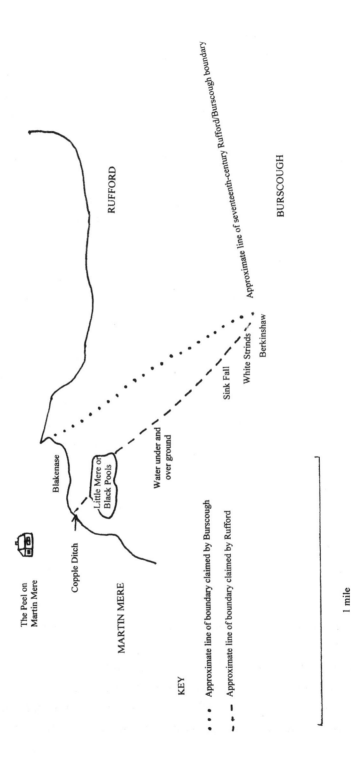

The Peel on
Martin Mere

Copple Ditch

Blakenase

MARTIN MERE

RUFFORD

Little Mere or
Black Pools

Water under and
over ground

Sink Fall

White Strinds

Berkinshaw

Approximate line of seventeenth-century Rufford/Burscough boundary

BURSCOUGH

KEY

• • •   Approximate line of boundary claimed by Burscough

– – –   Approximate line of boundary claimed by Rufford

1 mile

Fig. 6.2 *Map showing minor place-names on the late seventeenth-century township divide between Burscough and Rufford, based on LRO, DDHe 122/1.*

scough had right of turbary in the former place (LRO, DDO 5/2). This arrangement cannot, however, be older than the creation of Tarlescough hamlet in the sixteenth century (see below). Turf was the principal fuel in those townships in the Lancashire Plain where mossland was extensive, and carting turves was often one of the boonworks due from tenants. For example, the 'leadinge of two sufficient Taske of Turves' or payment of 2s. 0d. was an obligation included by James Scarisbrick in his lease to Edward Sumpner, husbandman, in 1668. Turf may have been an abundant commodity but its exploitation was carefully regulated. The township officers known as moss reeves were expected to ensure that the commons were not grazed by animals from other townships and that turf rooms (individual peat-cutting areas) were allocated for, and correctly used by, local inhabitants (LRO, DDO 5/20). In Scarisbrick in 1672 Thomas Wright was fined for laying his turf on Henry Blundell's 'roome' without his consent; Richard Holme was fined for delving a new 'roome' without consent; and several tenants were before the manor court for not 'mendinge' the moss when appointed to do so by township officers (LRO, DDSc 10/23). Grazing animals could also damage peat-cutting areas. For instance, an order in the Scarisbrick manor court in 1713 charged the moss reeves with ensuring that no tenant allowed his animals to trample the turves down. In 1703 the same court had ordered that no inhabitant was to turn out cattle or sheep into the turf moss between 1 May and 25 July unless 'they keep a tenter to keep them out of the turves' (LRO, PR 2816/1). This indicates that cutting peat in Scarisbrick took place when the peaty soils were drying out in late spring and high summer. Local custom may have restricted the activity to that particular time of year, but undrained organic soils surrounding Martin Mere would be impossible to dig in the wetter months. In Cumbria peat was cut in May and, as in Scarisbrick, May Day was the most common date from which digging was allowed (Winchester 2000: 128–29).

The mosslands around Martin Mere were conspicuous landscape features. For example, those in the north of Burscough in 1536 encompassed 100 acres (TNA, DL29 158/33), and eighteenth-century Ottersties Moss and Wood Moss in Scarisbrick were said to cover in excess of 150 acres and 200 acres respectively (Liverpool RO, 920 PLU 3). In fact, the true extent of these places could be considerably greater if these figures represent the large customary acre, which equalled more than twice the statute measurement. The improvement of common pasture and turbary could be traumatic for lord and tenant alike. For instance, when the Plumbe family tried to enclose the commons of Aughton, their efforts were thwarted by the freeholders for almost a century (Coney 1987). The Plumbes claimed manorial rights in Aughton but were freeholders in Scarisbrick. That being so, it is intriguing to find one of them, in the role of freeholder, earnestly opposing William Scarisbrick's enclosure of Scarisbrick commons. This improvement took place in the early 1740s and affected the greater part of the commons, including both Ottersties Moss and Wood Moss. The manorial lord, William Scarisbrick, had kept some of the newly enclosed land in his own hands and rented out the remainder to tenants. His freeholders strongly opposed this for they should, by rights, have been allotted shares in the newly enclosed ground. Consequently, in 1748 Plumbe of Aughton drew up a draft agreement on behalf of Scarisbrick freeholders. This document deplored the loss of the commons, and recorded how 'time out of mind' the charterers and inhabitants and their ancestors had enjoyed common rights of pasture and turbary for their own use and as occasion required. Enclosure was regarded by the freeholders as an invasion of property that lessened the value of their estates. It was their intention to employ one or two people to pull down the enclosures and lay open the commons again. They also resolved to fund, relative to the size of their estates, the costs of any suit that might ensue (Liverpool RO, 920 PLU 3). The question of what happened next requires further research.

Martin Mere's hay meadows were far less extensive than its pastures and turbaries. They were present, however, in certain places around the rim of the lake; in the vicinity of Long Meadow and Langleys Brook in Burscough; and within the Wyke in North Meols. Ownership of 12 acres of meadowland within the Wyke, the old western outlet of the mere, was under dispute during the 1550s. The tenant, William Stopford of Martin in Burscough, had leased this land from Thomas Gorsuch of Scarisbrick.

He now complained that a 'multytude' of men had cut his hay and that several days later another gang (his estimate suggests more than fifty persons) armed with swords, bucklers, daggers and so on had carried away a hundred loads of hay valued at £50. Other deponents were to put the number of men involved at no more than twenty; the number of carts at ten; and to say that while one person carried a sword, the others had pitchforks and rakes. The defendant in the case was John Bold, manorial lord of North Meols. He explained that the only implements carried were those used to mow the grass. He also declared that this was marshy ground and that he hired eight men to cut all the hay in one day while the weather was fair. It seems, though, that he lost the case (Farrer 1903: 34–36).

The need to manage meadowland is borne out by evidence given in a dispute concerning Long Meadow and Battleholme in Burscough. Portions of these meadows were included in a seventeenth-century grant of Martin Hall and demesne from the Earl of Derby to John Breres. Other portions were exploited by Burscough's tenants-at-will, who were accustomed to take hay from several parcels of land in Long Meadow and from two parcels in Battleholme. In 1622 it seems that they took the best of the crop. Breres complained that he had little return from the residue and described Long Meadow as barren and fruitless and worth only 5s. 0d. per acre. Long Meadow adjoined the mere but there were no defences against flooding and the area was often inundated by water from the lake. Ditches and watercourses were neither scoured nor cleaned and there were no gutters by which the water could drain away. Breres seems to have blamed the poor condition of Long Meadow on the fact that numerous tenants had interests there. Apparently, few tenants were inclined to make a concerted effort to improve fertility. Breres contrasted the condition of Long Meadow with his adjoining meadow which, it seems, was wholly in his hands. This was in a state of good husbandry, protected from the mere, and yielded 38s. 0d. to 40s. 0d. per acre.

Trees were another commodity in relatively short supply around Martin Mere by early modern times. That Robert Scarisbrick could show the 'Crow tree' as a marker on one of his sketch maps of the mere (see for example Fig. 4.5) indicates that woodland was less than plentiful along this part of the seventeenth-century shoreline (LRO, DDSc 143/23). There was, however, rather more woodland in earlier centuries in other places. The ancient woodlands around Holmeswood Hall and *Byrchynschaw* on the Burscough/Rufford boundary have already been mentioned (see Chapter 5), and Burscough's Walshaw Wood and Tarlescough Wood continued to be part of the mereside landscape until the sixteenth century. In fact, the hamlet of Tarlescough (Plate 5.5) owes its entire existence to the creation of three new farming units on land cleared of trees only after the dissolution of Burscough Priory (LRO, DDSc 143/23).

Depredation of the former monastic woodlands of Walshaw and Tarlescough began just a few years after the demise of the priory in 1536. At the Dissolution, Walshaw Wood had contained four acres of oaks, ash and underwood. Tarlescough Wood, twice this size, was composed of young oak saplings and underwood (TNA, DL29 158/33). Both were Crown property in 1543 when John Withington, keeper of the king's woods, complained that William Stopford, king's bailiff, had cut down Walshaw Wood, used the timber to build a new house, and created a new tenement on the demesne for his brother. Stopford had lived at Martin Hall, the former grange of Burscough Priory, since about 1539 and was said to have regarded the king's timber growing on the demesne as his property. He, in turn, charged Withington and others with a two-year period of woodland destruction. He said that Withington felled four score (80) trees to make a new house for himself while the old building was 'suffycyent and yet standyng'; added a new bay to his barn; and constructed a new 'downe dubbyng'. This was only the first of a long list of accusations of trees cleft, sawed into parts or boards, or used to make items such as barrels, axle-trees, spokes and even a kiln. Manorial tenants, of course, had the right to take wood for making implements and for house repair. Stopford himself said that when he first arrived at Martin Hall the house was in ruins and 'standyng apon proppes'. But the apparent scale of this woodland depletion seems far above what would normally be expected for 'housebote' and 'ploughbote'. In fact, some timber from Walshaw and Tarlescough went to people who were not even tenants of Burscough (TNA, DL29 158/30). This woodland never regenerated. Resentment on the part of the local community of the dissolution of the priory and of the new royal regime was perhaps a prime factor in its demise.

The felled timber was either carted away or loaded into boats moored on the Tarlescough shore and ferried across the mere. When Henry Smolt went to Tarlescough Wood to select a tree for new stocks for the township, he found two people felling and sawing wood there and three others loading wood onto boats moored at the lakeside. Over the two years prior to 1543 Mr Aughton of North Meols received six boatloads of sapling timber; Lawrence Ball of Blowick in North Meols four boatloads of timber; Hugh Abram of Holmes a boatload of cleft timber; and John Watkinson a boatload of sapling boles. Ellis Rimmer of Birkdale was sent two whole trees by boat (TNA, DL29 158/30). Martin Mere clearly provided a useful means of moving heavy goods. Indeed, it would have been easier to transport a heavy load across the lake than to traverse muddy and rutted local routeways. The condition of sixteenth- and seventeenth-century roads in Lancashire, and those across mossland in particular, often left much to be desired (Crosby 1998). The route from Ormskirk to North Meols over Ottersties Moss fell into this category. In the seventeenth century it was said to be so worn out and decayed that it was impassable in wintertime (LRO, DDSc 149/12).

This large-scale and apparently wanton destruction of the woods of Tarlescough and Walshaw is atypical of general economic practice in the area. Elsewhere, the abiding impression of how Martin Mere's resources were organised is one of controlled fenland management. This landscape was fully exploited, yet strictly regulated. Those who broke its code of conduct, be they tenant or manorial lord, could expect some kind of retribution. As far as the lake itself was concerned, its resources were available to only a few, the principal beneficiaries being the holders of the adjacent shoreline and their lessee fishermen. In reality, these resources filtered through to the wider community. Fish, fowl and eggs were sold at local markets and reeds provided thatch for homesteads and farm buildings. The islands in Martin Mere could provide only limited grazing, but meadows and mosslands surrounding the lake provided generations of tenant farmers with grazing, hay and turf.

Draining Martin Mere set in motion an ecological disaster for wildlife and the passing of a fenland way of life for lessee fishermen. History does not record what these fishermen felt about this, nor does it tell how the sudden depletion of wetland resources affected the economy of a rather wider area. We do know, though, that there was a duck decoy in Scarisbrick before 1714 (Fig. 4.6a, b). The numbers of birds caught in this device are unknown but the highest record in any one year for the Hale decoy, which seems to have been very similar, was in excess of 1000 birds (Mitchell 1885: 141). Plate 6.8 shows what the Scarisbrick duck decoy might have looked like.

The end of Martin Mere was foreshadowed by a document, dated 5 April 1694, drawn up between Thomas Fleetwood and the other owners of the soil, water and fishing: William, Earl of Derby; Robert Hesketh; Richard Bold; William Dicconson; Robert Scarisbrick; Barnaby Hesketh; Peter Ashton and Ann his wife; and Roger Hesketh. This document contained proposals and agreements for draining the lake and for converting it into dry and useful land. The parties agreed that within twenty months they would execute a lease of the lake to Thomas Fleetwood and that Fleetwood should have liberty to make sluices and drains. The actual lease is dated 22 August 1694 and was ratified by Act of

Plate 6.8 *Part of a duck decoy, provenance unknown.*

Parliament the following year. Fleetwood, the then manorial lord of Holmes, accomplished his mission to drain Martin Mere about 1697, a date based on the evidence of several witnesses in the court case in 1714, who said that the lake had been drained seventeen years earlier. Yet the waters had scarcely drained away before Fleetwood found himself and other proprietors defending eighteenth-century litigation initiated by the Earl of Derby and Robert Scarisbrick. The root cause of contention was the method of apportioning the lake basin. The defendants contended that the mere's proprietors never knew nor agreed the erstwhile fishery boundaries. The plaintiffs, on the other hand, were keen that these divisions be confirmed. The Earl of Derby and Robert Scarisbrick viewed these divisions as representing extensions of the various lakeside manors. They believed that the greatest share of the mere had belonged to them and that their own former fisheries now contained the best quality soil. They asserted, though, that other landowners had obstructed their attempts to define boundaries across the newly drained land. They also accused the defendants of adopting delaying tactics because many potential witnesses who could relate the boundaries of the fisheries were old, ill and not expected to live much longer. In fact, litigation apparently continued until the 1720s when a Special Commission was instituted so that the boundaries could finally be determined. The decree of 1723 indicates that many township divisions set by the commissioners differed little from those of the fisheries (LRO, DDSc 143/23). Indeed, modern township bounds still tend to follow their courses fairly closely.

The first homes on the mere – Mr Berry's House, Wiggins' House, Lowe's Little House and Lowe's Great House – were built in the mere basin rather than on the former islands (Fig. 6.1). Their locations reflect the prevailing optimism that Fleetwood's drainage would long be successful. Although the court case of 1714 is itself testament to the great achievement of the venture (Virgoe 2003: 37), these new houses were surely inundated when the scheme began to fail only a few years after completion. Despite the belief that Martin Mere was capable of being drained and turned into arable land, cultivation must soon have become impractical. Richard Latham's account books contain a few entries for 'score' of horses, colts and heifers on Martin Mere between 1733 and 1763 (see Weatherill [ed.] 1990: 25, 28, 31, 88, 93, 112) and this stinted grazing reflects the best use of this land. In fact, by the time that Fleetwood's lease expired about 1750, the mere was of little value, under water all winter, and liable to be flooded by even light summer rains. Thomas Eccleston's drainage improvements of the early 1780s gave some respite. By 1785 Eccleston was able to prepare 'two hundred large acres' for oats and barley, and to pronounce himself extremely satisfied with the results. Barley sown on land that had previously fetched no more than 4s. 0d. per large acre now sold at £11 17s. 6d. per acre. Oats from land that was once worthless fetched £10 17s. 6d. per acre. Grazing results were also good. Areas that formerly sustained only very poor pasture, even in the driest of summers, now supported several head of Scottish cattle. Indeed, Eccleston considered that these animals did better than any fattened on the best grazing lands in the neighbourhood (Aikin 1968: 320, 324; LRO, DDSc 143/23). His confidence in his drainage scheme, however, proved to be short-lived. In November 1787, a letter to Eccleston from John Codd referred to 'those floods you've had' and to the unfavourable season for ripening late-sown corn. Furthermore, Codd also reminded Eccleston that he must not put any sheep on land that had been overflowed with water at this time of year: it would 'certainly rot them – in the spring it will not do so' (LRO, DDSc 9/243). In 1789, after both the River Douglas and the Leeds and Liverpool canal inundated Martin Mere, Thomas Eccleston more or less decided to abandon arable agriculture in favour of grazing. The coarse grass and weeds of the softest land suited horses the best, so this entrepreneur accordingly increased his stock of 'those animals of the coach kind'. Suckling lambs did well, but ewes got out of condition and old sheep fell victim to foot rot. Black cattle were not successful, because many calves went down with a disease called 'the hyon'. Eccleston did, however, obtain good results from a flax crop harvested before autumn floods arrived. He discovered, too, that a mixture of grass seeds and rape provided useful fodder for his lambs (Aikin 1968: 325). The mechanics of Fleetwood's and Eccleston's schemes are examined in Chapter 7, in which later drainage improvements are also investigated.

CHAPTER SEVEN

Draining the Mere

W. G. Hale

Over the centuries fluctuating levels of the mere allowed piecemeal enclosures to develop around its rim and flooding of these areas was frequent. Because of the fisheries and the practical difficulties of draining the mere, no serious consideration was given to such a venture until the latter part of the seventeenth century. Draining the mere required the agreement of the various landowners concerned and it was probably in the early 1690s that Thomas Fleetwood of Bank Hall first proposed that the area should be leased to him for this purpose. Agreement was reached between Robert Scarisbrick of Scarisbrick; William, Earl of Derby, who held Burscough; the Hesketh and Bold families, who held North Meols; another Hesketh family who owned part of Tarleton and Rufford; and Thomas Fleetwood himself, who held Holmes in Tarleton. The lease, dated 22 August 1694, was confirmed by Act of Parliament in 1695 (LRO, DDSc 143/23).

Thomas Fleetwood was faced with the choice of either draining the mere into the Douglas, by deepening the channel between the two, or draining it into the sea. At times of flooding in the mere, its waters flowed over into Fine Jane's Brook (now part of the Three Pools waterway), via the ring-ditch and the Pool (Fig. 4.2), and the outlet of this to the sea is shown on the 1845–46 Ordnance Survey map just south of the present location of the Crossens pumping station. What is now referred to as Crossens River clearly existed as a stream outlet long before any attempt to drain the mere, though the discharge from the pumping station has greatly increased its size. Fleetwood chose to drain the mere onto the Crossens foreshore, into the bed of the Pool and Fine Jane's Brook, first because it was a lower point than the meeting of the mere with the Douglas, and secondly because only during periods of high tide would water re-enter any drainage channel.

From a point on the western shore of the mere, near to what is now Ainscough's Covert, a channel was dug in a north-westerly direction for some 1.5 miles over 'valuable improved land, both arable, pasture and meadow grounds […] then meeting and falling upon a rampart or Sea Cop (called Crossens pars cop) made to defend the said improved land from being overflowed by the ordinary spring tides of the sea' (Anon. 1760). The channel was dug some 24 ft wide and 'of a depth sufficiently lower than the mere', and it is said that as many as 2000 men were involved in the dry season to cut it. When the channel had been dug as far as the sea cop, this was breached and floodgates built at this point, which allowed the floodwaters to pass out but prevented the influx of seawater to the mere at high tide (Fig. 7.1a). Seaward of the floodgates the channel continued some quarter of a mile 'through the marshy ground below the Hamlet of Crossens […] then meeting with a Brook and uniting therewith called the Old Pool [and] falleth through the white sands into a lake called the Old Pool [Crossens Pool] thence into the open sea by the landfalls of [the] Ribble' (Anon. 1760). Once the sea wall was breached the mere, which was nowhere deeper than 10 ft (3 m), drained away in a few weeks.

The channel, known subsequently as the Sluice, was continued along the lower parts of the mere from the point where it cut into the mere shore near Banks, in a south-easterly direction but at an angle of c. 20°. The excavations produced a number of interesting artefacts including eight logboats (three more were found subsequently), several bronzes and 'human bodies entire and uncorrupted' (Leigh 1700) (see Chapter 5).

The floodgates erected by Thomas Fleetwood were designed in such a manner that they remained open so long as water was draining from the mere, but closed when the tide rose to a point where the water level was higher on the seaward side. This meant that the gates operated only on the highest tides and remained open at all other times.

The cutting of the channel from the mere to the sea affected several roads and pathways and necessitated the construction of bridges at these points. Of most significance was the highway between North Meols and

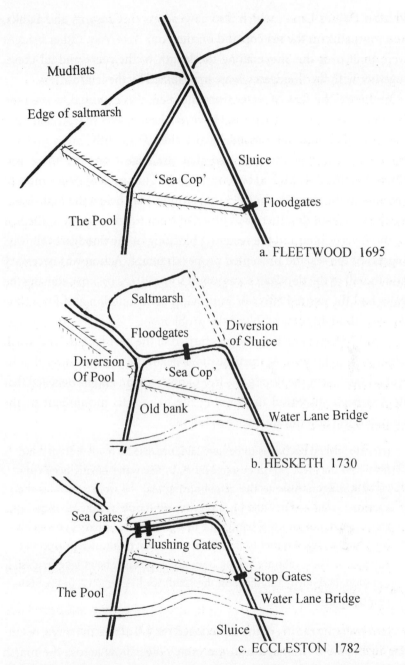

Fig. 7.1 *The exit to the sea of the Sluice waters as a result of different drainage plans: (a) Fleetwood 1695; (b) Hesketh 1730; (c) Eccleston 1782. Initially the Sluice met the waters from the Pool on the salt-marsh but subsequent plans resulted in the Sluice being diverted west to join the Pool at a more southerly point, thus creating the present Crossens River.*

Preston (Water Lane), which also gave access to Crossens and Banks, and footpaths on the sea cop and on the Four Acre Way. Other bridges were built over the Sluice along the length of the mere and all these, together with the floodgates, were maintained by the landowners.

In theory, the flow of water from the mere was expected to keep the floodgates clear of obstructions. However, the flow was so slow that both drifting sand, and silt carried by the tide, frequently prevented the proper function of the gates, so that drainage from the mere was impaired. By 1714 this had become a significant problem. Since most of the area of the mere (some 10.5 square miles) lay below the high-water mark of spring tides, there was little fall from the floodgates to the bed of the River Ribble and the resulting blocking of the floodgates allowed ingress of the sea and prevented proper drainage. Action was necessary and the sill of the floodgates was raised some 20 ins (0.5 m). Raising the gates had the desired effect of improving their function and for a time this was thought to have solved the problem.

In 1717 Fleetwood died and was buried in the parish church of North Meols (Churchtown). At the time of his death the new measures that he had adopted kept the floodgates free of obstruction and he believed that he had been successful in draining the mere. His monument in the church is in Latin but translates as follows:

> [...] He wished his bones to be here laid, because he made into dry and firm land the great Martinensian Marsh, by the water having been conveyed through a fosse to the neighbouring sea, – a work which, as the ancients dared not to attempt, posterity will hardly credit. He likewise constructed, not far off, a handsome bridge over the estuary at no small cost, from a regard rather to the public good than to his own prospective advantage. These labours having been accomplished, he at length, alas! too soon, laid down and died, on the 22nd April, A.D. 1717, in the 56th year of his age.

However, the raising of the sill reduced the fall across the mere, resulting in impaired drainage, and the even slower flow across the marsh failed to clear blown sand and deposited silt. Winter flooding took longer to clear in spring and the arable and meadow lands that had been created on the mere depreciated in value as water lay on them for longer periods of time. Eccleston, in his account of the draining of the mere, wrote that 'the Marshlands for many years were only made use of as a poor, fenny, watering pasture for the cattle of the neighbourhood, and that for a part of the summer months only' (Eccleston 1789).

Problems with the draining persisted and these appeared to be as much associated with the run-off on the seaward side of the floodgates as with the floodgates themselves. In an attempt to clear the seaward channel of mud and blown sand, Roger Hesketh, in 1730, diverted the course of the Old Pool westward some quarter of a mile (400 m) before its confluence with the Sluice. This gave it a shorter passage onto the foreshore and through the white sands. Shortly afterwards the proprietors and managers of the mere lands considered that diverting the Sluice into the new bed of the Old Pool would result in better drainage of the mere. The direction of the Sluice was diverted westward, some 200 m (40 rods) below the floodgates, to join the Pool at the point at which it had been diverted westward (Fig. 7.1b). The old channel of the Sluice running directly north over the flats is shown clearly on the 1736 map of Fearon and Eyes (Fig. 7.2), as is the westward channel of the diverted Sluice. Initially, this diversion had the desired effect of creating a better channel through the sands.

Some halfway along the newly cut Sluice from the old floodgates, a new set was erected with walls of stone, and the sea wall (sea cop) was moved to either side to prevent inundation. In addition to repairing and maintaining the bridges and roadways, the owners of the mere undertook to maintain the sea cop some ten yards either side of the floodgates. For some years, in this way, the mere was better drained.

The Sluice extended down towards the mere to its lowest point some 200 yards (180 m) west of Berry House (see Fig. 4.2) and there divided into two smaller drains extending eastward to Rufford and southward towards Burscough. Into these drained numerous ditches which over the years became blocked as the main sluice was neglected and not cleaned out, as Fleetwood's lease neared maturity.

Fleetwood's lease expired in 1750 and the responsibility for the lands of the mere reverted to the original estates from which they had been leased. Further neglect of the sluices was compounded by the destruc-

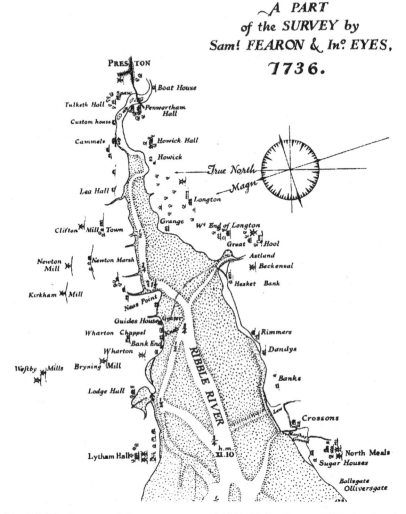

Fig. 7.2 *The Fearon and Eyes survey map of 1736–37 (in Barron 1938) showing the channel of the old course of the Sluice waters across the salt-marsh and the new course down the Crossens River.*

tion of the walled floodgates in 1755 when they were breached and broken down by very high tides coinciding with storm conditions. Necessity requiring, the various agents of the landowners met and appointed the Revd John Armetriding as agent to oversee the repairs. These were carried out and the costs paid by John Armetriding. However, in Articles of Agreement quoted in Betham's report on the drainage of the mere (Betham 1893), he had not been reimbursed by the landowners in August 1769, by which time, due to neglect, the mere flooded frequently.

The gates commissioned by John Armetriding were fourteen feet wide and, while an improvement on the old gates, they still required upkeep. Armetriding's interest subsequent to their replacement was limited to attempts to recoup his financial outlay from the landowners, and the state of the drains and the Sluice deteriorated. The Sluice was not cleared and the gates were still liable to be blocked by deposits carried in by the tide, which affected the heights of the outfall. The mere was covered by water all winter and flooded by small amounts of summer rain, and the land became again of little value: 'In this condition the best Mere lands let for a few shillings the large acre only' (Eccleston 1789).

In 1778 Thomas Eccleston settled at Scarisbrick Hall and immediately took a significant interest in the mere lands, which constituted a large part of his estate. Having ascertained that a significant fall could be achieved between the mere and the low-water mark he consulted and employed Mr Gilbert, the engineer involved in the construction of the Bridgewater Canal, to examine and restructure the drainage system of the mere. With Gilbert's advice in hand, Eccleston sought a lease of three lives from the other four landowners of the mere lands in order to be able to implement Gilbert's system. In 1781 he obtained leases from three of the four landowners, and began work in that year.

Gilbert's plan involved the erection of three separate pairs of flood-gates (Fig. 7.1c). The first and outermost of these were the sea gates, and within the same walls as the sea gates a pair of flushing gates were built, which opened in the opposite direction to the sea gates. Half a mile (800 m) up the Sluice towards the mere were erected the stop gates, and at low tide all three pairs of gates were open to allow the mere waters to drain into the sea. The stop gates were effectively a safety measure to prevent the ingress of the sea, should damage occur to the sea gates, which were closed during high tides. The stop gates, however, performed a second function. When the flow of water from the mere was small, and this was particularly the case in summer, there was insufficient flow to keep the channel clear on the seaward side of the sea gates. In these circumstances, the sea gates and flushing gates were allowed to remain open at high tide, brackish water thus filling the Sluice as far up as the closed stop gates. At high tide the flushing gates were closed, thus retaining a high level of water between them and the stop gates. Each of the six gates was equipped with four paddles, each 3 ft in length and 2 ft in depth at their bases, these paddles being raised by screws. At low tide, the raising of the paddles on the flushing gates allowed the water between them and the stop gates to rush out and flush the channel seaward of the sea gates, thus maintaining (at least in theory) the fall in level and the free movement of the sea gates. The raising of the paddles while the gates remained closed allowed the bases of the gates to be flushed and any obstruction or sedimentation to be washed away by the flushing effects generated.

Gilbert's final design involved a lowering of the sill of the sea gates by some five inches (12.5 cm) and building the sea and flushing gates some two hundred yards further out on the open marsh (Fig. 7.1c). This was, then, the third position in which the seaward floodgates had been placed, 1100 yards (1 km) seaward along the Sluice from the site of the original floodgates. The location on the salt-marsh required the extension of the sea cop as far as the new position of the gates, while on the seaward side an embankment was built and continued towards the mere as far as the stop gates; this increased the volume of water, and thus the flushing efficiency, available for clearing the channel at low tides. Because of the repositioning of the sea gates further out on the marsh, the sill was effectively five feet (c. 150 cm) lower than previously, the gates being some 18 ft (5.5 m) wide and some 19.5 ft (5.9 m) high.

While the gates were being built gangs of men were employed in deepening and widening the Sluice, which was some 6 yards (5.5 m) wide at the bottom, and on a dead level with the sill of the sea gates at the western end of the mere. In places the Sluice was 20 ft (6 m) deep and by April 1783 it had been dug out right up to the mere edge, where a dam had been constructed to retain the mere waters during the excavation. As a result of this damming the level of the mere was higher than it had been for some years and when the dam was released the success of the project was demonstrated by the waters running out in some five days, a process which would have taken as many weeks through the older system of drainage. Once drained, the rest of the Sluice towards the eastern end of the mere was deepened through to the same level, so that the cleared Sluice extended for nearly 5 miles (8 km) from the sea gates.

During the summer of 1783 the ditches on the mere were cleared and extended, so that there were over 100 miles (160 km) of such ditching. Drains into these ditches were cut by a guttering plough, drawn by eight or ten horses, which cut each day up to 8 miles (12.8 km) of drains some 20 ins (50 cm) wide at the top, 13 ins (33 cm) deep and 5 ins (12.7 cm) wide at the bottom.

In 1784 some few acres of the mere land were ploughed and yielded a tolerable crop of spring corn; some yielded a very inferior kind of hay; and the rest was pastured. The following year produced crops of barley selling for £11 17s. 6d. per large acre and oats at £10 17s. 6d. per acre, the former from land let at four shillings per acre, the latter from worthless land. Cattle were reared successfully on the mere and mowing gave some three pounds an acre and inferior grass letting two pounds an acre.

The ingenuity of Gilbert's design of the drainage cannot be denied, and Eccleston (1789) considered that 'the great obstacle to the perfect draining of Martin Mere is done away, which had baffled the many vain efforts of the proprietors for almost a century'. For his efforts in draining the mere Eccleston was awarded the Gold Medal of the Society of Arts, Manufacture and Commerce.

The success of Gilbert's drainage was short-lived. In the autumn of 1786 the failure of the bank of the River Douglas, at Rufford, at the eastern end of the mere, resulted in flooding that was both extensive and expensive, crops worth some £700 being lost. In the autumn of 1787 the bank of the Leeds & Liverpool canal broke and discharged water from a 28-mile length over the mere. Drained at one end, the mere was inundated at the other. Eccleston thus 'determined [...] to adopt, in great measure, the grazing instead of the tillage line' (1789). Once again, the watery origins of the great Martinensian Marsh adversely affected the designs of those who came to drain the peat lands.

For a few years the drainage was effective, but in 1813 the sea gates and the flushing gates were swept away by exceptionally high tides;

fortunately the stop gates held and the mere was saved from flooding. Thomas Scarisbrick, the son of Thomas Eccleston, had by this time inherited the estates. In 1814 he called in Mr Morris, who had been involved as engineer in the construction of docks in London and Liverpool, to re-examine the drainage system. Morris's solution was to replace the floodgates with cast-iron cylinders, three of 3 ft (90 cm) and one of 3 ft 3 ins (95 cm) in diameter, fixed under the bridge at Crossens at the end of the Sluice. Each cylinder had self-acting doors at the seaward end, but silting up of these doors immediately became a problem. White (1853) stated that '[t]hese cylinders [...] are obviously insufficient to allow the speedy escape of fresh waters, particularly during Winter and the consequence is that the portion of the Mere which depends upon this "natural" drainage alone, is submerged for weeks together'. Once again the measures taken to drain the mere were inadequate. The situation was compounded by the Douglas twice bursting its banks and by the sea breaking through at Hundred End and waterlogging large tracts of farmland. The water table formed affected that further inland on the mere. Consequently, the landowners were less disposed to spend money to keep the Sluice open, and matters grew steadily worse. Replacement of the floodgates by cylinders resulted in the loss of the flushing power of the former. In addition, the height of the outflow to the cylinders, 4.7 ft OD (1.40 m) for the 3 ft 6 ins cylinders and 4.83 ft OD (1.47 m) for the 3 ft cylinders, ensured that on all but the lowest tides, outfall from the Sluice stopped for a considerable time over the high tide period.

In 1826 William Miller proposed draining the area of the mere by means of discharging water at Birkdale, but his idea of making a waterway through the 'sandy mountains' received no support from the landowners (Miller 1826 [LRO, DDHe 1154]).

In 1843 Charles Scarisbrick, of Scarisbrick Hall, purchased his North Meols estate, thus owning land on both sides of the Sluice, in North Meols and Scarisbrick. He devised a scheme for draining the lands to the west of the Sluice by a new system, thus diverting water from the Sluice and consequently improving the drainage of the remaining lands draining into it.

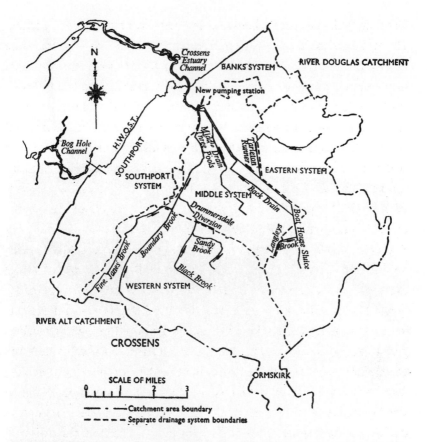

Fig. 7.3 *Drainage channels on the mere in 1963, after the new pumping station had been built (after Prus-Chacinski and Harris 1963).*

To the west of the Sluice the lands draining into the mere were higher and near Ormskirk as high as 200 ft (60 m) OD. The three streams draining this area were referred to as the 'high-level' watercourses. Fine Jane's Brook, Sandy Brook and Drummersdale Drain (Fig. 7.3) collected water from the south and west of the mere, and originally drained into the Old Pool which ran into the tidal channel below the floodgates. Diverted from the original course, it now formed the Three Pools System which, because of its height, would always run out at low tide at Crossens, without recourse to pumping. The streams were terminated by four new cylinders each 6 ft (182 cm) in diameter and placed 2 ft 2 ins (66 cm) OD. Fine Jane's Brook and Drummersdale Drain were each

Plate 7.1 *Cylinders under the roadway at Crossens draining the high-level waterways. The old pumping station, originally a corn mill, can be seen in the background.*

terminated by a single cylinder, whereas Sandy (Middle) Brook had two cylinders (Plate 7.1). A trunk joined the latter two brooks to maintain a similar water level in each. However, as before, the cylinders were closed for upwards of six hours out of twenty-four, and water could not escape during these periods. The new cylinders were situated under the roadway at Crossens.

In addition to this work in the western part of the mere, the high-level watercourses, a low-level watercourse subsequently known as the Back Drain was constructed which ran right through the mere on the western side of the sluice and parallel to it (Fig. 7.3). This took water from the lower-lying land, and pumps were installed at Crossens to carry the water from it into the Drummersdale Drain. The pumps were situated in what became known as the Crossens Pumping Station, a building erected in 1843 as a corn mill, and initially this housed a chain pump and a small centrifugal pump driven by steam. This work on the western and middle system drainage was completed in 1853.

The Crossens pumps were, however, not the first to be used on the mere. On 9 April 1850 the pumping station on Wiggins Lane (Plate 7.2), on the lowest (eastern) part of the mere, started operating. This was the brainchild of Mr Boosie, agent to Sir Thomas Hesketh, who 'conceived the project of relieving that gentleman's property by means of a water wheel driven by steam power, which should discharge the water as fast as it accumulated' (Neilson 1850). Mr. Boosie visited various projects in Lincolnshire and Cambridgeshire, on occasion with his friend Mr Robert Smith, an engineer from Manchester. The latter provided specifications for a engine of 20 horse-power and a wheel 30 ft (9 m) in diameter, both of which were built by Benjamin Hick and Son of Bolton. The wheel lifted water from the drain into the Sluice and in winter the height lifted was some 7 ft 1.5 ins (215 cm). Fig. 7.4 shows levels at various points on the mere in 1852. There are close similarities between the pumping station and wheel at Wiggins Lane and that preserved at Stretham near Ely in Cambridgeshire. While the former wheel and steam engine are long gone, the latter are lovingly preserved by the Stretham Engine Preservation Trust and can be seen at almost any time (Plate 7.3; Fig. 7.5). However, the engine house, now containing a diesel

Plate 7.2 *The pumping station on Wiggins Lane which drained the eastern end of the mere; the wheel was housed in the tallest part of the building.*

engine, still stands to the east of Wiggins Lane, though its chimney has been felled (Plate 7.4) and its wheel dismantled, as water is now pumped from one level to another.

While these measures again improved the drainage of the mere at the time, the very fact of removing water from the area caused peat shrinkage, so lowering the ground level and making the area more subject to flooding. Again, no measures had been taken to improve the run-off on the seaward side of the sluice, so it was not long before an increased pumping capacity was required to deal with renewed flooding. It was also necessary to bank the main drainage channels and not all landowners were keen to cooperate in expending further capital on drainage. Such lack of cooperation was probably the single main factor in the frequent flooding of the mere.

In 1881 Edward Garlick, engineer to the Ribble Navigation, made further recommendations on the draining of the mere area. Among these was the proposal to take two siphons under the Sluice to remove water from the north-east into the Back Drain on its southern side. This recommendation was eventually implemented but Garlick's proposal to divert the Crossens tidal channel in order to gain a better fall to the river failed to gain support. However, this was largely counteracted by the installation in 1882 of three new centrifugal pumps at the Crossens Pumping Station, the largest being capable of lifting 70 tons (18,000 gallons/81,827 litres) of water per minute and the two smaller ones 45 tons (11,570 gallons/52,603 litres) per minute. The large pump was so effective that the smaller ones were used only in times of flood. The cost (£60,000) was borne by the Scarisbrick Trustees; the Lords Lilford and Derby did not share the cost, so their lands continued to flood in winter.

It was, therefore, no surprise that the next report (Betham 1893) on the drainage of Martin Mere was commissioned by their lordships and

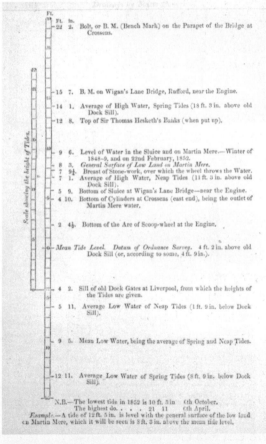

Fig 7.4 *Levels at various points in the mere in 1852. These heights do not correspond to present-day tide heights, as these are now measured in Liverpool from a point 4.93 m below OD (Newlyn) (after 1853).*

Plate 7.3 *The scoop wheel at Stretham in Cambridgeshire, which is almost identical with the mere wheel.*

Fig 7.5 *Plan of the scoop wheel installed in Wiggins Lane in 1850 – the first mechanical means of removing water to be used on the mere.*

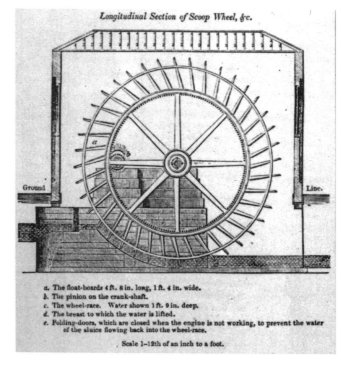

Longitudinal Section of Scoop Wheel, &c.

Ground

Line.

a. The float-boards 4 ft. 8 in. long, 1 ft. 4 in. wide.
b. The pinion on the crank-shaft.
c. The wheel-race. Water shown 1 ft. 9 in. deep.
d. The breast to which the water is lifted.
e. Folding-doors, which are closed when the engine is not working, to prevent the water of the sluice flowing back into the wheel-race.

Scale 1–12th of an inch to a foot.

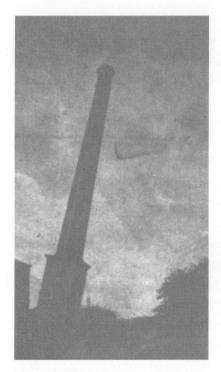

Plate 7.4 *The felling of the chimney associated with generating steam for the engine which originally turned the wheel in Wiggins Lane pumping station.*

Plate 7.5 (a) *The junction of the Sluice (left) and the Three Pools (High-Level) Waterway (right) at Crossens prior to the building of the new pumping station in 1961.*

was produced for their 'private use' on 17 June 1893. The main recommendations were that the old cylinders at the end of the Sluice be replaced by floodgates and that stop gates functioning in the same way as those of Thomas Eccleston be built. It was recommended that a new channel be dug straight out to the Ribble on a line with the Sluice and that the sea gates be installed in the new sea wall being built at the time (1890–95) to enclose Crossens Marsh. It was suggested there was no reason to 'meddle with' the outlet through the new 6 ft (182 cm) cylinders of the high-level watercourses, which should continue to flow into (and form) Crossens River. Other recommendations involved strengthening banks of drains on the mere, but all, once again, depended upon the agreement of the various landowners. Once again, it was not forthcoming and little resulted from Betham's proposals. Eventually, however, in 1907 the cylinders on the Sluice were replaced by a new floodgate, but it continued to empty the mere waters into Crossens River and no new channel was cut across the marsh. The new outlet was in the form of a culvert some 13 ft (3.96 m) wide and 8 ft (2.44 m) high with a sill level at 11.5 ins (28.7 cm) OD. Again, the consulting engineer (W. H. Wheeler) recommended a new seaward channel to the Sluice, similar to that recommended by Betham, but again no agreement was gained from the landowners. Wheeler recommended dredging the Crossens Tidal Channel, and from 1914 to 1918 a bucket dredger was employed along a length of the channel from the outlet of the high-level watercourse cylinders to some 1050 yards (c. 1000 m) downstream. Eventually the dredging was abandoned because the silt washed back into the channel and the dredger was difficult to manipulate, particularly during high tides. In 1927 the idea of dredging and straightening the Crossens Channel was resurrected by Mr Clayton, a consultant engineer, but Mr Eaton, later a surveyor with the Catchment Boards in Lancashire, put forward the alternative of pumping.

A factor which for a long time was seen as contributing to the silting up of the Crossens Channel was the discharge of the sewage works below the junction of the Sluice and the high-level watercourse outlets (Plate 7.5a). However, in 1928 the public analyst, H. E. Davies, went on record denying this. The Borough Engineer at the time, A. E. Jackson, found that in that year the bed of the tidal channel was higher than the cylinder inverts for 1.5 miles (2.4 km) seaward, and only 100 yards (91 m) downstream it was 3 ft (91 cm) higher. In 1930 G. E. Gregson, a surveyor, recommended a single new tidal sluice near the existing site, the dredging and training of the channels and abandoning 600 acres inland to flooding. In 1931 consultant engineers A. Havelock Case and E. C. Bartlett proposed a new sluice at the junction of the sea embankment, the building of a flushing basin and a training channel for 3 miles (4.8 km) downstream. Once again, lack of cooperation and an unwillingness on the part of the various landowners to provide the necessary financial support resulted in no action being taken. In fairness to the landowners of the mere it should be clearly understood that this was no problem unique to them. Throughout, the country landowners, who lived on higher land from which water passed onto lower land (resulting in flooding), escaped making any contribution; it was this fact, and the lack of cooperation among landowners in general, that resulted in the Land Drainage Act of 1930.

The Act provided for contribution to drainage of lower lands by those in higher areas, and divided the whole country into catchment areas. The mere was the responsibility of the River Crossens Catchment Area, some 38,000 acres (15,379 hectares), within which was a smaller area

Plate 7.5 (b) *The three brooks forming the Three Pools Waterway flowing towards Crossens; from left to right, Drummersdale Drain, Sandy Brook and Fine Jane's Brook.*

Plate 7.6 *1957 floods on the mere; farm machinery was often submerged at this time.*

(18,000 acres/7285 hectares) called the Drainage Area, controlled by the Drainage Board, consisting of members elected by the ratepayers. Five of them sat on the Catchment Board together with five persons nominated by Lancashire County Council, five by the County Borough of Southport and one person nominated by the Ministry of Agriculture. The Board was to be responsible for the main rivers, 34.5 miles (55 km) in length, notably the Crossens Channel, the Sluice, Boathouse Sluice, Langleys Brook, Broad Ditch, Tarleton Runner, Sandy Brook (in Birkdale), Fine Jane's Brook, Boundary Brook, Sandy Brook (in Scarisbrick), Black Brook and the Three Pools.

With the formation of the Catchment Board in 1930 further surveys of the area took place. These established that the Crossens Channel carried only one quarter of the water it should carry and the inland channels only one quarter to one half. Further, the pumping capacity required was double the existing provision. Since a pumping scheme would have cost some three times as much as a dredging scheme, the latter was initiated in 1933. A. E. Jackson reported as consultant to the Board, and over the subsequent years he maintained a close interest in the drainage of the area (Jackson 1938).

In 1933 dredging of the channel was begun by two dragline dredgers, purchased by the Catchment Board, and after fifteen months was completed except for the new cut (to straighten out three bends) which took place later. A distance of one mile (1.6 km) along the salt-marsh was dredged and then the dredgers moved inland to clear the Sluice and some of the other brooks. In addition, the three separate waterways (Plate 7.5b) which ran alongside each other (Fine Jane's Brook, Sandy Brook and Drummersdale Drain) were converted to a single waterway, the Three Pools Waterway, which ran for three miles to the outlet and was some 50 ft wide. An artificial 'wash' was constructed near Crossens to take excess floodwater (two other 'natural washes' were present at the time near Boathouse Sluice and the Tarleton Runner).

The Drainage Board was constituted in 1933 and diesel pumps were brought in to replace the old steam pumps at Crossens, increasing the pumping capacity from 140 tons per minute to 240 tons (52,794 gallons/240,000 litres) per minute. The machinery – three subsidiary pumping stations, two at Holmewood and one at Kew – was improved, and a fifth pumping station was built at Kew. These extensive works resulted in improved drainage and greatly reduced the possibility of flooding. Farms that had been unable to find tenants because of bad drainage were brought back into cultivation and the work was almost entirely completed by the outbreak of war in 1939.

Until the mid-1950s work on the mere drainage was limited to maintenance, but three disastrous floods over a period of four years made further action necessary. In 1954 the rainfall was 45.74 inches at Southport (compared to a yearly average of 33.3 inches), and at Crossens Pumping Station the rainfall (42.9 inches) was the highest recorded to that date. The mere was waterlogged for much of the summer (Plates 7.6 and 7.7) and crops were ruined. In August 1956 the mere was reborn after nine inches of rain fell in a month and again crops were spoiled (Plate 7.8). The third flood, on 1 November 1957, was not during a period of exceptional weather. The breaching of the Broad Ditch after heavy rain resulted in a gap 20 feet wide appearing in the bank and water from the ditch spread over a large area (Plate 7.9). Three floods in four years were too much for farmers to bear and swift action was taken by

Martin Mere

the then Ministry of Agriculture and Fisheries, resulting in the initiation of a costly scheme of improvement (Prus-Chacinski and Harris 1963). It was decided to abandon gravitational drainage, which up to 1961 removed the mere waters from the Three Pools Waterway and the Sluice. The decision to pump out all the water, first suggested in 1927, was taken because of the poor drain-off in Crossens Channel, which continually silted up, and because of the falling land level due to agricultural practices and drainage. A new pumping station (Fig. 7.6; Plates 7.10 and 7.11) was officially opened on 21 July 1961, and this housed thirteen pumping engines, five of them over thirty years old, having been moved from the old pumping station. These pumps had a capacity of over 14 cumex (cubic metres per second), i.e. 840 tons (184,88 gallons/84,000 litres) per minute, nearly four times the capacity of the previous machinery. This greatly reduced the likelihood of flooding.

On land as low-lying as the mere there can be no guarantee that farmland will never again be flooded. The float that was installed in the Sluice to ring a bell in the pumping station superintendent's house when danger levels were reached has now been replaced by a computerised system which can be programmed to maintain particular levels of water

Plate 7.7 *1957 floods threatened the return of the mere*

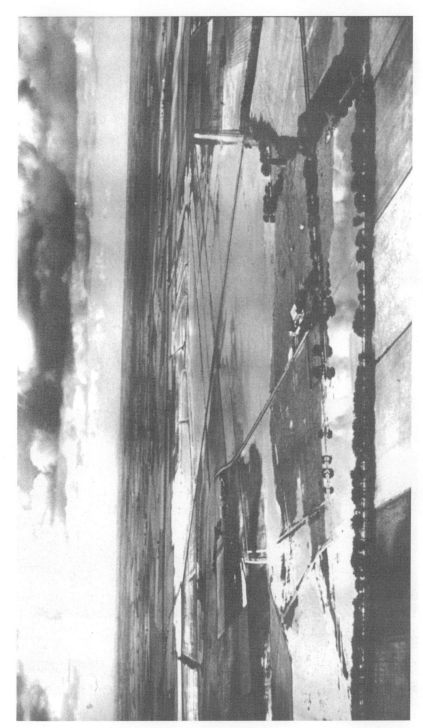

Plate 7.8 *Flooding in August 1956; Little Peel and Great Peel form a single island.*

Plate 7.9 *The breaching of the Geldhey Bank in November 1957 caused extensive flooding of the surrounding fields.*

Plate 7.10 *The new pumping station, completed in 1961, at Crossens.*

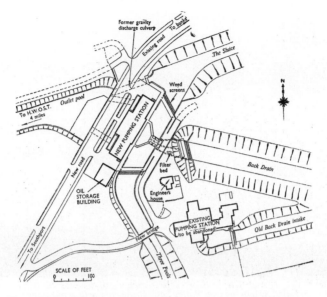

Fig. 7.6 *Plan of the new pumping station built at Crossens in 1961. The Sluice enters the system top right, the Back Drain from right middle and the Three Pools from the bottom of the diagram (after Prus-Chacinski and Harris 1963).*

on the mere. Effectively, draining is now almost automatic and the pumps can cope with almost any inundation. This sounds almost too good to be true, after some three hundred years of problems caused by floods – and it is! So efficient are the pumps that the shrinkage of the peat since the opening of the new pumping station in 1961 has been roughly equivalent to that of the previous 260 years. The ground is a metre lower than it was in 1961 and two metres lower than in the 1690s. The lower it is, the more likely it is that flooding will occur. In 1997 more new pumps were installed and a total of twelve electric pumps and four diesel pumps made up the final complement of sixteen. Five of the electric pumps now serve the Back Drain, two the Three Pools waterway and two the Sluice. In addition, there are three supplementary electric pumps and four diesel pumps, two associated with the Back Drain and one each with the Three Pools waterway and the Sluice. In total they are capable of 28.27 cumex (that is, 1696 tons, 373,000 gallons or 1,696,000 litres per minute). The consultants were not being unduly pessimistic in putting in pumps capable of removing nearly 1700 tons of water per

Plate 7.11 *Aerial view looking over Water Lane Bridge to the new pumping station and the Crossens River. The Back Drain, which runs parallel with the Sluice for most of its length, can be seen turning towards the pumping station and the Three Pools Waterway, between Water Lane Bridge and the salt-marsh. Roddons are visible to the left of Water Lane.*

minute; they were being realistic, and in 2000 it became necessary for the first time to run all the pumps simultaneously to full capacity. But more pumping means more shrinkage – and consequently more pumping. So the cycle continues until some time in the distant future, with the possibility of global warming and rising sea level, when the pumps may no longer be able to cope with an encroaching shoreline and increasing run-off from the land and, like the returning cavalier, the mere may well come into its own again.

CHAPTER EIGHT

The Natural History of the Mere

W. G. Hale

Because the mere was drained in times before the systematic recording of most aspects of natural history, there is little relevant first-hand information in the literature concerning its flora and fauna. The fisheries clearly flourished and according to Leigh (1700: 17–18), in the mere 'were found great quantities of fish as Roach, Eels, Pikes, Perch and Bream and the like'. This suggests a well-balanced freshwater ecosystem. On the other side of the Ribble the same author records the presence on Marton Mere of 'vast quantities of fowls, such as Curlews, Curleyhilps, Wild Ducks, Wild Geese and swans, which are there sometimes in great numbers'; it is almost certain that Martin Mere was also a haven for these birds.

The mere itself was largely surrounded by reeds and evidence of this is found in the micro- and macro-fossil evidence of the presence of *Phragmites* (reed), *Typha* (bulrush) and *Cladium* (great fen sedge). At the time of the draining of the mere, reed beds were extensive and the collection of reeds for thatching was an important aspect of the economy of the mere. Remains in the peat indicate the presence of reed fringes from the earliest times of biogenic sedimentation in the mere, some 6800 BP (Tooley 1977). From then until the mere was drained it provided an environment of open water bordered by reed margins with areas of *Sphagnum* cover, the whole being initially surrounded by woodland of one type or another which over the years was burned and felled until only small areas were left.

Whereas throughout this period the pollen preserved in the sediment gives an indication of the varying plant cover, the first sign of animals in the area is found in footprints exposed in eroded muds on the present-day shore which originated in the Sub-Boreal climate of the late Bronze Age, some 3500 years BP (Roberts et al. 1996; see Chapter 3). However, while concrete evidence is lacking for the presence of animals in the region of Martin Mere before this time, some speculation can be justified on the basis of records from elsewhere and knowledge of the changing climate.

Peatlands other than those of West Lancashire, particularly those in Southern England and the Fens, have provided interesting assemblages of bones, not surprisingly mainly the larger waterbirds. Of these, the remains of Dalmatian pelican (*Pelicanus crispus*) (see Colour Plate 8.1 following p. 80) are perhaps the most interesting, reflecting the warm climate of the Atlantic Period. Pelican remains from as far north as Hull suggest that the species may well have been present in West Lancashire around 4000 BP when the climate probably reached its post-glacial optimum; indeed pelicans may well have bred on Martin Mere.

Since it was not until Neolithic times, during the Atlantic Period, that serious felling of the wildwood began, areas of freshwater with adjacent open ground (to the west in the case of Martin Mere) must have been relatively few and afforded important habitat for water birds in general.

Much of our knowledge of previous avifaunas comes from the middens of old cultures, and pelican bones were present in refuse found in the Iron Age village of Glastonbury dating from around 250 BC. At this time pelicans were still breeding in Britain, as evidenced by the bones of fledglings from Glastonbury, which was a lake village with a surrounding habitat that would have resembled Martin Mere closely. Fisher (1966) records dabchick, shearwater, pelican, cormorant, shag, bittern, heron, mallard, teal, scaup, tufted duck, pochard, red-breasted merganser, greylag, mute and whooper swans, goshawk, kite, white-tailed eagle, crake, corncrake, coot, barn owl, carrion crow and a variety of passerines from the lake village excavation. While it is possible that all these species were killed in the region of the lake, some species, for example shearwater and shag, suggest Iron Age excursions to the coast.

A very similar assemblage of bones was collected from excavations of lake dwellings at Lagore, Co. Meath, Ireland, which date from AD 750 to AD 950, so that it is not unreasonable to assume a similar species spectrum of birds at Martin Mere. Among the bones from Glastonbury were those of crane (*Grus grus*), and that this was a common bird in the region of Martin Mere some 3500 years BP is shown by the presence of numerous footprints (Plate 8.2) on the shore at Formby in Holocene silts. These are associated with footprints of wading birds (*Scolopacidae*), deer, cattle and humans in what is interpreted as being brackish to freshwater lagoonal conditions associated with a sandy foreshore (Plate 8.3). The footprints of crane are extremely common, which suggests that many birds were present in the area, and the presence of Martin Mere within some 15 km of these lagoons would have provided an excellent nesting area for the species. It is likely that other freshwater pools, behind the emerging shore dunes, would have provided suitable nesting habitat for cranes, but the extensive reed beds around the mere at that time would have provided the most likely breeding location. Nowadays cranes are found in wetlands with or without scattered trees, in bogs, fens and reed beds along rivers or lakes – a description exactly covering the habitat around the mere at that time. In the Irish bogs cranes were still present a few hundred years ago, so that they may well have been common in the region of the mere over a period of several thousand years.

Associated with the bird footprints are those of several species of mammal. Both red deer (*Cervus elephas*) (Plate 8.4) and roe deer (*Capreolus capreolus*) occur frequently, often associated with human tracks which appear to be following them. These were possibly made by hunters, a suggestion supported by the fact that the following tracks show an increase in speed, as though the hunters were in pursuit of the deer.

The tracks at Formby occur in two different sediments, the higher and more recent dated as 3649 ± 109 years BP, the lower and older being as yet undated. Tracks of small-footed cattle and small unshod horses are associated with the younger sediments and such livestock probably indicate human settlement in the area. The presence of mammalian foot-

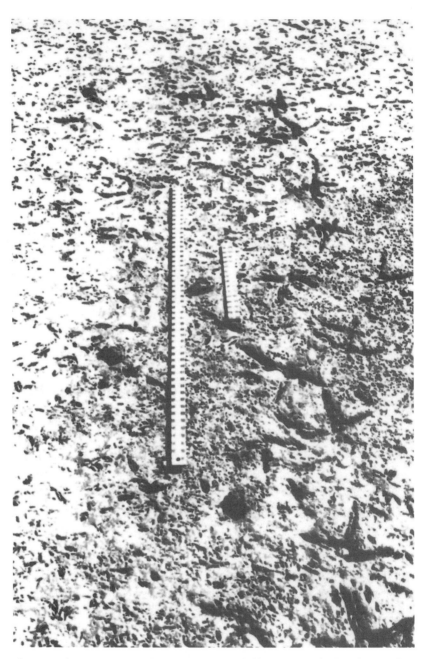

Plate 8.2 *The common crane* (Grus grus) *was probably a common bird in the area three thousand years ago, as its footprints on the beach at Formby show (photograph by G. Roberts).*

Plate 8.3 *Beds of peat-like silts on the shore at Formby contain numerous footprints of birds and mammals; of particular significance are the human footprints – some 150 trails have been recorded.*

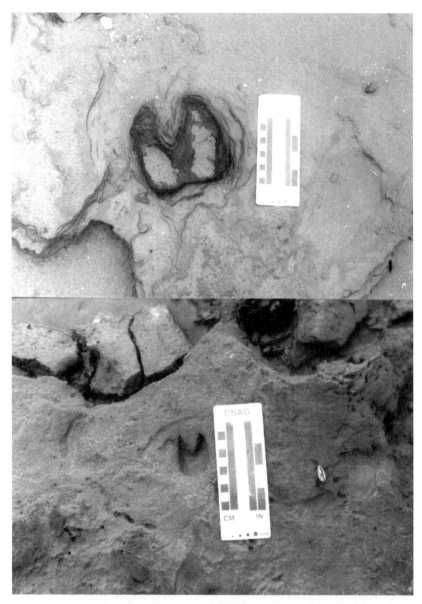

Plate 8.4 *Tracks of (a) red deer* (Cervus elephas) *and (b) roe deer* (Cervus capreolus). *Tracks of the latter are the more common on the shore at Formby, often associated with human footprints, suggestive of hunting (photographs by S. Gonzalez).*

prints superimposed on those of wading birds suggests either a fore-shore habitat or, more likely, a freshwater drinking area where wading birds were driven to roost during high-tide periods. The presence of several species of wader together at the same time suggests a high-tide roost and footprints similar in size to those of oystercatcher (*Haematopus ostralegus*), knot (*calidris canutus*), dunlin (*calidris alpina*) and plovers (*Vanellus/Pluvialis*) are recognisable. The presence of a freshwater source, such as a stream entering a lagoon, is indicated by other stratigraphic features.

While the imprints of auroch (*Bos primigenius*) (Plate 8.5) can be recognised infrequently in the younger silts, their massive prints are much commoner in the lower and older sediment, where they are twice the size of the younger cattle prints. Clearly, for a long period of time deer and wild cattle (Plate 8.6) roamed the areas surrounding Martin Mere. In both sediments prints of wolf (*Canis lupus*) – or possibly a very large dog (*Canis familiaris*) – have been found, and further west, at Hightown, bone finds dated to 4545 ± 90 BP include boar (*Sus scrofa*) and sheep (*Ovis ovis*). The antlers of red deer were found buried in the sand off Lifeboat Road, Formby, and these were dated at 4425 ± 45 BP (carbon 14 date, G. Roberts pers. comm.).

There are no references in the literature to the natural history of the mere in the period up to its draining. Perhaps the oldest recorded mammal from Martin Mere is an elk described by Leigh (1700) as having been found below the peat, at 'Meales'. Since it had antlers some 'two yards across' it was almost certainly the European elk (American moose), *Alces alces*. Leigh's general comments are the first to appear in print and shortly after this, about 1714, the records of litigation (LRO, DDSc 143/23) refer to swans nesting on the south side of the mere close to Greening Point. In evidence given in 1714, Mary Hesketh referred to the great numbers of 'geese, ducks and other wildfowl' which bred on Great Peel and Wet Holsome. It is possible that the geese referred to were breeding greylag (*Anser anser*), as this species was formerly much more widespread in Europe than it is now. The ducks were probably mainly mallard (*Anas platyrhyncos*), teal (*Anas crecca*), shoveller (*Spatula clypeata*) and possibly tufted duck (*Aythya fuligula*); all these species

Plate 8.5 *Auroch* (Bos primigenius) *footprints occur more commonly in the older beds (photograph by S. Gonzalez).*

Plate 8.6 *Auroch may have been present in what is now West Lancashire for a longer period of time than in other areas of England.*

have bred in the area in recent years, long after the draining of the mere. It is also likely that the black-headed gull (*Larus ridibundus*) bred on islands in the mere and large numbers still breed on the nearby salt-marsh, where local people still take eggs for food in spring.

Although it is over three hundred years since the marsh was drained, for one reason or another large areas have remained water-covered in winter for much of the time and the establishment of the Wildfowl and Wetlands Trust Reserve has ensured the continuation of some wetland habitat. It is not surprising, therefore, that waterbirds in particular continue to visit the area. The earliest reliable documentation of their presence comes from the correspondence of Lord Derby with John Riddiough, an Ormskirk taxidermist, in the early 1800s.

Riddiough collected and mounted specimens for Lord Derby. A letter dated 6 March 1812 contains a list of birds found in the Ormskirk area, the ordering being based on Pennant's eighth edition of *British Zoology*. Among the diurnal birds of prey Riddiough lists a white-tailed eagle (*Haliaetas albicella*) frozen to the shore at the western end of the mere at Crossens, hen harrier (*Circus cyaneus*) at Scarisbrick and hobby (*Falco subbuteo*) as 'frequently taken in autumn by the Lark catchers in their nets'. The common buzzard (*Buteo buteo*) is described as very common on the sandhills, though surprisingly no mention is made of the marsh harrier (*Circus aeruginosus*) (see Colour Plate 8.7 following p. 80), which some fifty years later (c. 1860) was shot from the nest on Martin Mere by one of the gamekeepers, John Cookson. Of the owls, Riddiough states that the short-eared owl (*Asio flammeus*) was very common on the mosses in winter. The barn owl (*Tyto alba*) was common, whereas other species of owls, including the tawny owl (*Strix aluco*), were scarce.

The grey heron (*Ardea cinerea*) was recorded on Martin Mere and at Bank Hall, 'where they bred among the Rooks, carrying on perpetual warfare'; bittern (*Botaurus stellaris*) (see Colour Plate 8.8 following p. 80) was listed as breeding on the mere (Riddiough 1812), but Mitchell (1885) records it as absent as a breeding species from the mere by 1865, when one was shot. Pennington's annotation in Mitchell (1885) records a specimen shot by Robert Blundell, head keeper to Sir Talbot Scarisbrick, on the west end of Martin Mere (the 'Blacks') in 1907, and two more were shot in 1929 (Oakes 1953). Of other waterbirds, the water rail (*Rallus aquaticus*) was recorded by Riddiough as common, while the spotted crake (*Porzana porzana*) occurred on the low meadows but was a very scarce bird; the cornrake (*Crex crex*) bred commonly on the mere.

Perhaps the most surprising aspect of Riddiough's account of the birds of Martin Mere concerned the distribution of waders. He was clearly familiar with the area from his own personal experience and describes the lapwing (*Vanellus vanellus*) as breeding there in great numbers but deserting the area in winter; of the common snipe (*Gallinago gallinago*) (see Colour Plate 8.10 following p. 176) he writes that 'a few breed there – I have seen their eggs and young ones'. Ruff (*Philomachus pugnax*) (see Colour Plate 8.9 following p. 80) 'formerly frequented the mere in great numbers in the month of April but since the late Mr. T. Eccleston drained and improved it [in 1781], they have deserted the place': both bar-tailed godwit (*Limosa lapponica*) and black-tailed godwit (*Limosa limosa*) were said to be 'very scarce [and] come at uncertain times'. Surprisingly, the redshank (*Tringa totanus*) (see Colour Plate 8.11 following p. 176) was recorded only from Crosby marsh 'along the seashore, very scarce'. Mitchell (1885) states that its nest has very seldom been found within the county limits, and its apparent absence from the mere as a breeding bird in the early nineteenth century supports Oakes' (1953) contention that this bird has increased and spread to a remarkable degree during the twentieth century.

While it is difficult to overlook the redshank the same cannot be said about the ruff. A record of nesting on the mere, supported by a clutch of eggs taken there on 20 April 1910 and exhibited by P. F. Bunyard at the British Ornithologists' Club, is, in fact, the only record from the mere. The rediscovery of breeding ruff on the Ribble salt-marshes in 1976, however, and certain or probable breeding records in most years since, suggest that there may well have been a continuous presence in the area, particularly since the ruff is so reclusive during the breeding season. This is supported by Mitchell's reference to mere-men still living in 1885, who remembered birds staying all summer and had seen them lekking, and by the records of two males in full breeding plumage shot around 1840 and young birds, unable to fly, caught by one William Parker of Crossens.

One of Riddiough's letters to Lord Derby (6 March 1812) casts some light on the first record of glossy ibis (*Plegadis falcinellus*) in Lancashire. This was shot by a man named Westhead, known to Riddiough, in November 1798 on the shore near the north of the Alt. It was sent to market in Liverpool and purchased by Riddiough's brother who passed it on to Riddiough to mount. By this time it was in poor condition and could not be sexed, though its weight was given as 28 ounces. At the time of writing the letter the ibis was in the possession of Lord Derby, and is almost certainly the specimen referred to by Wagstaffe (1935) as from Ormskirk and in the Liverpool Museum, from Lord Derby's collection.

There is little information in Riddiough's letter on the different species of gulls in the area. Mention of large numbers of black-headed gulls (*Larus ridibundus*) breeding on the estuary of the Wyre suggests that the mere and salt-marshes lacked a large colony of the species, though they probably bred on the islands when the mere was in existence and certainly for a long time the local people have gathered gulls' eggs from the salt-marsh at Banks.

Perhaps the group of birds for which the mere had the most attraction was the Anseriformes – the swans, geese and ducks. In winter Riddiough recorded 'wild swans' on Rufford and Croston Low Meadows (effectively the mere) in large flocks. By Mitchell's time (1885) both whooper swan (*Cygnus cygnus*) (see Colour Plate 8.12 following p. 176) and Bewick's swan (*Cygnus bewickii*) were rare in South Lancashire. That this may well have been due to Eccleston's draining in 1781 is supported by their return in large numbers following the creation of suitable winter habitat by the Wildfowl and Wetlands Trust.

One of the most interesting of Riddiough's records is that relating to the wintering wild geese. At the time of this letter to Lord Derby, the commonest species recorded in the area in winter was the barnacle goose (*Branta leucopis*), which was said to occur 'in large flocks on the marshes below Crossens and on Langton Marsh near the Ribble – very difficult to become near'. This is a marked contrast to the pink-footed goose (*Anser fabilis brachyrhynchus*), which at that time occurred occasionally in winter at Altcar. Pink-feet became the most plentiful species of goose in Mitchell's time (1885), and subsequently increased in numbers to the point at which today over thirty thousand (a third of the world population) may be present in this area during winter. The increasing food supply in the form of unharvested potatoes lying on the fields has played a large part in the increase in numbers. However, the more northerly wintering of geese, probably associated with milder winters, has probably resulted in the species change in the area. Barnacle geese now have their winter headquarters on Islay (this is the Spitzbergen breeding population). The build-up in winter numbers of pink-feet has taken place largely over the past forty years, since Oakes (1953) quotes 2200 as a maximum winter figure.

Other geese recorded by Riddiough as frequenting the mere area are white-fronted goose (*Anser albifrons*) and brent goose (*Branta bernicla*), but other species were said to be rare. Nowadays, both species are seen occasionally with the pink-feet, as are bean goose (*Anser f. fabilis*) and snow goose (*Anser caerulescens*). Greylag goose (*Anser anser*) breeds on the mere in semi-feral conditions, and it probably bred in the fully wild state in the past.

Of the duck recorded by Riddiough, only the mallard (*Anas platyrhynchos*) and shelduck (*Tadorna tadorna*) are recorded as definitely breeding in the area, though of the other species he mentions, teal (*Anas crecca*), shoveller (*Anas clypeata*) and tufted duck (*Aythya fuligula*) may well also have bred. Visitors to the mere in Riddiough's time included red-breasted merganser (*Mergus serator*), smew (*Mergus albellus*), pintail (*Anas acuta*), wigeon (*Anas penelope*) and velvet scoter (*Melanitta fusca*).

At the beginning of the nineteenth century the kingfisher (*Alcedo atthis*) was a common breeder in the area of the mere, and the nightjar (*Caprimulgus europaeus*) was described by Riddiough as ubiquitous on 'all the moss sides'. The wryneck (*Jynx torquilla*) was described by Mitchell as nearly extinct as a breeding bird, whereas Riddiough's notes list the species as 'common, breeds here, but leaves us very early'. Clearly, the demise of the wryneck has nothing to do with the draining of the mere, and it is now rare throughout the British Isles.

As a taxidermist, Riddiough handled many specimens of rarer birds shot in the area of the mere, and he refers to two hoopoes (*Upupa epops*) shot not far from Ormskirk and a live bird from Liverpool market which he had in his possession. Of particular interest are Riddiough's notes on the rose-coloured starling (*Sturnus rosaceusi*) as these shed some light on comments made by both Mitchell and Oakes. Lord Derby was clearly interested in obtaining a specimen of the species and was prompted to enquire of Riddiough on the basis of Donovan (1794–1818), who states that the species visited the region of Ormskirk annually. According to Riddiough only a single specimen had been shot, the male of a pair observed on 14 August 1783 by Mr Paul Jump at Ainsdale 'on a sandy copse near the mill'. This specimen remained in the possession of Riddiough in 1812 and he sent a drawing of it to Donovan, since that illustrated in the latter's book was 'so very imperfect, both in the colouring and particularly the crest [...] but he never acknowledged the receipt of my letter or the drawing. I believe that the one I had was the only one ever seen in this neighbourhood in the 40 or 50 years past.'

A letter from Riddiough to Lord Derby dated 25 September 1816 records a second rose-coloured starling, a description of which had appeared in a Liverpool paper. As a result, Riddiough had numerous people to see it, and he placed a high price on it (£5.00, mounted in a case) as 'six days indefatigable diligence and pursuit' had been required to obtain it. Apparently Lord Derby did not want the case, and the bird was subsequently offered to him at £3 (letter, 22 October 1816).

Another bird well known to Riddiough, and now extinct in the area as a breeding bird, was the woodlark (*Lullula arborea*), found 'all around us, particularly on poor dry grounds'. Red-backed shrike (*Lanius collurio*) was recorded around Ormskirk and great grey shrike (*L. excubitor*) on Martin Mere; ortolan bunting (*Emberiza hortulana*) was taken by Riddiough 'at my back door' and he records crossbill (*Loxia curvirostai*) 'at Hurleston Hall [Scarisbrick] – shot many from fir trees'. In winter hooded crow (*Corvus cornix*) was recorded from fields near the sea shore, and starlings (*Sturnus vulgaris*) 'congregate among the reeds in vast multitudes'. Turtle dove (*Streptopelia turtus*) was recorded at Halsall in all winters but was said not to breed, whereas now the species breeds not uncommonly in south Lancashire.

Two other species are worthy of mention: first, red grouse (*Lagopus lagopus*), which occurred formerly on the mosses but by Riddiough's time was nearly extinct; and, secondly, a single record of little bustard (*Otis tetrax*), which Riddiough believed to be the only specimen taken in Lancashire (at Burscough) at the time and which was placed in the Leverian Museum at Alkington Hall, Prestwich, the contents of which have since been disposed of at sale.

Another source of unpublished information on the mere is Pennington's copy of Mitchell (in the author's possession), which contains many hand-written marginal notes by the former. Among these is a reference to hoopoe shot on Tarleton Moss (probably that mentioned in Oakes as taken in 1905) by Mr Cookson, keeper to Lord Lilford; in the notes in the catalogue of the Pennington collection the specimen is said to have been in the possession of either Cookson or Lord Lilford. While he makes no comment on the fact, Pennington probably recorded the first little owl in Lancashire in the early 1900s at Holmeswood, Rufford, 'but did not get a chance to procure it' (pencil annotation in W. G. Hale's copy of Mitchell 1885).

Gamekeepers on the mere were responsible for several of Pennington's marginalia. Langdon, a keeper on the Scarisbrick marshes, shot a marsh harrier around the turn of the century and a hobby (*Falco subbuteo*) at Sixfield Convert; the latter was misidentified as a red-footed falcon (*Falco vespertinus*) and is now in the possession of the Liverpool Museum. An osprey (*Pandion heliaetus*) (see Colour Plate 8.13 following p. 176) recorded by Mitchell as shot on the Scarisbrick Estate in April 1880 was, according to Pennington's notes, shot by a Mr Gradwell on Black Otter Farm (the site of the previous Black Otter Mere, near Halsall).

Wildfowl receive some attention in Pennington's marginalia and he mentions pink-feet as numbered in thousands on the Ribble in 1913; his specimen of brent goose was shot at Crossens in January 1911 and he also mentions a case of two specimens of barnacle goose at 'Braids Farm, shot by [his] father about 50 years ago' (i.e., around 1860). He also notes that wigeon were so common 60 years earlier (c. 1850) at Banks that no flight shooter would fire at any but a flock, and that Hine (a Preston taxidermist) shot seven tufted duck (*Aythya fuligula*) one night between the lake and the drain, by the electric light off the promenade. Also mentioned are teal nesting behind Formby Hall and at Rufford, and shoveller nesting on the mere.

Two other of Pennington's marginal notes are of interest: first, the specimen of quail (*Coturnix coturnix*) in his collection was shot out of a

flock of rooks at Holmeswood, Rufford, on 1 October 1913; and, secondly, alongside black tern (*Chlidonis niger*) he wrote 'Sooty [tern]
Sterna fuscata shot at Halsall Down'.

Other interesting records from the mere appear in R. Wagstaffe's
'Birds of Southport' (1935). Two Pallas's sand grouse (*Syrrhaptes para-
doxus*) were shot out of a group of five at Winacre Farm on the mere
'towards the end of the year 1890' by Nathan Ainscough; previously, in
1863, two male birds had been shot by a gamekeeper from a flock of fifteen birds on a field of spring oats on the Scarisbrick estate. The only
record of squacco heron (*Ardeola ralloides*) for Lancashire also comes
from the mere area, an adult bird being shot by Mr John Ryding at
Marsh Farm, Banks, in August 1930.

Great crested grebe (*Podiceps cristatus*) (see Colour Plate 8.14a following p. 176) and dabchick (*Podiceps ruficollis*) (see Colour Plate 8.14b
following p. 176) would have been common breeders on the mere and
are now to be seen again in the Mere Sands Wood Reserve. Little is
recorded of the commoner birds and, by their very nature, most of the
old records are of relatively rare occurrences. With the draining of the
mere new habitat would be created for birds preferring marshy areas,
and lapwings and snipe became common breeding birds. Oakes mentions the mere as an old nesting haunt of the dunlin, but it has not been
known to breed there since 1916, when several nests were found. Probably it began nesting on the mere area after the draining, though it may
have nested previously on the mosses. Reed warbler (*Acrocephalus scir-
paceus*) still breeds not uncommonly on the mere area, as does the sedge
warbler (*Acrocephalus schoenobaenus*), and both species have probably
been much commoner in the area than Oakes suggested. The grass-
hopper warbler (*Locustella naevia*) lost its last stronghold at Mere Brow
with the destruction of the breeding habitat in the 1970s, but a few pairs
remain to breed on the mere.

Until the creation of the 'Leisure Lakes' at Mere Brow, the advent of
the Wildfowl Trust at Burscough and the creation of the Mere Sands
Wood Reserve at Rufford, no open areas of water existed except at times
of flooding, but for the Sluice and the drainage channels feeding it.
Once new open areas of water were created and new reed beds estab-

lished, many of the water birds which must have nested on the mere in the past returned to breed. Great crested and little grebe are not uncommon breeders, and of the wildfowl, mute swan, greylag goose, shelduck, mallard, gadwall, shoveller, tufted duck, pochard and golden-eye have all bred. Moorhen and coot are common and water rail has been recorded as a breeder, though it is possible that this last species has always bred somewhere on the mere. Because of the presence of the Wildfowl and Wetland Trust Reserve, it is difficult to be sure which species of wildfowl are incoming wild birds, though clearly the breeding of whooper swan, Canada goose and ruddy duck can be attributed to feral birds.

The presence now of species on the mere area is not evidence of their having been there in the past. The redshank, for example, nests commonly in the area but in Mitchell's time (1885) its nest had seldom been found within the county limits. Its footprints have not been identified among those found in the Bronze Age sediments on the shore, and if the species eventually proves to be absent from that environment there is a possibility that the species had not extended as far north as Iceland at that time. Clearly there have been changes in the fauna over the years which cannot be attributed to the draining of the mere, but few records exist. Riddiough's notes concern his observation and specimens brought to him for mounting. These latter were mainly birds and mammals which had been shot by keepers and 'sportsmen', but a few came from the professional bird catchers. Many methods of trapping birds, both for the cage and to eat, were used on the mere and in surrounding areas from time immemorial until well into the twentieth century.

For larks and finches clap and cymbal nets were used (Plate 8.15), often with tethered decoy birds. These were set on open ground, and baited if decoys were not used. Once the birds were in the area, often attracted by caged 'call birds', the nets were pulled over by the catcher and 'in favourable weather an average of eight or ten dozen a day, of which eighty per cent will be alive, can be taken' (Mitchell 1885). The best weather for this was in the autumn, and a return might be expected of 1s. 3d. to 1s. 6d. per dozen birds as food items or up to 6s. a dozen for males as cage birds.

Plate 8.15 *Clap nets were used on the mere for catching larks and finches.*

Particularly in the area of the mere, snares, known as 'pantles', were used to catch snipe. These took the form of lines some 12 yards long woven of horse hair, twenty hairs in thickness, with loops two hairs in thickness at intervals of some three inches. The lines were fixed some twelve inches above the ground and snipe and teal were caught mainly during the night. Trampling of the vegetation along the line of the pantles gave the impression of water cover in semi-darkness, and supposedly attracted waterbirds. There is one record of a drake scoter taken in a pantle on the mere at Tarleton. Smaller pantles were used for catching larks.

On open ground and on mud-flats, ring or fly-nets (the old equivalent of mist nets) were set, usually in the dark, and often on areas previously covered by the tide. The nets were set so that the mesh formed diamond shapes and they were allowed to bag on poles some ten to twenty yards apart. On the Lune these were set some three feet above the ground, whereas on the Ribble the bottom of the net was allowed to touch the ground. Waders, ducks and geese were regularly taken, though sometimes groups would break through the netting and escape.

Also on the flats dowker nets were set to trap diving ducks. Nets of some four inches mesh were stretched horizontally between posts, some fifteen inches above the mud in areas where ducks had been feeding on the previous tide. During the tide cover, ducks and other diving birds such as grebes and divers were taken by becoming trapped in the mesh of the nets and drowning. 'Half a cartload' was considered to be a normal day's catch by Mitchell.

The wildlife of the mere played a considerable part in its economy, and after its draining the decoy described in Chapter 4 was built. How successful this was is unknown since no records survive, and presumably it fell into disrepair during the nineteenth century.

Nowadays, what is known as 'the mere' is once again an important wetland, due to the activities of the Wildfowl and Wetland Trust and the Wildlife Trust for Lancashire, both of which have important reserves on what was once the mere bed. Open areas of water once again attract wildfowl to the area. Where once barnacle geese wintered, thousands of pink-feet (Plate 8.16) are now attracted, not only by the wetland features, but by the root crops, the inefficient harvesting of which leaves plenty of food for them. It is very unlikely that the numbers of barnacle geese ever approached the present-day counts of pink-feet, and this

Plate 8.16 *The pink-footed goose* (Anser brachyrhyncus) *is now the most significant bird of the mere, with nearly a third of the world's population wintering in the area.*

goose is undoubtedly the most significant bird of the mere and the reason for the establishment of the Wildfowl and Wetland Trust Reserve. This reserve has also attracted large numbers of duck, but perhaps the swans which it has attracted are the most significant addition to the mere in winter. Both whooper and Bewick's swans have visited the Ribble marshes in small numbers for many hundreds of years but numbers have increased very significantly over the years since the arrival of the Trust. The geese and swans show the more dramatic aspects of the conservation story on the mere, but the Mere Sands Wood Reserve (Wildlife Trust for Lancashire) gives a hint of what the mere was once like. Open areas of water, surrounded by reeds and woodland, create an environment similar to that of the old mere, though it may lack the grandeur of the old vast areas of open water. Despite its smaller scale, the reserve provides more than a hint of the past when the 'great Martinensian marsh' extended from Rufford to the western skyline. Here visitors can see for themselves much of the natural history of what was the largest lake in England.

CHAPTER NINE

Rural Life, c. 1840–1950

Audrey Coney

By the mid-nineteenth century Martin Mere was essentially a country-side of fields, deep ditches, some fringing woodland, and the occasional game covert (OS 6 ins, 1845, sheets 75, 76). Although this diversity provided habitats for birds of open country, woodland and water (see Chapter 8), the vagaries of an unreliable drainage system (see Chapter 7) provided challenging conditions for agriculture. The wetland landscape could, and frequently did, return. This chapter describes aspects of Martin Mere's local society and rural life between about 1840 and 1950. It places particular emphasis on one mereside family, the Seddons, who farmed Old Midge Hall and New Midge Hall in Scarisbrick. The family was long established in the area, but Robert Seddon's retirement to Southport in 1988 brought the family's long association with this part of Scarisbrick to an end. Robert was the third generation to farm New Midge Hall and his experiences are supplemented by anecdotes and papers passed down from parents and grandparents. To this corpus of material must also be added details from diaries written during the 1930s by Frederick Holder, an accountant and well-respected amateur naturalist. These diaries provide a wealth of information on rural life, local flora and fauna, and conditions on the mere. Holder married the daughter of a Scarisbrick gamekeeper, William Langdon, who lived at the Shooting Box near to New Midge Hall, and the insight that his diaries also provide into the gamekeeper's yearly routine is described in Chapter 10. There are, in fact, Seddon family connections with the Shooting Box. This was once the home of Robert Seddon's maternal grandfather, the gamekeeper William Mayor.

A farming family

Both New Midge Hall and the Shooting Box are relatively late compo-
nents in Scarisbrick's settlement pattern. Neither place existed when
William Yates published his map of Lancashire in 1786, and both are
absent from the township's tithe map of 1839 (Yates 1786; LRO, DRL
1/71). In the late eighteenth century there were just two farmsteads in
this locality, Wyke and Midge Hall. They lay in close proximity to the old
basin of Martin Mere, recorded on Yates's map as dry only during
summer months. Half a century later the remoteness and dampness of
the area were undiminished, for the tithe map could still describe the
Scarisbrick portion of the old lake as marsh used as summer pasture.
This map depicts Wyke farmhouse as lying within a nook of land at the
extreme northern tip of the township, an area probably known as Otterhouseholme in medieval times (see Chapter 3). By the mid-nineteenth
century Wyke Farm was bounded by the former basin of the mere, by
the drained Wyke outlet towards the west and by enclosed mossland.
Midge Hall, almost a mile to the south-east, occupied a sliver of land
between other mossland enclosures and the former brink of the mere.
Both tenements comprised a mix of older fields and later allotments of
mossland. In 1839 the final improvement of the waste in this part of the
township was perhaps a relatively recent undertaking: the tithe map left
many fields unnamed and a few of those attached to the Wyke estate
even remained in their natural heathland condition. At this time neither
the Wyke nor Midge Hall held any part of Martin Mere. That area
remained in the hands of Charles Scarisbrick (LRO, DRL 1/71) and in
1845 horses and cows were agisted there at weekly rates of 3s. 0d. and
2s. 6d. per animal respectively (Bailey 1992: 87). Land from the old lake
basin perhaps passed into tenant hands when Midge Hall tenement was
divided in the 1870s. After this division the original farmhouse became
known as Old Midge Hall. Its daughter settlement, New Midge Hall, was
constructed about a quarter of a mile to the north-west (Fig. 9.1). This
part of Scarisbrick retains its sense of isolation even today. Wide vistas
over farmland are interrupted only by coverts for game, and access to
lonely homesteads is difficult over rough road surfaces. Those farm-
houses that lie within the old mere basin are linked by a network of

meanygates – narrow commonways, frequently bounded by deep ditches and often poorly maintained. The occupancy of these isolated homes has changed in recent years: several are now owned and lived in by families no longer dependent on agriculture (see Chapter 11).

The intricate bonds of kinship and family support that linked the older agricultural community are well demonstrated by the complexity of Robert Seddon's own family history since the mid-nineteenth century. In 1839 James and Thomas Seddon were tenants of Wyke and Midge Hall farms respectively (LRO, DRL 1/71). By 1876 Wyke Farm was occupied by the Howard family, but the original Midge Hall perhaps

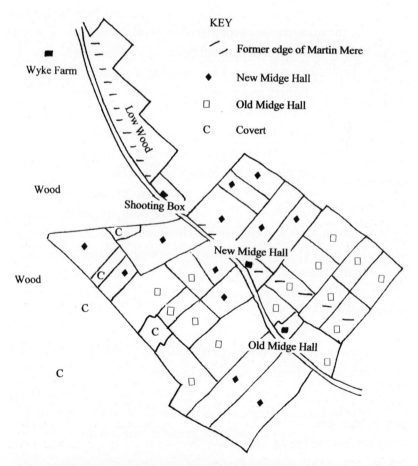

KEY

↗ Former edge of Martin Mere

◆ New Midge Hall

◻ Old Midge Hall

C Covert

Wyke Farm

Low Wood

Wood

Shooting Box

New Midge Hall

Wood

Old Midge Hall

Fig. 9.1 *The fields of New Midge Hall and Old Midge Hall in 1957, based on a plan for the sale of the Naylor-Leyland Estate (in possession of Robert Seddon).*

continued to be farmed by Thomas Seddon (LRO, DDSc 122/68). Thomas Seddon had four sons: James (Robert Seddon's grandfather), William, Thomas and Nathan. William eventually became tenant at Old Midge Hall while James ultimately acquired both this farm and New Midge Hall. There was, however, no opportunity for Nathan and Thomas Seddon to continue the family farming tradition. Instead, Nathan trained as a blacksmith, and later went to America on behalf of the government to buy horses for the Boer War. Thomas, a joiner and wheelwright, helped in the construction of New Midge Hall and in due course founded the Southport firm of Seddons Undertakers (Robert Seddon pers. comm.).[1]

James Seddon's acquisition of Old Midge Hall and New Midge Hall was due to the misfortunes encountered by previous occupants. At Old Midge Hall, William Seddon suffered financial problems: at New Midge Hall, the first tenant was evicted for shooting a pheasant (see below). Both James's son, Robert, and grandson, also Robert, were born at New Midge Hall. Robert Seddon senior was born in 1879, and he and his wife were over forty by the time that their son arrived in the world, a circumstance that led one family friend and neighbour to describe the new arrival as 'a very late hatched 'un'. Robert had an older sister, Ellen, who continued the family's agricultural traditions by marrying a local farmer. She lived at Mere Hall, a farmstead built within the drained lands of Martin Mere and close to her childhood home. Robert Seddon senior died in 1945, leaving his wife and young son and namesake to take over the running of New Midge Hall. Into this long-established local family there came in the aftermath of World War II a most unlikely newcomer. German bomber pilot Karl Herold had been captured during the allied invasion of Normandy and was sent initially to America as a prisoner-of-war, but spent the latter part of the war in England. After peace was declared he chose not to return to his former homeland in what was now East Germany. He ultimately arrived at New Midge Hall, where he became almost one of the family. When Robert's mother died in 1967, Karl was to say sadly but proudly, 'She was my mother, too'.

---

[1] All the anecdotal information contained in this chapter comes from the authors' personal communication with Robert Seddon unless stated otherwise.

Plate 9.1 *New Midge Hall, front elevation (photograph in possession of Robert Seddon).*

Karl Herold would have found the flat, windlashed landscape and wet climate of lowland Lancashire markedly different from either Germany or America. Homesteads around Martin Mere inevitably suffered from the permeating dampness of the general atmosphere and, as one local farmer put it, 'Yer went to bed to get out of t'dew'. Soil surfaces around New Midge Hall lie only 2 m above sea level, and it was to counteract this all-encompassing wetness that the foundations of the 1870s farmhouse were raised to a height of just under 3 m OD. The house (Plate 9.1) was warmed by coal fires, but Robert Seddon remembers it as extremely cold in winter. Built of locally made brick, the farmstead initially comprised a parlour, a kitchen, a lobby or hall, and four bedrooms. One of the bedrooms was later converted into a bathroom.

The first occupier of New Midge Hall was Philip Ascroft. He appears in estate accounts for 1870–71 under the name of Philip Ashcroft. In that account year the Scarisbrick Trustees paid out several sums of money for work on new buildings on Martin Mere and in the moss-lands. They include reimbursements to James Houghton for casting clay, for making bricks and for sugar bags to cover the bricks. More specifically, in August 1870, John Tomlinson was paid £100 for building work at Philip Ashcroft's. The following April he received a further £443 10s. 7d. for constructing Philip's farmhouse and buildings on Martin Mere (LRO, DDSc 79/1/45). Ascroft's tenancy of New Midge Hall was brief: it terminated abruptly after his eviction for shooting a pheasant. With shooting rights exclusively reserved for the lords of Scarisbrick, their friends and authorised gamekeepers (Mutch 1988: 26), tenant farmers could clearly expect harsh punishment if they infringed this code of conduct. In a more lenient era, though, Robert Seddon was assured by *his* landlord, Roger Fleetwood Hesketh, that history would not be repeated. Fleetwood Hesketh purchased several farms on the fringe of Martin Mere in 1957 and New Midge Hall was among them (Foster 2002: 127–28).

Philip Ascroft's downfall provided Robert's grandfather, James Seddon, with an unexpected opportunity to acquire the tenancy of New Midge Hall. The pitfalls and insecurity of tenant farming in the late nineteenth century are demonstrated, however, by the difficulties suffered by James's brother, William. In 1886 William Seddon was forced to surrender Old Midge Hall after he encountered serious financial problems. He was in arrears with his rent and had not, for the past three years, paid the agreed proportion of expenditure incurred on new farm buildings. In September 1886 his debts amounted to £423 19s. 4d. and the estate agent prepared a notice to distrain his goods. Soon afterwards, on 11 November, William Seddon surrendered Old Midge Hall to the Scarisbrick Trustees (LRO, DDSc 79/1/49). In return he received £123 19s. 4d. which was to be considered as a gift back out of the rent and arrears. This amount was also to operate as a settlement for work done for the Trustees (LRO, DDSc 79/1/45).

William had carted building materials. Among sixteen items listed were deliveries of 50,000 bricks, 42 tons of pavers, 91 tons of foundation flags, 195 tons of cinders for foundations and 1040 loads of ashes. The total cost was £132 11s. 8d. (LRO, DDSc 79/1/45). With his farm taken from him William Seddon was forced to find alternative accommodation and work. He moved to a cottage with a small amount of pasture land in Wood Moss Lane in Scarisbrick and operated a milk round.

Plate 8.10 *The snipe* (Capella gallinago) *was probably a common breeder on the bogs surrounding Martin Mere; while it is still to be found breeding on the mere it is no longer common (photograph by J.D. Drakeley).*

Plate 8.11 *The redshank* (Tringa totanus) *now breeds on the mere area but is probably a recent arrival (photograph by J.D. Drakeley).*

Plate 8.12 *The whooper swan* (Cygnus cygnus) *is an increasingly common winter visitor to the area, where it probably bred in immediately post-glacial times.*

Plate 8.13 *While there is no evidence that the osprey* (Pandion heliaetus) *ever bred on the mere, it was probably a regular visitor to what would undoubtedly have been a good feeding ground for the species.*

Plate 8.14 (a) *The great crested grebe* (Podiceps cristatus, *above) and* **(b)** *the dabchick* (Podiceps ruficollis, *below) were almost certainly common breeders on the mere until the time of the drainage in 1697 (photographs by J.D.Drakeley).*

Plate 9.2 (b) *Wetland soils to the front of New Midge Hall.*

Plate 10.2 *The Shooting Box and part of the adjacent woodlands.*

Plate 10.6 *Low Wood near the Shooting Box; site of the 1930s pheasant hatchery and pigeon-trap.*

Plate 11.2 *Windblow over Rufford mere and mossland.*

Plate 11.6 *A few of Hubert Pilkington's finished articles.*

Plate 11.7 *The Martin Mere Wildfowl and Wetlands Centre in Winter.*

Plate 11.8 *The former game covert at Mere Sands Wood Nature Reserve.*

Plate 11.10 *The Causeway Heys in Rufford in winter.*

James Seddon was more successful with his tenancy of New Midge Hall. Indeed, after his death at the age of 85, he was described as an excellent farmer who 'thoroughly understood the conditions under which he laboured on that vast and fertile area' (newspaper cutting in possession of Robert Seddon). The deaths of both his wives, however, must have ushered in traumatic periods in his life. He employed a housekeeper in the interim between first and second marriages, and again after the death of his second wife. The housekeeper, Mary Ashcroft (no known relation to Philip Ashcroft), proved to be extremely strict. During the day her employer's sons were banished to the 'back kitchen', a building attached to the washhouse in the farm yard. They were denied access to the farmhouse until bedtime. Mary Ashcroft's special *bête noire* was dust on linoleum floors. This was difficult to avoid when boots were removed after a long day in the potato fields, and Robert's father's solution was to shake his socks into his bed. The youthful memories of Robert junior are more pleasant. They include cycle rides along the meanygates of Martin Mere and picnics among gorse, heather and birches in Six Fields Covert in the midst of the old lake basin.

Farming the land

On the wetland soils of the Martin Mere area, mixed farming was the traditional type of agriculture until the second half of the twentieth century. Then, rising rents and greater profits from growing crops paved the way for the largely arable landscape of today. The older mixed farming practice is well portrayed by the Scarisbrick tithe map and award. In 1839, of 54 fields on Thomas Seddon's Midge Hall holding, 26 were down to arable and the remainder were used as meadow or pasture. The old-established fields supported the major portion of the unploughed land. Arable agriculture was mostly in evidence in mossland enclosures (LRO, DRL 1/71). As yet, of course, this farm held no land in the old lake basin.

The lease of New Midge Hall from the Scarisbrick Trustees to James Seddon in the early 1880s provides important information on farm management (document in possession of Robert Seddon). As with other leases described below, this was a printed document and its clauses probably applied to other holdings administered by the Trustees. James Seddon's tenancy began on 2 February 1882, ran from 'year to year', and was terminable on twelve months' notice by either party. The annual rent for the 98 acres was £117, payable on 1 June. A commencement date of 2 February is interesting. This is Candlemas, an ancient festival of candlelit processions celebrating the formal opening of spring and 'the month which drives the darkness from the afternoon' (Hutton 1997: 139–45). This time of anticipation of better farming weather was an appropriate date for the beginning of a new tenancy. Furthermore, it allowed for final preparation of the ground before the growing season.

James Seddon would be acutely aware, however, that his tenancy could be terminated if he became insolvent, was in arrears with his rent for more than 21 days, or breached his agreement. There were countless ways in which this agreement could be broken. The Scarisbrick Trustees retained all rights to minerals, timber, underwood, pollards and saplings. They also reserved exclusive rights to shooting and fishing and to the preservation of game, rabbits, snipe, wild duck and other wild-fowl. James could ferret and net rabbit burrows on the farm between August and February but he could not, in theory, shoot over his land nor fish in his ditches. He must endeavour to prevent trespassers entering his land; keep his farmhouse, buildings, gates, fences and roads in good repair; and maintain his watercourses. The Trustees undertook to pro-vide raw materials for any repairs but cartage was the tenant's responsi-bility. The extent to which James adhered to the terms of his lease agreement is unknown, but some laxity on the part of his landlord is evi-dent from the way some stipulations were not, even at the outset, fol-lowed through by the Trustees themselves. For example, the tenant was expected to manage and crop his fields according to a schedule attached to the agreement. Yet the information as to which fields were to be farmed as arable, meadow or pasture was never entered on his copy of the document.

There is no doubt, though, that many conditions of this lease of New Midge Hall were aimed at good husbandry. Each spring James Seddon was expected to level molehills and anthills and endeavour to destroy all moles and vermin on the tenement. Every year before the month of August he was to eradicate weeds, thistles, docks, rushes, whins and brambles growing in the fields and alongside adjoining roads. If he burnt the peat or heather on his land without the consent of the Trustees or their agent he could be penalised at the astonishing rate of £60 per acre in additional rent. Similarly, consent was required before he could sow two white straw crops in successive years or convert meadow and pasture to arable. The latter offence carried a penalty of £20 per acre in additional rent. Manure produced on the premises could neither be sold nor removed and one-third of the hay and half of the straw produced on the farm must remain there. If hay and straw *were* sold off the farm, two-thirds of any sales had to be expended in 'the purchase of good natural or artificial manures or cake [animal food] to be bestowed on the premises'. Similar clauses regarding the selling of hay and straw are a feature of many eighteenth- and nineteenth-century leases on the south Lancashire plain (see for example LRO, DDM 21/52; 21/54; 21/57). They reflect the interdependence between urbanised Liverpool and its rural hinterland. Because of an abundance of human and animal manures in that hugely overcrowded town it was possible to set aside the canon of the Norfolk system of agriculture, whereby hay and root vegetables were consumed only on the farm and straw was trodden into manure by livestock. The farmers of south Lancashire grew produce for Liverpool's inhabitants and provided hay and straw for its animals. In return, their delivery vehicles returned home laden with copious quantities of town manure (Coney 1995). This practice allowed rural fields to be fertilised without the need for large numbers of farm livestock. In 1885 the winning farm in the Liverpool Prize Farm Competition had 160 acres of arable land but just 6 acres of grass. Cows were kept only for home consumption (Edwards 1885). The Scarisbrick Trustees in 1880 clearly had a more cautious attitude towards extensive conversion of pasture to arable. In fact, they required James Seddon to keep a 'sufficient' number of horses, cattle, sheep and other stock. He could not, however, take in any 'score' cattle without the consent of the Trustees or their agent. This last measure was presumably aimed at preventing over-grazing.

Conservatism on the part of the Scarisbrick Trustees is evident in other clauses in James's lease. For instance, the tenant was expected to perform three boon days annually with his horses when required or else pay an additional rent of 10s. 0d. per horse for every neglect or refusal. He was also obliged to attend the manor court of Scarisbrick and to submit to its rules and regulations. Despite such obligations there is no evidence that yearly boons, or even payments *in lieu* of cartage or ploughing duties on the demesne, were still extracted in Scarisbrick in the late nineteenth century. Nor is there documentation to show that the manor court still operated.

James's lease agreement also outlines the procedure to be observed at the end of the tenancy. He must leave at least 120 tons of good farmyard manure 'properly cast up in the middenstead' for the benefit of the Trustees or the incoming tenant. If he sold items intended to be used on the premises (for example, one third of the hay, half of the straw and all the manure) he would incur fines of £5, £3 and £1 per ton respectively. For their part, the Trustees agreed to abide by the terms of the Agricultural Holdings (England) Act of 1875 and allow compensation for drainage work, watercourse improvement, erection or enlargement of buildings, and the laying down of permanent pasture. They also agreed to pay for half of any wheat crop, provided that it was sown on well manured and properly prepared potato or other root ground. In fact, if wheat was sown on land previously well manured and summer-fallowed, they would pay as much as two-thirds of its value. In order to qualify, though, a land valuation would have to be made in July before the crop was sown.

James Seddon acquired another lease for New Midge Hall in 1899 (document in possession of Robert Seddon). In all probability the underlying reason was enlargement of the tenement to 101 acres and increase in rent to £123 17s. 4d. The clauses in this lease are broadly similar to those of 1882. By now, however, responsibility for repair of main building walls, principal timbers and roofs had passed to the Scarisbrick Trustees, with the tenant maintaining items such as windows, pumps and water pipes; gates and fences; and roads and bridges on the tenement. The Trustees' disinclination to adopt the intensely arable agriculture practised by certain south Lancashire farmers is evident from their restrictions on ploughing meadow and pasture. On the other hand, cultivated land was to follow the 'four-course rotation' system, a method of farming that originated in east Norfolk. It actually comprised a complicated yet flexible six-course rotation in which tilled land lay fallow every third year. The aim was to produce fat stock from arable crops. Bullocks were fattened on turnips in winter and later on rye-grass and clover. The method certainly proved successful in east Norfolk: when farmers sold their beasts in May and June, beef from this district reigned supreme in the markets (Kerridge 1967: 296-98). The Scarisbrick Trustees doubtless hoped that their Lancashire farmers would be equally fortunate.

James Seddon's second lease continued to impose constraints on removing manure and now included a penalty of £2 per ton in additional rent. Increasing bureaucracy is seen in the tenant's obligation to produce samples and vouchers for any purchases of natural, artificial and farmyard manures and for any 'cake' (animal feed) used on the premises. James was also expected to provide evidence of the application or use of manure or cake if required to do so. Arrangements for the final year of the tenancy were broadly similar to those outlined above. Corn must not be grown where corn had grown the previous year nor should land sown with first year's clover and rye-grass be ploughed. In addition, the outgoing tenant must allow access to stubble once the crop was removed and provide free stabling and accommodation for the incoming tenant so that he could commence ploughing operations. There is no mention of boon services in James Seddon's lease of 1899. The tenant was, however, bound to attend the manor court of North Meols if required. This court continued to be held twice a year until 1926 (Pat Perrins pers. comm.).

The tenancy of New Midge Hall passed to Robert Seddon senior in 1914 (deed in possession of Robert Seddon). The acreage remained at 101 acres, but the rent increased to £150. There were still restrictions on ploughing meadow and pasture and on removing manure from the farm. The tenant was obliged to keep a sufficient stock of animals and provide documentation and samples for fertiliser and cake. Nevertheless, there is evidence of greater arable flexibility. It was sufficient that

Robert Seddon cultivate the farm in a good and husbandlike manner. He could not, however, use any part of the farm as a market garden or display advertisements.

On Robert Seddon's death in 1945 the lease of New Midge Hall passed to his son and namesake. Although his widow could have acquired the tenancy, both she and the Scarisbrick estate agent were keen to secure young Robert's future on the farm. If Mrs Seddon had succeeded her husband as named occupier of New Midge Hall, there would have been no guarantee that on her death the estate would pass to her only son. Robert's own lease agreement is missing. He remembers its clauses, though, as very similar to those in his father's lease and always regarded them as guidelines rather than absolute rules.

The fields of New Midge Hall straddle the interface between lake and mossland and overlie wetland earths with rather different origins. The soil behind the farmhouse is the Martin Mere Complex (Plate 9.2a). This formed on the bed of the lake and is richer in nutrients than most of Lancashire's organic soils. The surface is a friable black loamy peat. It overlies a black organic mud, laminated with deposits of silt and fine sand. This fertile soil can produce heavy arable crops, but adequate drainage is vital. Under cultivation there is also a tendency for the organic material to oxidise and for the peat to shrink. By contrast, the peaty soil to the front of New Midge Hall belongs to the Altcar Complex (see Colour Plate 9.2b following p. 176). It contains frequent remains of reeds and sedges. The plough layer, a friable, black, well-humified peat, can be slightly loamy because of marling, but in lower waterlogged horizons the peat is often a dark reddish brown. This soil also requires artificial drainage. Although never inherently rich in nutrients, it responds to the addition of fertiliser, and moisture-retentive properties allow plants to make steady growth. On the other hand, susceptibility to late frosts meant that many twentieth-century farmers on land such as this chose to grow maincrop potatoes, oats, peas and brassicas (Crompton 1966: 73–74; Soil Survey, sheet 75).

Both Robert Seddons clearly understood the advantages and limitations of the land. Their principal crop at New Midge Hall was potatoes – second earlies and maincrop varieties. By contrast, in the 1930s at

Plate 9.2 (a) *Looking over the mere near New Midge Hall (photograph in possession of Robert Seddon).*

Mere Brow on the sandy side of the mere, farm labourers and small-holders competed with each other to be first to produce new potatoes. Popular varieties at Mere Brow were Ninetyfold, Epicure and Sharp's Express. A late frost could be disastrous, but in favourable seasons potatoes could be lifted by early June. On mosslands at some distance from this hamlet, however, growing later maturing potatoes was the norm (Mere Brow Local History Society 1990: 15). Other crops grown at New Midge Hall included carrots; brassicas, such as sprouts, cabbages and cauliflowers; and spring-sown oats and barley. That it was eventually possible to grow wheat successfully on these frost-susceptible soils was due to the development of quick-growing strains that could be sown in spring. Older varieties required a longer period of growth. Carrots were difficult to grow before the advent of selective weedkillers, for it was all too easy to pull up the immature crop along with the weeds. The situation improved with the introduction of paraffin, the first selective weed-killer to be used at New Midge Hall. This killed weeds but left carrots unscathed. In the early years of his tenancy Robert Seddon senior sold his produce at Liverpool market, making the journey in his horse-drawn wagon. This age-old delivery method had lapsed before his son acquired the tenancy. About 1925 local produce merchants such as James Martland of Burscough began collecting goods directly from local farms. Yet smallholders in Mere Brow continued to use horse-drawn carts to take produce to Southport for door-to-door sale at private houses, boarding houses and hotels until World War II (Mere Brow Local History Society 1990: 15).

The Seddons' livestock comprised roan or dark-brown shorthorn cattle (Plate 9.3), pigs, horses, poultry and sheep. The last were usually ewes intended for the next season's breeding. In the decade after 1940 they were brought by truck from the Trough of Bowland to the Lancashire plain, where they remained for about four months before being returned to the uplands. Bowland farmers erected their own fencing on these lowland farms, but many sheep were attacked by local dogs. Most stock at New Midge Hall, however, was bred and reared on the farm. Goslings were often raised by broody hens and occasionally piglets neglected by the sow were bottle-fed. Many smallholders and cottagers around Martin Mere, however, kept just a single pig and this was usually slaughtered at Christmastime. After providing pork for Christmas dinner, the carcase was salted for two weeks on a large stone slab in the pantry and then hung up to dry in the kitchen. The head provided brawn, fat was rendered down and leftovers were made into sausages (Mere Brow Local History Society 1990: 15). New Midge Hall maintained a cattle herd of about twenty beasts. Bulls were rarely part of this herd and cows were put to the nearest available animal instead. The family's dairy requirements were supplied from just two or three cows, and Robert's mother and other family members helped with milking and butter-making. Milking could be a hazardous occupation at times, for cows can deliver a hefty kick. The number of shire horses was normally four (Plate 9.4). This was the number required to pull the self-binder at harvest – two in front leading two behind.

Before the advent of self-binders in the late nineteenth century, corn and hay were cut with a reaper or mowing machine (Plate 9.5). This had a 'flake' at the back next to the knives and, as soon as enough material for a sheaf was gathered, the operator put his foot on the flake to release

Plate 9.3 *Robert Seddon, senior, with shorthorn cow (photograph in possession of Robert Seddon).*

Plate 9.4 *Four of James Seddon's shire horses. The photograph shows James, second from left, with his sons and a farm worker (photograph in possession of Robert Seddon).*

the load. The corn was then gathered into sheaves and tied with bind-
ings made from the same material. Hay was left to fall in a swathe across
the field. The self-binder both cut the corn and tied it into sheaves which
were then set up to dry in stooks of six sheaves for about ten or twelve
days. When dry, the sheaves were either stored in a barn or built into a
stack. Stacks at Mere Brow were thatched with straw or reeds as protection against winter weather (Mere Brow Local History Society 1990: 15).
By the 1930s it was commonplace for farmers to arrange for a threshing
machine to separate the grain from the straw (Plate 9.6). Threshing
machines were owned by a contractor and the earliest ones were driven
by a steam-traction engine on coal provided by the farmers. That
threshing was hard and dusty work is clear from this account of threshing day at Mere Brow:

> On top of the stack two or three men would be feeding the sheaves into the
> machine. At one end the straw came out and went into the baler. Two men
> were required to take off the bales as they were pressed and form them into
> a stack. Another two men were at the other end of the thresher where the
> grain was fed into sacks. Some grain would be stored to be used for seed
> the following year, some would be used for feeding to stock, and the rest
> would be sent to the local miller to be ground into meal. The threshing
> contractor would have three men who travelled with the machine to the
> farms in the area. The farmer would need six more men to help out on
> 'threshing day'. (Mere Brow Local History Society 1990: 16)

The trend towards mechanisation in agriculture gathered pace in the
1930s. New Midge Hall acquired its first tractor in 1938 from Hesfords
in Ormskirk. The increasing sophistication of farming equipment
inevitably hastened the demise of local harvest customs. One of these,
prevalent in North Meols and surrounding districts, was called 'cutting
the neck'. In a time when reaping was done with sickles or reaping hooks
(Plate 9.7), the last stalk of the last field to be harvested on each farm was
cut by throwing one or other of these implements. These were not easy
tools to throw in a straight line. Holder's description of events indicates
that, while it was customary to allow younger men to have first try, the
prize of beer was likely to go to the veteran harvester (Holder and Frankland 1932–37: III, 12).

Plate 9.5 *The reaping machine with two seats. One man drives the horses; the other binds the sheaves. This machine could also be used for mowing hay (photograph in possession of Robert Seddon).*

Plate 9.6 *John Ball's threshing machine at Plough Farm in Crossens (photograph in possession of Harry Foster).*

Plate 9.7 *Harvesters at work on the North Meols portion of the mere – reaping, raking and making ties of twisted straw for the sheaves (Photograph in possession of Harry Foster).*

Martin Mere's farmers sometimes had to adapt agricultural equipment to suit their soft organic soils. Carts, for instance, needed extra wide wheels and, on newly improved earth, plough horses wore pattens – flat pieces of wood with leather thongs wrapped around their hooves. A heavy horse would often panic if it began to sink into soft ground. The animal then had be freed from the plough so that it could extricate itself. Organic earths contained other hazards. The well-preserved trunks and roots of prehistoric oak and pine frequently caught on the plough, and when this happened work usually halted abruptly. In order to deal with the problem the first tractors at New Midge Hall pulled ploughs with a special peg attached. This released the implement whenever it snagged on these remains. Bog oaks and pines were found most frequently in the mossland, but the timber was harder in specimens from the lake basin. In fact, so resistant were some of these ancient trees to disposal that farmers frequently resorted to blowing them up. Winter floods brought additional anxiety, for the waters of Martin Mere could return with a vengeance. Indeed, when Robert's grandparents were first married, it was sometimes possible to row by boat from Scarisbrick to Rufford across the old lake basin. In the 1930s Holder was to record how prolonged frost turned flooded fields and ditches into an icebound landscape, where local youths were quick to practise skating skills (Holder and Frankland 1932–37: I, 155–56).

In the 1930s a combination of inadequate drainage and deteriorating land quality resulted in rent reductions for some farms. Proposals put forward by the Catchment Board to improve the situation surprisingly failed to gain the full support of the farming fraternity. There were fears that deepening major drainage channels would cause water shortages for crops and animals. One tenant anticipated this by taking matters into his own hands and digging a deep hole in one of the lesser dykes (Holder and Frankland 1932–37: V, 225). Drainage improvement could even exacerbate the very problem it was designed to eliminate. Cutting the new Middle Drain caused the peat to shrink and the water table to rise. After the Seddons' tractor became bogged down in one of the consequent mires, Crossens Pumping Station was forced to lower the water table even further. Cutting the Middle Drain had other results that were more advantageous. Its excavation produced a fertile mountain of soil and this was spread across adjacent land in the following year. In the fields of New Midge Hall the next crop of King Edward potatoes produced tubers almost as big as turnips. There were other remarkable crops in the summer of 1976. A combination of hot, dry weather and a water table kept artificially high to prevent peat shrinkage caused Robert's sprout plants to grow virtually as tall as him.

The inadequate drainage of the 1930s was nowhere more apparent than at Lord's Mere, the local name for Lord Derby's Burscough portion of the old lake. This frequently waterlogged ground could support grazing for horses and cattle only when conditions allowed. Indeed, much of the place still resembled a bog when Holder visited the area in the spring of 1932. The fenland aura of this landscape was further enhanced by the materials and construction method used in building a barn and huts. Walls and roofs were thatched with reeds and 'props' were bog oak 'washed out of the mere during the winter floods'. This was the work of an old craftsman using the products of the wetland. Attempts to drain Lord's Mere in the years prior to 1932 had barely lessened the amount of standing water. Although Holder was concerned to find the bird population lower than on his previous visit in the 1920s, shoveller, reed bunting, sedge warbler and redshank were just some of the species nesting there. Among the rushes and reeds grew other moisture-loving plants such as cotton grass, bog bean, flag iris, marsh marigold, marsh violet and cuckoo flower. In the early 1930s wildlife conservation lay far in the future. Holder records the shooting of two otters in November 1931. A pair of bitterns suffered the same fate in August and September 1932 (Holder and Frankland 1932–37: I, 109–10; V, n.p.).

In those parts of the mere where drainage was more successful, constant ditch maintenance was essential. One aspect of this was mole-catching. The Scarisbrick Estate employed a mole-catcher because it feared that these animals would undermine and collapse the banks. The cost was apparently borne by individual farmers and was commensurate with the acreage of individual holdings. The list of 'mole rents' for North Meols and Scarisbrick in 1876 contains over 240 names with payments varying between 1d. and £6 0s. 5d. (LRO, DDSc 122/68). Moles were caught in pincer traps set in underground runs, and rows of skinned victims hanging on a fence were evidence that the catcher had done his work. These animals were a problem in the Shooting Box garden. On one occasion, after traps were placed in the burrows, ten moles were caught before tunnelling operations ceased. Trapping moles could be a lucrative occupation: when prices were high during the First World War, William Langdon received £15 for a consignment of moleskins (Holder and Frankland 1932–37: I, 197). The last mole-catcher on the Scarisbrick Estate was Tom Fazackerley. No-one undertakes this task at the present time.

The water in the dykes still supports an eel population. Formerly, these fish were caught with a share, a fork-like implement with serrated edges, and carried home in a bucket to be skinned before cooking. Another method of catching eels is described in Chapter 11. Eel pie was a favourite dish in the Seddon household. Rabbit pie was another delicacy. It was customary for Scarisbrick gamekeepers to invite local farmers to attend rabbiting days, when normally about thirty to forty rabbits were caught. Although the supply dwindled with the onset of myxomatosis, Robert remembers convivial evenings after the shoot when participants sat down to hot-pot and potato pie in the kitchen at New Midge Hall. The potatoes, of course, had been produced on the farm.

The mosslands of the Lancashire plain are famous for their potatoes. Local tradition even claims that North Meols was the first place in England to grow this vegetable. It seems that an Irish ship laden with potatoes was wrecked on the Lancashire coast in the seventeenth century and that local farmers were quick to take advantage of its bounty (Bailey 1992: 24). By 1700 potatoes were grown in several places close to Martin Mere (LRO, WCW William Barton of Tarlscough, 1690; Thomas Aughton of North Meols, 1691; Henry Blackhurst of the Holmes, 1700; Richard Ball of Banks, 1700).

In the twentieth century between 400 and 600 tons of potatoes were harvested annually at New Midge Hall. Each spring the seed potatoes were put into spritting boxes until the first shoots appeared. Initially, the crop was planted by hand, but this method was superseded first by the horse-drawn planter and then, in the late 1960s and early 1970s, by the auto-planter. In an attempt to combat weeds, the fields were harrowed with a drill harrow before the first potato leaves appeared above the ground (Plate 9.8). For many years the potato crop was hand-harvested. The arrival of the mechanical potato digger in the 1920s proved a mixed blessing, for it tended to scatter the crop instead of collecting it. Both farmers and labourers alike believed that it was quicker and cheaper to harvest tubers with a fork. Although the mechanical potato digger eventually improved in efficiency, the advent of the elevator, which deposited potatoes neatly in a row, provided a more satisfactory solution (Robert Seddon pers. comm.; Holder and Frankland 1932–37: III, 218).

Maincrop potatoes were harvested in October. Holder records the scene in the 1930s when lines of bent pickers, rows of hampers and horses straining with full loads over sodden soil were a common sight across the mere. Autumn squalls sent workers scurrying to shelters constructed from corrugated iron sheets on a wooden frame. Among many

Plate 9.8 *Farm worker Harry Wallbank, with drill harrow on the fields of New Midge Hall (photograph in possession of Robert Seddon).*

who doubtless sighed with relief at the day's end were the Irish harvest-men who appended their names to the comment 'Rest and be thankful' on a stable door (Holder and Frankland 1932–37: I, 34). The appalling state of local tracks and farmland in a wet autumn is well illustrated by Holder's photographs of October 1932, which show the sodden unpaved way between the Shooting Box and New Midge Hall merging into a background of flooded fields. Similar conditions existed in the lane near Winacre Farm in North Meols (Holder and Frankland 1932–37: I, 36).

Newly harvested potatoes were not normally despatched to market immediately. Farmers preferred to wait until the price was right (Mutch 1988: 15), and trade usually picked up around Christmas. The crop was bagged using wooden rather than metal shovels because this caused less damage to the tubers. In a time before the storage of potatoes in barns became commonplace, the crop was placed in field clamps, there to release the characteristic pungent odour of moist tubers onto the autumn air. The clamps were covered with straw and soil and quickly began to heat up internally. In order to combat this, drainage tiles were inserted into the sides to draw off the steam. In late November the clamps received an additional covering of discarded potato haulms as frost protection, and Plate 9.9 shows a cart heavily laden with these potato tops. Frosty weather provided farmers with the opportunity to cart manure onto fields otherwise too wet and difficult for wheeled transport. During the 1960s potatoes began to be stored in barns. The potato clamp, once a feature of the winter landscape, is now a distant memory.

Robert Seddon and his father normally employed three or four labourers and provided seasonal work for two Irish harvesters. The latter were paid on a piece-work basis, with payment at the end of each week. In the early 1940s the rate varied between 1½d. and 5d. per score (twenty yards) of dug potatoes, and Robert junior remembers helping his father assess the distance with the aid of a tape-measure. The Irishmen rose at daybreak and worked until dusk. Their midday snack frequently consisted of bacon sandwiches with inch-thick slices of bread and was followed by an evening meal with potatoes on the menu. The Irishmen prepared their own helpings and these were cooked by Robert's mother. Like most of their ilk, they were accommodated on the farm on which they worked. New Midge Hall's 'paddy shant' (the name

Plate 9.9 *Loading potato tops (photograph in possession of Harry Foster).*

given to accommodation for Irish labourers) was a single-storey building attached to the open-fronted washhouse in the farmyard. Occasionally, its occupants chose to seek alternative sleeping quarters over the
stable, where the heat from the horses provided extra warmth. The
Irishmen made their own straw mattresses, which they covered with
grey army-surplus blankets.

Most Irish harvesters returned to the same farm year after year, and
those who worked at New Midge Hall were no exception. They arrived
in England at the end of May, and travelled first to the hay country of
east Lancashire where cattle and dairy farms proliferated. After the hay
was gathered in, they usually wrote to the Seddons to ask if they could
come the following week. Later, the advent of the telephone made communication easier. Irishmen normally arrived on the Lancashire plain in
July in time for the corn and potato harvests. By November they were
ready for home, anxious to return as soon as possible, as they feared the
ferry crossing in winter storms. Home was normally Achill in County
Mayo, but two regular workers at New Midge Hall, Tommy and Tony
McFadden, eventually settled in Southport. When Tommy McFadden
first arrived in Liverpool he could hardly believe that such a place
existed. He was aghast to see a woman enter a public house and commented that if any female in Ireland had done the same she would have
been regarded as having gone to 'Old Nick' altogether.

Despite the reputation of many Irish labourers as unreliable, Robert
Seddon recalls only one occasion when they caused difficulties for him.
That incident took place shortly after the end of World War II, when
Robert was a relatively new tenant farmer. The harvesters in question
were thoroughly unsatisfactory workmen. When they also demanded
extra pay, the young farmer was forced to remonstrate with them. The
ensuing argument between Robert and one of the Irishmen ended
abruptly when Karl, the German bomber pilot, jumped off his tractor,
hit the man on the chin and floored him. The harvesters left Scarisbrick
that same day. Their uncouth behaviour was exceptional. Robert
remembers the majority as good workers who worshipped regularly at
St Elizabeth's Roman Catholic church in Scarisbrick. They took some
pride in their appearance and had their clothes laundered by local

women. In fact, after one cherished white shirt came back a striped one, the aggrieved owner cycled off in search of better service in the town of Ormskirk.

The network of rutted minor roads in the north of Scarisbrick could prove hazardous for wheeled transport. In the 1930s one vehicle en route for the Shooting Box with a consignment of broody hens had lost both doors before it reached its destination. Local farmers generally put much of the blame for the poor condition of the lanes on the heavy threshing machine. This precursor of the combine harvester was owned by people such as J. Ball of Crossens, Johnsons' of Banks and Heatons' of Halsall. It originally trundled around the area from farm to farm at the farmers' bidding. In winter, smoke from its engine spiralled above withy-encircled farms before even the full light of day, and wagons freshly laden with loads of straw were often outward bound to market by eight o'clock (Robert Seddon pers. comm.; Holder and Frankland 1932–37: I, 155, 198). Responsibility for repair of Scarisbrick's access roads lay with the estate, but this body was often lax in carrying out its obligations. One farmer, who encountered particular difficulty with his potato-laden wagons in 1934, threatened to withhold the use of his land for pheasant-rearing purposes unless the estate repaired the lanes. By 1937 these lanes were in good condition with a covering of red shale and the Scarisbrick Estate was clearly keen to keep them that way. It now dictated that all farmers must thresh within the same period, and that the threshing machine should visit farms in consecutive order without going backwards and forward at the farmers' whim. Naturally, this change was unpopular. Tenants again contemplated using the rearing field as a bargaining lever. 'One would think,' wrote Holder, 'the farmers ought to appreciate the disappearance of the old muddy and deeply rutted tracks' (Holder and Frankland 1932–37: III, 20; VI, 139).

Fred Holder's deep affection for the area is evident in every diary. He records a March walk through rushes and bracken on the old mossland; a September cycle ride over the misty mere; and winter skating on flooded fields and ditches (Holder and Frankland 1932–37: IV, 349; VI, 120–21). Sometimes the diarist revives older memories, such as the occasion when he found a corncrake's nest in Fishpond Covert. By also including details from his wife's diary, Holder adds an extra dimension to the minutiae of mereside life. These extracts date from Gertie Langton's single days as the gamekeeper's daughter. She records the occasion when the shooting tenant of Lord's Mere came to tea and commented favourably on the water cress: 'Great stuff for keeping pimples off the back of your neck'. Gertie's writing also demonstrates the gulf that can exist between country dweller and town person. On one occasion the local postman reached the back door at the exact time that keeper Langdon deposited three freshly killed chickens there. 'He said we were cruel', she wrote. Gertie was both amazed and amused at the postman's ignorance of wildlife. She was particularly intrigued by his belief that the mole was a kind of rabbit (Holder and Frankland 1932–37: V, 223).

This gamekeeper's daughter could be more perceptive than her husband on occasions. Holder describes the March day when he, his wife and the underkeeper, Ellis Tomlinson, disturbed a courting couple in fond embrace upon the turf:

> 'Nah, lad,' said the keeper, 'tha's started early.' I remarked to Gertie that the 'lad' seemed well over thirty, but she replied that Ellis meant the 'lad' was out on the grass early in the year. (Holder and Frankland 1932–37: VI, 121)

Anecdotes have figured fairly frequently in this chapter. They have a place, too, in Chapters 10 and 11. Such snippets of rural life broaden our understanding of rural society and add an extra dimension to agricultural history.

CHAPTER TEN

Gamekeeping and the Shoot

Audrey Coney

Local shooting records and Frederick Holder's description of the game-keeper's annual routine provide an insight into gamekeeping practices on Martin Mere between about 1920 and 1956. They also shed some light on how this remote part of lowland Lancashire was affected by economic depression in the 1930s and by the consequences of World War II.

There have been gamekeepers in Scarisbrick since at least the late eighteenth century. One, Joseph Glover of Prescot, was appointed by Thomas Eccleston in 1778 to kill game for Eccleston's own consumption in his manor of Scarisbrick. Glover was also authorised to seize any dogs and equipment kept and used by persons not entitled to kill hare, pheasant, partridge and rabbit (LRO, DDSc 26/41). Joseph Glover's tasks were undoubtedly less exacting than those of his twentieth-century successors. By the 1930s Scarisbrick had two head gamekeepers. One looked after the Scarisbrick Hall area, while the other was responsible for matters concerning game across the western half of Martin Mere and some of the surrounding mossland. This chapter is concerned with gamekeeping on the mere and mossland. Head gamekeepers for this area oversaw a territory that included the Scarisbrick portion of the drained basin and sectors of the former lake in North Meols and Tarleton. The whole contained 4720 acres of open shooting and 175 acres of coverts. In the 1920s and 1930s the Scarisbrick Estate Office managed this land for Captain C. E. Scarisbrick and Sir Edward Naylor-Leyland, and leased game rights to a shooting tenant (LRO, DDSc 79/1/10; RS).

Successful gamekeeping demanded a range of qualities. It required an affinity with the countryside; extensive knowledge of pheasants and their ways; tremendous stamina; good administrative skills; and the ability to mix with different levels of society. More than any other employee on a country estate, a gamekeeper was largely left to his own devices. He had to expect the unexpected and to take the initiative where poachers and vermin were concerned (*The Gamekeeper*, 1932, vol. 35: 313). In the 1920s and 1930s the head keeper for the western part of Martin Mere was normally supported by a staff of two underkeepers and one assistant (Plate 10.1). The head keeper, however, had ultimate responsibility for rearing and protecting pheasants, maintaining coverts and organising the shoot. His Scarisbrick home was a rent-free bunga-low known as the Shooting Box and constructed in the late nineteenth century. It lay surrounded by game coverts and beside a track leading along the former lake shore from New Midge Hall to Wyke Farm (see Colour Plate 10.2 following p. 176). This building replaced an earlier

Plate 10.1 *William Mayor and his gamekeeping staff about 1918. From left to right, William Mayor, Dick Parker, Dick Tomlinson and William Langdon (photograph in possession of Harry Foster).*

shooting box on the opposite side of the lane (LRO, DDSc 79/1/10; Robert Seddon pers. comm.).

Robert Seddon's grandfather, William Mayor, was head gamekeeper from the the late nineteenth century until 1926. His day normally began at 5.30 am and ended at dusk, but he was often up and about in the night as well. Mayor found his Scarisbrick landlord to be a hard taskmaster. Once, after a long working day, he was summoned to discuss shooting matters with Squire Charles Scarisbrick at Scarisbrick Lodge in Hesketh Park in Southport. It was three miles (4.8 km) from the Shooting Box to this part of the town, and on arrival the gamekeeper was ordered to wait until his landlord finished dinner. Yet this was no opportunity for rest. Mayor was despatched with a telegram to the post office, which in those days remained open until 10 pm. Shooting matters eventually concluded just before midnight, but the tired keeper was now charged with delivering a letter to the estate agent. Agent Betham listened carefully to Mayor's complaint that Charles Scarisbrick had little sympathy for his tenants. He commented that such people thought that a man was like a horse – never tired. He also warned that, if Mayor wished to keep his job, absolutely nothing could be done: landlords like the Scarisbricks would ensure that similar work was unobtainable locally. As later events were to show, William Mayor was not alone in his dissatisfaction. The following year Betham disappeared with the rent money (Robert Seddon pers. comm.).

Mayor was succeeded as head gamekeeper by William Langdon. Langdon came to Lancashire from Shropshire and was initially employed on the Scarisbrick Estate as a rat-catcher. He then worked as an underkeeper before eventually obtaining the post of head gamekeeper. During his time as underkeeper Langdon lived at Sluice Cottage in the midst of the old mere basin (Robert Seddon pers. comm.; Holder and Frankland 1932–37: V, 58). Plate 10.3 shows William Langdon, his wife and family in Six Fields Covert.

Plate 10.3 *William Langdon and his family (photograph in possession of Robert Seddon).*

The gamekeeper's year

The gamekeeper's year began early in April in advance of nesting time. The Scarisbrick Estate reared its own birds and April was a time for disposing of as many natural enemies of the pheasant as possible. Traps were set in the holes of rat, stoat and weasel in the coverts and also at the entrances to ditch drains. Individual keepers had their own methods of setting traps. Langdon, for example, always lubricated his with 'sweet oil' (olive oil). Rat, stoat and weasel were not the only animals caught by trapping, for accidental casualties included little owls, the occasional redshank and marauding cats. Keepers usually shot the latter on the spot (Holder and Frankland 1932–37: I, 195–96). April was also the month for driving rats from the shed where game food was stored. Fleeing rodents were normally shot on sight and those that escaped often ended their days in the vermin trap. The squeal of a snared rat often penetrated to the Shooting Box kitchen, but was soon silenced by the 'knobkerry' – a short stick with a knobbed head. On one occasion the underkeeper, Ellis Tomlinson, was inspecting his traps when he heard the distant squeal of a captured rat. He soon discovered that two of his feathered charges had reached the victim first, for he found a pair of hen pheasants pecking away at a large hole in the animal's back (Holder and Frankland 1932–37: V, 223).

The first half of April was generally a slack period for keepers. Nevertheless, long rows of sitting boxes needed coats of creosote and, as nesting time approached, coverts had to be protected from intrusion by humans and dogs. Bare places in the woods were planted with rhododendron. The initial supply of pheasant eggs was usually procured from 'wild' birds (that is, birds which had been reared on the estate and had survived the shooting season) during the first two weeks of April. By the third week of that month keepers were systematically searching coverts and lane verges. One foray by an underkeeper produced 174 eggs. Until the mid-1920s 'wild' hen pheasants were also caught during March and April and placed in an aviary within one of the coverts to lay. Their eggs were then transferred to the hatchery. The Shooting Box aviary was last used in 1926. It was abandoned after the netting fell into disrepair and the practice of buying in large quantities of eggs from a game farm became commonplace. The pheasants it housed were caught in pits known as 'catchers'. These had a drop lid supported by a stick and a scattering of corn at the base. Unfortunately, though, these pits often caught moorhens instead of pheasants. As a trapped moorhen ensured that no pheasants could be captured until the trap was re-set, exasperated keepers would often grab the unfortunate moorhen by the legs and knock its head against the nearest tree. The demise of the aviary and therefore of the need to trap 'wild' pheasants led to an unforeseen rise in the local moorhen population. In 1932 the head keeper of one neighbouring estate was so tired of these birds raiding his covert corn that he organised a moorhen drive. Almost one hundred birds were destroyed (Holder and Frankland 1932–37: I, 196, 198–200; V, 60).

Scarisbrick gamekeepers had, in fact, purchased pheasant eggs since at least the 1921–22 season, when 1420 eggs were acquired. Although this number reduced to 800 eggs in the following season, it increased to 2500 eggs per annum between 1928 and 1933 (LRO, DDSc 79/1/10). The game farm was changed each year in order to vary the stock (Holder and Frankland 1932–37: I, 199). The records of the Scarisbrick Estate contain catalogues from farms as far afield as north Oxfordshire, Berkhamsted and Petersfield in Hampshire, and Chichester in Sussex. The earliest-laid eggs commanded a premium rate. In 1932–33, for instance, those from Dwight's Pheasantries at Berkhamsted cost £6 per hundred if purchased before 12 May, but only £2 5s. 0d. per hundred at the beginning of June. Similarly, in 1934, one hundred freshly laid pheasant eggs from W. Harvey and Sons in north Oxfordshire cost £5 5s. 0d. if bought before 12 May. Yet the cost fell to £2 10s. 0d. for eggs purchased just before 2 June (LRO, DDSc 79/1/10).

The first consignment of bought eggs normally reached Scarisbrick about 27 April. Pheasants do not usually make good sitters, so their eggs were placed under broody hens in the hatchery. A shortage of broody hens was a source of anxiety for gamekeepers and whenever this happened local farmers were approached. It was a point of etiquette that keepers did not enter a farmyard while the farmer selected surplus broodies. Unfortunately, the price of protocol meant that most fowls acquired in this way were 'nowt but skin and bones'. Once settled in the hatchery, imported broodies were initially given a ceramic egg. With pheasant eggs costing a shilling each in the 1930s, a keeper could not afford to take risks with indifferent foster parents. The authentic eggs were aired in trays and turned daily before being placed under the hens and the ceramic eggs removed. Most hens took their eggs quietly but a sharp peck could bring blood to a keeper's hand. Because space was limited, broodies were taken off to feed in two batches, a process that lasted about two hours as each hen had to be pegged to a stick. This routine continued into May (Holder and Frankland 1932–37: I, 198–99, 201–202).

It was the custom for local tenant farmers to allow one of their fields to be used for pheasant-rearing. A different field was used each year in order to thwart the disease called gapes which, once present, could linger on for a season or two (Robert Seddon pers. comm.). Losses directly due to gapes were not especially heavy but affected birds were listless, failed to fly to roost and took little interest in their own safety. Consequently, considerable numbers fell victim to vermin, dogs and foxes. Outbreaks of gapes often occurred during rainy periods and, if allowed to run their course, would result in stunted flocks that failed to thrive. Gamekeepers were advised to keep their young birds on the rearing field for as long as possible and to dress them with a gapes remedy before removal to the covert. If disease then broke out, one course of action was to add Gapecuria or some other medication to the food. It was also advisable to fumigate affected and weak birds (*The Gamekeeper*, 1932, vol. 35: 319).

As pheasant chicks were also in danger of getting wet, lost, or eaten by stoats and foxes, rides about three metres wide were scythed in the long grass of the Scarisbrick rearing field. As soon as the coops were placed along these rides, the area was kept under watch at night, with either the head gamekeeper or an underkeeper observing the flock from May until harvest from a cabin in the field. It was also necessary to prevent the brood from wandering into the sporting territory of neighbouring estates. Roaming pheasants were a particular nuisance when the wind was in the east. This usually signified settled weather, and young birds would always walk against this wind and head away towards Lord Derby's Burscough portion of the drained mere (Robert Seddon pers.

comm.). The brood was usually transferred from rearing field to covert in July or August. The young birds still remained at risk from foxes and vermin, however, and good gamekeeping practice demanded that they did not wander far afield. Nearby fields of standing corn and other tall crops were an especial hazard, because pheasants were difficult to shepherd back to safety from such places. Harvesting machinery posed a particular danger (*The Gamekeeper*, 1932, vol. 35: 316). Within the relative security of the coverts the young pheasants were fed with corn on a daily basis. This practice ensured that they frequented those areas that in due time would be shot over by the shooting parties.

Scarisbrick gamekeepers were themselves expert marksmen. They often used the gun to scare wild geese away from the coverts or to obtain the occasional bird for the table. Local farmers in the 1930s were also allowed to shoot geese on their own farms, but many were poor shots. Holder records how one individual had been known to blaze away at birds on the wing 80–100 yards beyond range (Holder and Frankland 1932–37: V, 463). During the shooting season local farmers were sometimes invited to shoot woodpigeon in the coverts. Although the advent of pheasant-rearing time in April put a temporary end to this sop for the tenants, keeper Langdon would sometimes make a furtive foray alone to shoot woodpigeon. He was careful, though, to wait until the wind was in the right direction so that the sound of his gun was masked from the ears of the nearest farmer (Holder and Frankland 1932–37: I, 197). Woodpigeons consumed more than their share of pheasant food and caused enormous damage to crops. Holder records five hundred birds feeding on a single field on an autumn day in 1932 (Holder and Frankland 1932–37: I, 35). One method of controlling their numbers was trapping. Pigeon traps in the 1930s operated on the 'drop' principle, but Holder unfortunately provides no information as to how this worked. He does state, though, that keeper Langdon caught 21 pigeons in Low Wood trap in a single 'pull' in 1937 and that another keeper worked a similar device in Perch Pool Covert (Holder and Frankland 1932–37: VI, 478). Holder gives a more comprehensive description of an earlier method of catching pigeons in the coverts and also provides a sketch of the trap itself (Plate 10.4). This device consisted of a frame of logs and wood with the tops and V-shaped ends covered with wire netting. Lengths of cord netting along the open sides were concealed by fallen leaves and connected by strings to a hut in which a game-keeper waited for an opportune moment. As soon as several pigeons had entered the trap to eat grain strewn inside, the strings were pulled taut, the netting sprang up and the gamekeeper hopefully obtained his supper. But pigeons are wary birds, and these traps were only really effective during periods of snow or frost when the birds had difficulty finding food and lost just a little of their habitual caution (Holder and Frankland 1932–37: VI, 36–38).

Gamekeepers were also expected to keep the rabbit population in check and thus protect growing crops. One method of catching rabbits was to place muzzled ferrets in the burrows (Plate 10.5), and then to shoot the rabbits as they tried to escape. If ferrets were not muzzled, they would kill and eat any rabbits they caught underground. Rabbits were also caught by netting the entrances to burrows in the ditches. Once a rabbit was in the net, the gamekeeper usually wrung its neck. Game-keeping additionally involved keeping a vigilant watch for poachers.

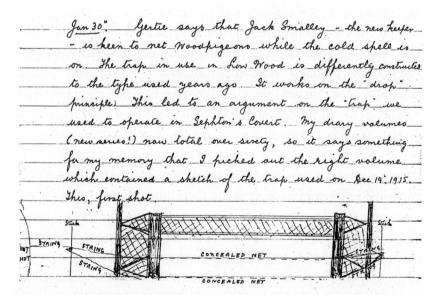

Plate 10.4 *Extract from Frederick Holder's diary and sketch of the pigeon-trap in use in 1915.*

Clauses in William Mayor's tenancy agreement allowed the gamekeeper to order local tenants to turn out day or night whenever assistance was required (Robert Seddon pers. comm.). Various deterrents were used against poachers during the 1930s. One method adopted by the under-keeper, Ellis Tomlinson, was to place trip wires at foot and throat height across the paths in covert glades. These wires were unbarbed and infi-nitely more humane than the barbed wires Ellis's own gamekeeper father had used for the same purpose. Scarisbrick gamekeepers also used trip wires to activate an alarm gun but these varied in their success rate. On one occasion the gun went off but the keepers failed to hear the report. The startled poachers escaped unscathed but left behind a bag containing several rabbits and a young hare. After this, the Shooting Box acquired a replacement gun with a 'shuddering roar', an idea culled from one of the underkeepers who had served in the trenches in World War I (Holder and Frankland 1932–37: VI, 119, 407). Another deterrent was the concealed pit. Extending across the width of a glade, it lay deep, half full of water and polluted with rotting rabbit paunches. Such pits were uncovered just before a shoot so that they could be visible to beaters. On one occasion, however, keeper Ellis missed his footing and fell victim to his own device in waist-deep water. He later commented to Langdon's daughter that 'it's an awful feeling, and any poacher who goes in at night won't want to come again' (Holder and Frankland 1932–37: V, 447; VI, 119). Poachers usually timed their first raid for just before the big November shoot in the Shooting Box woods. They frequently had advance notice of the occasion, even though the head gamekeeper and his staff were loath to reveal the date until it was necessary to notify the beaters. The keepers' concern was that raiding poachers would scatter the pheasants from woodland coverts into surrounding farmland. If this happened just before a covert shoot, there would be less sport for the shooting party. To combat this possibility, keepers often kept nightly watch from a hut in Big Wood and one gang of four poachers who blun-dered upon this hut found the full gamekeeping staff inside. The men escaped in the dark and rain but not before one of their number had received a charge of buckshot in his pants. A rifle and several shot pheas-ants were later recovered (Holder and Frankland 1932–37: I, 51; V, 455).

Plate 10.5 *Rabbiting with ferrets, dogs and guns. The bag contains the ferrets (photograph in possession of Harry Foster).*

The seasonality of poaching is well recognised by historians, who have related autumn and winter peaks in nineteenth-century poaching offences to times of higher unemployment and poverty. In considering poaching offences in East Suffolk, however, Osborne has suggested that economic and environmental factors underlay this seasonal pattern and that maturity of game, and availability and marketability of the quarry were often the key determinants (Osborne 2000).

The shoot

The shooting season was the culmination of months of hard work by the gamekeepers. Although there were several shoots in a season's sport, the most important occasion was the Big Shoot. This occasion, and that of 1932 in particular, is graphically described by Holder, who also provides a plan of the action (Holder and Frankland 1932–37: I, 51–67; Fig. 10.1). The Big Shoot was centred on woodlands by the Shooting Box (see Colour Plate 10.6 following p. 176) and was normally held in November.

Gamekeepers deemed this to be a far more auspicious event than the numerous 'rough' shoots over fields and outlying coverts. By early morning on the day of the Big Shoot those fields that would be shot over were bereft of farm animals, as the head gamekeeper had already warned local farmers of the event (Robert Seddon pers. comm.). Fields near the Shooting Box were also largely empty of game, for most pheasants had been driven into the coverts. Other birds were driven in later as beaters converged on their starting positions from outlying underkeepers' cottages. Beaters were hired on an *ad hoc* basis. That the number of men in search of work could exceed the number required is clear from an entry in Gertie Langdon's diary for 1930:

> Beaters are getting a nuisance, for at 8 am there were three waiting on the Drive for Dad, but he has got all he wants. More came later, and Dad took on one for tears were flowing down his cheeks as he talked to Dad. He had a wife and two children and no work. This man was genuine but some of the beaters can pitch the tale [...] Farming is going down at present for there are farmers' sons and farmers themselves after jobs as beaters for a few shillings, and some do look down and out, too. (Holder and Frankland 1932–37: V, 447–48).

Two dozen beaters were hired for the Big Shoot of November 1932, and one of the head gamekeeper's many tasks was to ensure that these men were used to the best advantage once shooting commenced. Some beaters acted as 'stops' to prevent game wandering far afield, but their main objective was to converge on the coverts during a drive and so send the birds forwards and upwards over the trees to the waiting guns. Once his beaters were in position Langdon returned to the Shooting Box in time to greet the shooting party and to discuss driving methods for the day. By about 10.30 am, with guns unpacked and cartridge bags filled, the eight sportsmen, their loaders and a handful of beaters set out behind the game wagon. The 'guns' rarely brought their own dogs to the Big Shoot: those present normally belonged to the resident underkeepers. The shooting party included the shooting tenant and a specially invited guest (Holder and Frankland 1932–37: I, 51–67). This guest sportsman was allowed to take part in all covert shoots, and was either a man nominated by the lessor of the shooting rights or someone chosen

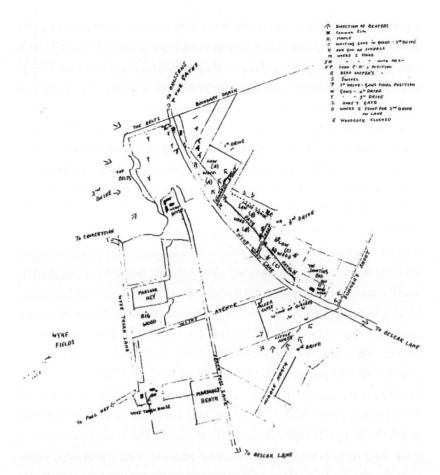

Fig. 10.1 *Frederick Holder's 'Map of the ground beaten during the annual Big Shoot on Martin Mere' in 1932.*

by the nominee (LRO, DDSc 79/1/10). Occasionally, the guest was accompanied by his own gamekeeper who acted as loader, but more frequently his chauffeur assisted. Scarisbrick keepers were guarded in their approach to a visiting gamekeeper. He was, for example, free to join chauffeurs, loaders and Scarisbrick gamekeepers for lunch, but he was usually offered a chair away from the table, where he sat throughout the meal and 'kept his own councel' (Holder and Frankland 1932–37: I, 65).

As the morning's drive commenced the pheasants were driven out by the beaters and flew towards the waiting sportsmen at intervals. Some birds, however, skulked amidst the rhododendrons in the coverts and had practically to be trodden out. For safety reasons it was important to have a good rise of game. In order to encourage pheasants to rise Langdon devised his 'swivel' – a length of cord to which scores of white rags were attached. With one end of this cord tied to a tree, the other was pulled up and down to give a dancing motion. The degree of shooting expertise varied. While there were some excellent shots, in November 1932 a man referred to by Holder only as 'Mr T' blazed away but never a feather left his birds. Mr T also fired at a passing starling. He missed. A covey of thirteen partridges also escaped intact (Holder and Frankland 1932–37: I, 51–67).

After three drives it was time to recover fallen game and return to the Shooting Box for lunch, where strict social segregation governed dining arrangements. Separate rooms were set aside for beaters; for chauffeurs, loaders and underkeepers; and for the shooting tenant and his party. During lunch the keepers supervised the transport of game to the larder before joining chauffeurs and loaders for sandwiches and coffee in the kitchen. The shooting party dined on hot-pot and held a sweep on the quantity of shot game. At the Big Shoot of 1932 the lunchtime bag was 331 pheasants, four partridges, eight hares and two rabbits. After two or three further drives in the afternoon, and a final game tally of 461 shot game, the guns fell silent about 4.30 pm. Cattle and poultry, penned in since the previous night, could now be released. There was time, however, for the 'guns' to have a final toast in their room while chauffeurs and underkeepers filled their game baskets. As the 'guns' tipped their helpers, head keeper Langdon collected his beaters together for a drink (pints of Bass were much in demand) and gave each one the day's pay of six shillings. Langdon then re-engaged the best beaters for the next shoot. Finally, the head gamekeeper was free to join his underkeepers for tea, the evening's discussion on the day's sport greatly enlivened by half a bottle of Green Stripe in a can of hot coffee (Holder and Frankland 1932–37: I, 51–67).

The number of shoots in a season varied. For example, the 'guns' were out on 28 occasions in season 1921–22 and on 17 occasions in season 1929–30. By 1933 the average annual bag over the previous five years was 1431 pheasants, 136 partridges and 460 hares (LRO, DDSc 79/1/10). In some seasons it was deemed necessary to preserve the stock of hen pheasants. Only cock birds were shot during a shoot in January 1934, and on that occasion pheasant shooting was supplemented by a hare drive. The total bag was 108 hares (Holder and Frankland 1932–37: III, 10). Occasionally the weather curtailed sporting activities. For instance, conditions were so poor in January 1937 that the last drive of the day was abandoned. The party returned early to the Shooting Box and, after a 'good windup', some of their number returned to their chauffeur-driven cars 'not too steady on their legs' (Holder and Frankland 1932–37: VI, 35).

Unsurprisingly, shooting and pheasant-rearing sometimes conflicted with farming activities. The shooting tenant and his party had access to local fields and the potential for damage was considerable. A tenant farmer could not prevent shooting over his land, but he could eventually claim damages from the shooting tenant. Another problem was pheasants 'basking' in dry summer soil in fields of potatoes. The birds fanned the earth with their wings and the exposed tubers then turned green and unsaleable (Robert Seddon pers. comm.). At New Midge Hall in 1927 Robert Seddon senior observed such damage to his crop of Red King and King Edward potatoes several months before the crop was harvested. Unfortunately, he failed to notify the estate office until the October day that he began to dig the tubers. By then one field of almost ten acres was almost completely spoiled. Independent valuation made on the farmer's behalf put the damage to eight acres at £60. By contrast, a second valuation made for the estate office calculated the damage at no more than £25. The agent naturally regarded the first claim as excessive. He also informed the farmer that the problem should have been reported when first noticed, rather than on the day that harvesting commenced. Seddon's response was to refuse the £25 offered in compensation. He said that he would not take less than £50 and that 'if he didn't get it he would see that they did not get much shooting over his land and would drive everything off it with his dog' (LRO, DDSc 79/1/10). The shooting tenant, Mr Harrison, eventually offered £30, or more if the farmer supplied a rearing field for the 1928–29 season. Ultimately, the agent paid out £35 on Harrison's behalf. For his part, Robert Seddon senior agreed to provide a rearing field, for which the shooting tenant would pay half a year's rent at the rate per acre of the farm. With the field in question amounting to 4.705 acres and the rate per acre to 39s. 7d., the farmer received a further £4 12s. 4d. (LRO, DDSc 79/1/10). There was at least one other occasion when the shooting tenant was obliged to pay compensation for pheasant damage to the potato crop at New Midge Hall. In 1935, Harrison paid the farmer £5 after keeper Langdon verified that this was a fair claim (Holder and Frankland 1932–37: IV, 399).

Frederick Harrison of Wavertree and Woolton in Liverpool was shooting tenant for the western part of Martin Mere and parts of the surrounding countryside in the 1920s and the 1930s. A shipping magnate, his company was the Harrison Line. Leasing shooting rights was an expensive undertaking as, in addition to the cost of the rights themselves, the lessee was accountable for expenses associated with gamekeeping and shooting. In the season 1929–30, for example, total outgoings were £1761 4s. 10d. The rents and wages of the gamekeepers amounted to £697 4s. 6d.; payment for an assistant keeper and watcher to £121; and rates and taxes to £152 4s. 3d. Pheasant eggs, rearing food and corn cost £414 7s. 1d., and expenditure on hospitality and payments for beaters' wages and the game cart disposed of a further £148 12s. 6d (Fig. 10.2). Harrison defrayed these outgoings by sharing the shooting with other 'guns' and by selling game to dealers and others (LRO, DDSc 79/1/10).

By 1933, however, the deteriorating economic climate was threatening the viability of game preservation and shooting on Martin Mere. Harrison encountered difficulty in finding other 'guns' to share the costs and his lease expired in February of that year. The following month he wrote to the agent for the Scarisbrick Estate stating that 'there are two of us and if we could find a third suitable gun we could be ready to talk but can't afford the expense of only two'. Harrison asked the agent to look out for a third party. Agent Booth's response was that he would like Harrison to carry on and hoped that he would find someone to share the costs. He suggested, however, that he (Booth) should advertise the shooting. In the event, advertisements in the *Liverpool Daily Post* and in *The Field* attracted few enquiries and no new lessee (LRO, DDSc 79/1/10).

PAYMENTS.

Stock:- Pheasant Feeders &c.	11.18. 9
Legal Expenses	13. 1. 0
Rents	697. 4. 6
Rates & Taxes	152. 4. 3
Assistant Keeper and Watcher	121. 0. 0
Pheasant Eggs (2,500)	150.14. 4
" rearing Food & Corn	263.12. 9
Hens for sitting	34. 4. 0
Keep of Dogs	29. 3. 0
Hire of Land for rearing	22. 0. 0
Wages Luncheons, Beaters/& Game Cart	111.10.10
Whiskey, Beer, Minerals &c.	37. 1. 8
Insurances	3.19. 6
Gratuities to Keepers & Others	34.10. 0
Management	50. 0. 0
Sundry:- Cartridges, Carting, Dog Licences, Keepers Suit, Coal & Bank Commission.	29. 0. 3
Total Expenditure	1,761. 4.10
Balance	77. 2. 3
	£1,838. 7. 1

TO ARRIVE AT COST PER GUN.

Total Expenditure		1,761. 4.10
Deduct:- Game sold to Guns	94.12. 0	
- do. - Dealers & Others	244. 6. 5	
Sundry Receipts	21.10. 8	360. 9. 1
		£1,400.15. 9

NETT EXPENDITURE - £1,400.15. 9

Divided between 4 Guns =	350. 3.11	
Deduct - Amount paid on Account to F. Harrison.	300. 0. 0	
	£50. 3.11	- Balance due from each Gun to F. Harrison, to which add each Game Account as per list.

Fig. 10.2 *Payments shown in the Statement of Accounts for shooting year 1929–30 (LRO, DDSc 79/1/10).*

By early April, Sir Edward Naylor-Leyland, co-owner of the shooting rights, was alarmed at the prospect of contributing to three gamekeepers' wages from his own pocket. This absentee landlord admitted to knowing nothing about the lie of the land nor of gamekeepers' requirements. Yet, when O. J. Humbert, his London advisor, wrote to the agent for the Scarisbrick Estate, he recorded that his client seemed determined that one keeper must be dispensed with. Sir Edward had even asked if just one man could keep down the rabbits and look after the woods. Alternatively, he wondered whether keepers' wages could be reduced if the men were employed solely on rabbit-catching and looking out for poachers. Humbert expected Booth to answer that one man could not carry on alone: there were lots of rabbits to keep down and the shoot, being near Southport, would be overrun with poachers if it was thought that only one man was looking after it. As to the question of reducing keepers' wages, Humbert's comment was that wages were not large and a cut of a few shillings a week would make little difference to his client. 'Would it be possible,' he asked instead, 'to knock off the suit of clothes this year?' This was a reference to outfits annually provided for the head gamekeeper and his two underkeepers, a cost normally borne by the shooting tenant. In reply, agent Booth wondered if the two underkeepers might share their time between their present job and necessary estate repairs (the estate was soon to be involved in drainage improvements) (LRO, DDSc 79/1/10).

In fact, Booth was continuing his efforts to keep gamekeeping and shooting a viable part of the Scarisbrick Estate's economy. He wrote again to Frederick Harrison asking if they could come to some arrangement. Booth was doubtless extremely relieved when the shipping magnate succeeding in finding two extra men who agreed to take half a 'gun' each, an arrangement he described as 'significant of the times'. Harrison agreed to pay the rents and wages of the three keepers as before and also £50 for the shooting rights (LRO, DDSc 79/1/10). Shooting across the western part of Martin Mere was now secured for a few more years, but by 1936 Harrison had reached the age of 65 and was becoming stiff in the arm. In a January shoot in the following year he only managed to bag one bird, and his loader commented that he had to 'do everything for him except put him to bed'. It was widely expected that when the shoot-ing tenant retired this would mark the end of game preservation on the mere in its present form (Holder and Frankland 1932–37: V, 122; VI, 35). Harrison finally relinquished his shooting rights at the end of 1939. Agent Booth informed Humbert, his landlord's advisor, that no rearing was expected next season, and in April 1940 Langdon drew up an inven-tory of his gamekeeping equipment:

1 double section dog-kennel	£10 0s. 0d.
20 sitting boxes	8s. each
2 sitting boxes, new	10s. each
80 coops with floors	5s. each
12 coops with floors, new	8s. each
12 runs for coops	1s. each
1 portable boiler	30s. each
3 brass alarm guns	7s 6d each
7 doz. traps	7s. per doz.
1 meal mincer	5s.
1 dusting bellows	5s.
22 beaters' cups	5d. each
92 drinking pans (enamelled)	2d. each
1 doz. large enamel plates	5d. each
1 doz. small enamel plates	3d. each
7 glass tumblers	3d. each

Langdon also added a note to the effect that the 22 sitting boxes accommodated 168 hens (LRO, DDSc 79/1/10). The end of an era was now a probability. Furthermore, England was at war.

In fact, the sport did not cease completely during World War II. Although the numbers of shot game were drastically reduced, there were often four guns out on the mere and mosslands. Changed circumstances are evident, however, in a letter signed by T. Scarisbrick concerning a shoot at Low Wood in November 1940. Scarisbrick made the suggestion that it would be better if he and the five other participants brought their own provisions 'as with rationing these days it is difficult to provide lunch for them'. There were other indicators of altered fortunes. For instance, the twelve beaters were half the contingent of 1932 and the number of pheasants shot was only 37 in total. On the other hand, there still seems to have been a token attempt at game preservation: Ellis Tomlinson's rent and wages appear in accounts of the early 1940s; and the head gamekeeper was still in occupation of the Shooting Box in 1941 (LRO, DDSc 79/1/10). In fact, William Langdon was to continue working in his beloved coverts until he was 80 years of age. When organised shooting restarted in the 1950s, however, he was told that he could continue as gamekeeper only if he was deemed fit to do so. Of course, this was an impractical proposition for a man of his age and Langdon was forced into retirement (Robert Seddon pers. comm.).

World War II had a more direct impact on Martin Mere than merely reducing shooting to a shadow of its former self. Four bombs exploded near Six Fields Covert in the middle of the mere on 7 April 1941 and, in another episode during the following week, both the Shooting Box and New Midge Hall were damaged. Subsequent repairs to the Shooting Box included renovating the front wall, propping up part of the gable, making good the foundations and brickwork, and re-plastering. Floorboards and guttering also needed attention. In August 1942, high-explosive bombs caused damage in the middle of the mere at Sluice Farm (LRO, DDSc 79/1/10). There were many German prisoners of war working on farms around the mere. Enid Pimblett, who lived in the Mere Brow area during World War II, remembers how a lorry laden with about twenty prisoners would call at local farms to ask how many labourers were required (Enid Pimblett pers. comm.).

It was perhaps 1956 before the shooting rights were leased again. The lessors were now the Smalley Estates, and the land in question covered parts of Scarisbrick, Burscough, North Meols and the borough of Southport. The lessees were a consortium of five men: Winston Blamire of Longton near Preston, John and Peter Holland of Southport, Duncan Marsden of Midge Hall near Preston, and Harold Sutcliffe of Hebden Bridge in Yorkshire. Under the terms of the lease agreement, this consortium had to ensure that ground game was kept down in order to prevent damage to plantations, crops and pasture; offer at least two-thirds of the number of shot hares to farm tenants; agree to invite a nominee of the lessor to take part in all covert shoots; indemnify the lessor against claims for damage to tenants' lands; and at their own expense to employ two gamekeepers. But the lessees were required only to endeavour to maintain a reasonable stock of game (LRO, DDSc 79/1/10). This was a different world from that of the 1920s and early 1930s. The heyday of shooting over Martin Mere was gone. Men of the calibre of Mayor and Langdon were part of a vanished era.

CHAPTER ELEVEN

Towards Today

Audrey Coney with Bill Pick

'There is nothing on the mere but farms', said Collins in the 1950s (1953: 62). He viewed the area as 'a life apart' and a place where few strangers went down the long, straight and stony roads between the parallel fields of Martin Mere. He recounted his visit to a farm where the piped water supply was only then in the process of being supplied, where hams hung from ceiling hooks and where the living room still retained its stone flagged floor. Geese and turkey fattened in the orchard, the butcher arrived once a week and the land supplied everything else. This farmer's wife was the third generation of her family to live on the mere. Her grandfather had come to the land when it was being ploughed for the first time and had seen the bricks carted for the farmhouse (Collins 1953: 62–63). There are echoes here of the Seddon family (see Chapter 9). Indeed, there are still several farms on Martin Mere that have been held by one family for three or more generations, and the area remains essentially a landscape of agricultural fields. On the other hand, the old order is changing: some farmsteads are occupied by people from non-farming backgrounds; amalgamation and diversification are in the ascendant; and wildlife reserves and leisure amenities increasingly attract visitors to the area.

Because of the sheer size of Martin Mere it is almost impossible to view the area in its entirety. The area is, in fact, divided into two quite distinct sections by the main drainage channel, the Sluice, and by its feeder drain, Boathouse Sluice. These watercourses run in a north-westerly direction towards Crossens Pumping Station, and most recreational and wildlife reserves are located north and east of this divide. Access to and through this area is by paved road, narrow meanygate and footpath.

For example, the route from Rufford through Holmeswood to South-port passes close to the former shoreline in places; the road from Burscough to Holmeswood crosses the old mere basin and the former islands of Great and Little Peel; and the footpath through the Leisure Lakes at Mere Brow takes the walker to the Sluice in the midst of the old mere. How different then is the prospect south and west of the Sluice and the Boathouse Sluice. Here, it is easy to lose direction, and approaching even the edge of the old mere basin can be difficult without a map. Frequently, there is no public access at all. In Burscough a foot-path does lead down from Derby Farm towards the Wildfowl and Wet-lands Trust at Martin Mere, but there is no right of way to the edge of the mere in the opposite direction until Scarisbrick. In Scarisbrick, the road leading towards the wetlands from the hamlet of Bescar becomes appre-ciably more stony as it approaches isolated farms near the old lake fringe. It meets eventually with a single-track road with passing places coming from the Southport direction. Within the old mere basin a vast grid of drainage ditches and meanygates links other isolated farms. These meanygates are unpaved and their bordering ditches are deep. Small woods and coverts lie scattered throughout the area. There is just one public footpath across this part of the old lake basin and cultivated fields do little to remove the enduring feeling of solitude. Those few out-siders who pass this way may even feel that they are intruding. They will certainly find it hard to appreciate that the sprawling fringe of urban Southport lies only one and half miles distant.

Farming

Controlling the former wetland of Martin Mere and its immediate envi-rons has never been a simple task. Watercourses, verges and meanygates require constant maintenance (Plate 11.1) and strong winds forging across dry, ploughed land can literally blow the soil away (see Colour Plate 11.2 following p. 176). Currently, agriculture is affected by low food prices and farmers have to adapt the way they use their land to suit market forces. Growing the more profitable types of produce helps to sustain good returns. Some farmers have turned to diversification.

Others have increased landholdings by acquiring extra acreage. For example, smallholdings set up after the war are now generally absorbed in larger farms.

Donald Sephton, of New Berry House on the former island of Great Peel, is pleased, however, that his elder son has taken over the family farm. Currently all the fields are in hand, although some were recently rented for £250 per acre per annum. Donald Sephton is the fourth generation of his family to farm here. Prior to the family's arrival from Halsall, some time before 1904, New Berry House did not exist as a farmhouse. It was previously three cottages providing homes for 'scorers' – men who oversaw the numbers of cattle and horses grazing the drained lands of Martin Mere (Donald Sephton pers. comm.).

Donald Sephton's father followed the mixed farming traditions of the area. Donald recalls the great quantity of hay that was grown on the land when he was young. This was sold as animal fodder to Liverpool or to places such as Mellor near Blackburn. A crop of hay rested the field, put fibre back into the ground and opened it up. Donald himself kept pigs and just one Jersey cow for milk for home consumption. For the past twenty years, however, the farm has been wholly arable. Hay is no longer

Plate 11.1 *Maintaining the waterway verge.*

profitable: the peaty fields of New Berry House are classed as Grade One agricultural land and arable crops – grain and potatoes – give better financial returns. Yet this farm provides an example of successful farming in sympathy with the environment. The Sephtons grow wheat, barley and potatoes under a system of crop rotation. Although artificial fertilisers are applied to the land annually, individual fields are down to potatoes about every six or seven years and these are manured before planting. The manure arrives on a tractor and trailer from a dealer in the Longton area, is applied at the rate of 30–40 tons per acre as required, and helps to maintain the moisture content of the land in dry seasons. Because insecticides are only used when necessary, beneficial spiders and ladybirds proliferate. A wide variety of woodland and farmland birds helps to keep less welcome insects under control. Ornithologists who survey this farmland report favourably on the variety of bird species present. Among them are woodpecker, long-tailed tit, thrush, corn bunting, goldcrest, owl (both barn and tawny) and buzzard. Saturday shoots in February control the numbers of woodpigeon, and consequently these birds do not constitute a particular problem. This farmland also supports newts, water voles, foxes and rabbits. There is obviously a need to watch the rabbit population, but the buzzards and foxes keep numbers down.

The Sephtons see no particular need to diversify. There is, however, a fishing lake for anglers and there are plans to convert some farm buildings into housing. The intention is that these new homes will be rented out rather than sold. Given the high cost of housing in the area, they will no doubt be eagerly sought after.

Clay Brow Farm in Burscough is a further example of a wholly arable holding. Farmer Hugh Caunce now lives in Newburgh, and when he first began to farm this land in the 1960s he kept cattle and poultry. These 70 acres, however, have been down to arable since 1972. There was an epidemic of fowl pest in that year and, because the price of eggs was low, Hugh never restocked his poultry flock. At one time the range of produce grown in his fields included potatoes, cereals, and vegetables such as spring onions, lettuces, cabbages, cauliflowers and leeks. With declining profits from growing greens, however, the farmer concentrated on wheat and potatoes. Sugar beet is a recent introduction, and six acres are currently 'set-aside' land (Hugh Caunce pers. comm.).

By contrast, David Slinger of Windmill Farm on the former Little Peel island farms wet soils that are not at all suitable for arable agriculture. Although potatoes were grown during World War II, since that time the farmers have concentrated on livestock – principally dairy and beef cattle. The land now supports sheep and cows and provides hay for the flourishing Windmill Animal Farm (see below). David Slinger's grand-father bought Windmill Farm and Holcroft's Farm from the Earl of Derby about 1940 for £500, and the land passed down through his son and grandson (David Slinger pers. comm.).

Much of this land has defied all efforts to drain it successfully. Some fields could only be used between May/June and October. David Slinger well remembers the times when they needed a boat to rescue sheep stranded by winter floods, and how this boat was always kept near the old windmill for that purpose. On land such as this a tractor might begin to sink if left in one place for any length of time. Consequently, whenever a cow fell into a ditch it took an army of men to extricate her. Often a crust of drier earth would form over permanently waterlogged soil. Sometimes, if hooves penetrated this surface layer, the animals might find themselves stranded in the underlying morass. Galloping animals could even cause the land surface to undulate. David well remembers the time that a Polish workman set out to herd the cattle, only to see the land rippling towards him 'like the skin on a rice pud-ding' as the cows galloped across it. In the belief that he was about to be overtaken by an earthquake, the terrified man threw himself prostrate on the pasture. The only occasion on which land like this dried out was during the drought of 1976, when it was possible to mow it for hay. Fields like these were only productive if water could be pumped away. As was the case with most farmers in West Lancashire, the Slingers employed Irish workmen. Brothers Paddy and John Dunn lived all year round in the old wash-house at Holcroft's Farm, which contained little more than a bed and a kitchen range. Their employers supplied them with bread, bacon, salt and potatoes. But they also begged potatoes from other farmers and caught rabbits to cook in an old paint pot. Paddy and

John were clearly less fastidious than the Irishmen who worked at New Midge Hall (see Chapter 9). David Slinger remembers that their bed was infested with rats. They also tended to disappear in the direction of Preston's public houses as soon as they were paid. On several occasions the police of that town telephoned the Slingers for verification of the Irishmen's good character. Yet, when sober, John and Paddy were extremely hard workers. John in particular was strong as a horse. He never seemed to feel the cold, worked in his shirtsleeves all winter, and could pick up hay bales with ease. He helped David's father, Matt, to milk 150 cows daily, and would check both cows and calves each night and perambulate the whole farm boundary. The combined acreage of Windmill Farm and Holcroft's Farm comprised a large unit of 600 acres. In 1971, however, Matt Slinger sold Holcroft's farmhouse and all but 100 acres of land to the Wildfowl Trust. In the deteriorating economic climate of the 1980s, this reduced acreage proved too small to be viable. The family considered diversification. David and his wife, Gill, now run the successful Windmill Animal Farm (see below).

Several other farmers have also diversified their interests. For instance, on the Holmeswood portion of Martin Mere, John Hinchcliffe set up Redblades Mowers in the early 1990s. He now sells and repairs grass-cutting equipment and lawnmowers. The fields formerly attached to this farm have been sold, but the family is still involved in poultry farming (John Hinchcliffe pers. comm.). In Burscough, the Travis brothers decided to concentrate on their packaging business. They retained their farm buildings at Wood End Farm, but sold fields in the old mere basin in 2003 to the Wildfowl and Wetlands Trust (see below).

In the past, farming life in the Martin Mere area depended to no small extent on service industries located in local settlements beyond its fringe. For example, Churchtown in North Meols, Mere Brow in Tarleton and Holmeswood in Rufford all had their smithy and adjacent wheelwright's shop. This juxtaposition of trades was an extremely common arrangement, and, in fact, the two trades complemented each other. For example, the wheelwright made the wooden felly (rim) and spokes for the wheel and the blacksmith produced its iron tyre. Plate 11.3 shows the Churchtown smith at work about 1945. Mrs Alice Yates of Holmeswood recalls how her grandfather was the Holmeswood wheelwright and local joiner. As he also made coffins, he was effectively the local undertaker. Of his fifteen children, two sons became joiners and three became blacksmiths. The demise of carts and wagons lessened the need for these skills, but a cousin of Mrs Yates used the former wheelwright premises in Smithy Lane for his joinery business and often sold nails and other small items. He later derived extra income from a large range of greenhouses behind the building (Alice Yates pers. comm.).

Mrs Yates is now over ninety years old and has always lived in the Mere Brow/Holmeswood area. She worked as a dinner lady in the local school at Holmeswood. The school, like the chapel, is still in being, but Mrs Yates feels that there is rather less of a community atmosphere today. Contributory factors may well be the closing of the two village shops (one of which also served as a post office), and the demise of both blacksmith and wheelwright. Places like these were a vital part of rural life. They did not merely perform a service: they were meeting places where local news could be exchanged and discussed. At the Mere Brow smithy local men even had their hair trimmed by the blacksmith,

Plate 11.3 *The Churchtown smithy (photograph in possession of Harry Foster).*

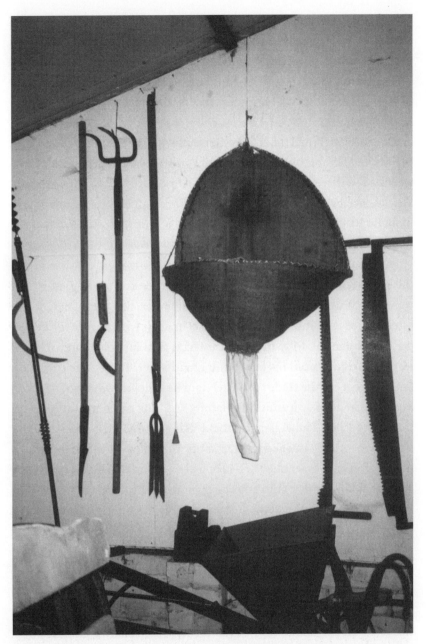

Plate 11.4 *'Bobbing bag' used by Alice Yates's husband. Once the eels were in the narrow tube at the end of the bag, they could not escape. The forked implement in the photograph is an eel spear.*

although it is said that he could only cut one style. This smithy is still a forge today, but gates and garden ornaments rather than horseshoes are now the norm. The Holmeswood smithy in Smithy Lane was turned into garages about ten years ago, and there are plans for a house conversion. Next door, the wheelwright's shop is currently undergoing conversion to a home.

Mrs Yates well remembers how her husband went 'bobbing' for eels in the Sluice. His bait was a bunch of worms tied to a piece of string, weighted with a plumb, and attached to a pole about five feet in length. He caught 'loads of eels' by this method and put the catch into a large 'bobbing bag' (Plate 11.4). Mrs Yates also recalls how the raw material for basket-making was grown in local willow beds.

Hubert Pilkington is the last of several basket-makers who worked in the Holmeswood area. His father, grandfather and great-grandfather were all basket-makers. His great-grandfather had been taught the essentials of the craft by an Irish basket-maker, who came over during the potato famine to work on local farms as a farm labourer. Hubert learned his skills from his father and grandfather. There were many different aspects of the trade to master, and he followed what was in effect a seven-year apprenticeship. The family was long based in Smithy Lane, but in the 1950s Hubert and Mabel Pilkington moved to their present home, where they opened a retail shop. Until the 1970s they also sold their basketware to wholesalers. Like several of his ilk, Hubert combined basket-making with poultry-keeping, housing his hens in a shed near his shop. He retired in 2000, but still retains the tools of his trade and many finished examples of his craft (see Plate 11. 5 and Colour Plate 11.6 following p. 176).

The different processes involved in basket-making are all labour-intensive and some of this labour was supplied by family and local people. The raw material came from nearby willow beds, one of which was sited on the damp edge of the former lake basin in Holmeswood. The cut willows, known as 'twigs', were harvested in January and February before the leaves unfurled. They were first laid out on the ground, then tied into sheaves and left to dry throughout the summer. After the potato harvest was over, the dried twigs were bundled together into

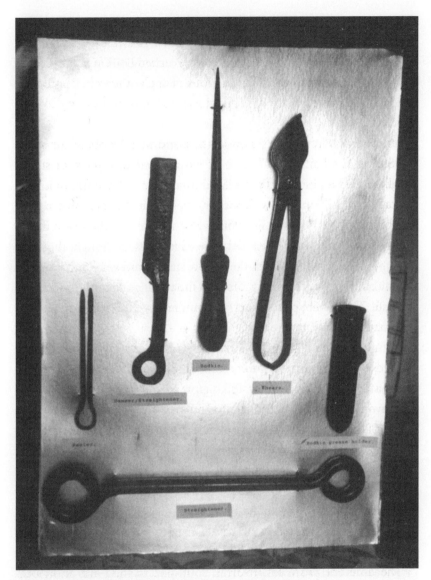

Plate 11.5 *Hubert Pilkington's tools of his basket-making trade*

'bolts' in preparation for boiling. A 'bolt' was an inexact measurement, but generally equated with the number of twigs that would fit within a rough circle of about 18 inches diameter. Each bolt was secured by a willow twig and placed in batches in two large boilers at the rate of one bolt per container. The boilers were large receptacles with lids so heavy that lifting was done by pulley wheels. Two boilers were needed for the process. One dealt with a bolt of willow twigs while the other was brought to full heat. As soon as the water reached boiling point the bolt of willow twigs was lifted steaming out of the container. The process softened the bark, which was nicked with a knife, and then peeled by hand using a twig peeler made by the local blacksmith. As many as fifteen women could work at this task at any one time. They were recruited from as far away as Hesketh Bank on the opposite side of Tarleton. The freshly peeled twigs were then placed in a barrel for grading into 6 ft, 5 ft, 4 ft and 3 ft lengths, with the largest, thickest twigs removed first. After grading, the willows were placed in outside stacks and left to dry for at least a year. Smaller lengths were never wasted, though: those 2 ft in length were used to thatch the willow stacks, and smaller trimmings were taken home for kindling. Nor did the peelings from the willows go to waste. These were pushed into the butt ends of the stacks so that the rain would run off more easily.

Holmeswood willow beds supplied the raw material for a wide range of articles. The Pilkington family sometimes operated a sort of 'putting out' system, whereby Hubert Pilkington made the willow frame and other workers provided the finishing touches to the baskets in their own homes. The range of baskets was diverse: clothes baskets, shopping baskets, bicycle baskets, pram baskets, and even prams, cots and chairs. From the 1920s onwards some of these wares were despatched from Rufford station to places as far afield as Scotland and the Isle of Man. Large willow chairs were taken to the station by horse-drawn vehicle or lorry. The bread-and-butter line of basket-making, however, was potato-picking baskets for local farms. There was, in addition, great demand for cycle baskets and pram baskets from Southport in the 1960s and 1970s. In fact, the demand for 'leaps' from local shrimpers on the coast continued almost to the present day. This style of basket had long remained the same. It was a deep and slightly kidney-shaped basket, and strapped easily to a fisherman's back. The Pilkington family also made shallow rectangular baskets in which the catch was laid out.

The supply of local willow twigs began to dry up during World War II. Hubert Pilkington then began to buy in his raw material from

Somerset. Some even came from as far away as Argentina. Latterly, baskets were bought in ready-made from Poland and, in fact, foreign competition helped to hasten the decline of local basket-making, as similar products could now be made using cheaper labour in far-flung lands. Today there are no basket-makers in Holmeswood. There is, however, a craftsman at work in Mawdesley.

Conservation and recreation

The special conditions that created the inherently damp soils of Martin Mere have also been harnessed by schemes for wetland conservation and water sports. The Martin Mere Wildfowl and Wetlands Centre at Burscough (see Colour Plate 11.7 following p. 176) was founded in the early 1970s at the eastern end of the old lake basin on fields at Holcroft's Farm (NGR SD 4214). Some of this land had defied every attempt at drainage, although it did sustain a flora of wild flowers, grasses, sedges and rushes. In summer redshanks and lapwings nested, and insects proliferated in numbers rarely seen today. In autumn geese arrived in their thousands (Underwood 2002: 19–21, 23).

The centre owes its inception principally to the inspiration of Sir Peter Scott, founder of the Wildfowl Trust, and to the high-profile and successful fund-raising of Peter Gladstone. Sir Peter, who believed that education was vital to wildlife preservation, recognised the ecological and educational potential of the site. He realised that a wildfowl reserve with its own education department in Burscough would be easily accessible for large numbers of people, as it lay close to large centres of population. The land was purchased from Matt Slinger of Windmill Farm and the transfer was completed in July 1971. The process did, however, involve complex negotiations over agricultural tenancies, boundaries, access, and footpath diversion. It also entailed the acquisition of shooting rights in perpetuity, thus creating a shooting-free buffer zone (Underwood 2000: 17–23). In 2003, the reserve expanded its horizons with the purchase of further land from the Travis brothers of Wood End Farm.

The basic plans for the original reserve were drawn up by Sir Peter Scott and developed as three distinct areas. The Waterfowl Collection comprised pens, lakes and paddocks for tame and free-flying waterfowl from many countries. The Mere, or Swan Lake, was home to decoy wildfowl kept to attract wild birds. The Wild Area, later known as the Marsh, comprised 262 acres of grass and open water where wild populations of swans, geese and waders could feed undisturbed. Well-positioned hides ensured that birds remained visible to observers (Jackson and Ogilvie 1975: 15). The preparation phase necessitated a great deal of work. The site was cleared of farming and domestic debris; new paths through the reserve were laid down on a bed of hardcore from the demolished buildings of Holcroft's Farm; and pond areas were excavated. But the soft organic earths were several metres deep in places and there were occasions when heavy digging machinery began to sink. Furthermore, as all new buildings had to be inconspicuous from the air, the entrance to the reserve from the car park comprised a wooden building capped with a turf-covered roof. The curator's house was of similar construction (Underwood 2002: 21–28, 35).

The reserve opened to Wildfowl Trust members in April 1974 and to the public in March the following year. Wardens undertook the day-to-day management, with routine labouring tasks performed by the ground-staff team. The wardens were responsible for bird care, managing the Marsh for wild birds, ground maintenance, erection of fences and pest control. Their work is ongoing: dead vegetation has to be cleared away, nettles and rushes kept in check and water levels carefully controlled. The grass on the Marsh is cut for hay or kept short by grazing cattle. Reed-beds, created in 1984, form stilling ponds to filter out bird excrement, plant debris and peat particles in water issuing from the reserve. The result is a flourishing wetland flora that includes the northern marsh orchid and the common spotted orchid. Since the reserve was established, there has been a considerable increase in the numbers of migrant birds. When Sir Peter Scott first visited this area, about 14,000 pink-footed geese roosted here in winter but there were no migrant swans. In 1990, there were over a thousand Bewick's swans and the nine whooper swans recorded in 1977 had increased to 473. In fact, so successful was the Martin Mere Wildfowl and Wetlands Centre in attracting migrants that it became a Ramsar Site in 1985 on account of its numbers of overwintering geese and swans. This meant that it was included in the List of Wetlands of International Importance (the name 'Ramsar Site' derives from the intergovernmental treaty adopted in February 1971 in Ramsar in Iran). The Wildfowl and Wetlands Centre is also a Site of Special Scientific Interest (SSSI) and a Special Protection Area. The purpose of SSSI designation is to safeguard for posterity a series of sites of high national heritage importance. Special Protection Areas are places specially protected for wild birds. Although its status means that the Martin Mere centre is one of the finest sites for wildlife in England, huge numbers of migrant birds have the potential to do enormous damage to agricultural crops. At Martin Mere suitable bird food is put out regularly in an attempt to minimise this (Underwood 2002: 35, 38, 57–61, 323).

In addition to attracting many species of wildfowl, this reserve now attracts whooper swans, Bewick's swans, pink-footed geese, wigeon and pintail in internationally important numbers (Underwood 2002: 263). For several years the Trust focused principally on wildfowl conservation, but now adopts a wider perspective. The new policy led to a change of name to the Wildfowl and Wetlands Trust. A basic tenet of the Trust, however, and one that echoes the thinking of Sir Peter Scott, is the importance of scientific study in promoting the cause of conservation. This includes aspects such as waterbirds as individuals and as populations; wetland ecosystems; patterns of waterbird and wetland biodiversity; the human element of wetland use; and the result to which research results are put (Underwood 2002: 242).

Sir Peter also believed that education, and that of children in particular, was vital to wildlife conservation. Educating children has been an important aspect of work at Martin Mere for more than 25 years, and three quarters of a million children have benefited. In fact, the reserve was designed with education in mind. As early as 1975 it contained a lecture theatre, two field study rooms, a laboratory and a darkroom (Jackson and Ogilvie 1975: 19). The exhibition hall once had displays of local geology, history, natural history and archaeology, and even a logboat found in the old bed of the lake. By 2000, however, this had become a gallery concentrating on arts, books and crafts (Underwood 2002: 39, 51–52, 64)

The success of the extension into land once owned by Wood End Farm depends in no small measure on carefully controlled water management. When this was farming land excess water was removed by a pumping system. The current plan is to continue to use the pump, but to reverse the flow into rather than out of the area. The vision is of an extended wetland habitat: a series of lagoons with 70 acres of seasonally flooded meadow and 70 acres of reed-bed where bitterns might be encouraged to stay, rather than to remain a while in winter as they do at present. To this end 140,000 plugs of phragmites from nursery-grown stock of British provenance have been planted. The seasonally flooded meadows will be reasonably deep in winter, with island refuges where swans and geese can roost. By dropping water levels in spring and summer, however, the ground will become damp with water splashes and islands dry enough for waders to breed. In 2005, visitors to the area will find an ambitious new hide – a kind of soil amphitheatre – and areas set aside for interpretation of the flora, fauna, history and archaeology of this wetland (Martin Mere Wildfowl and Wetlands Centre, and Pete Bullen and Charlie Liggett, pers. comm.).

This ambitious project has not been achieved without mastering a number of problems. First, in order that birds should have safe flight-lines, overhead power cables were re-routed below ground. Secondly, the footpath that once followed the perimeter of the older portion of the reserve now lies within the extended area. The proposal is to re-route it around the new extension.

On the opposite side of the mere in Rufford, the Nature Reserve at Mere Sands Wood (frontispiece) comprises 42 hectares of woodland, lake and heath (NGR SD 4415). This reserve is owned and managed by the Wildlife Trust for Lancashire, Manchester and North Merseyside and is a Biological Heritage Site, nationally important for the numbers of teal and gadwall that winter here and for the breeding assemblages of dragonflies and damselflies. It is also a Site of Special Scientific Importance for its geological interest. The soils of Mere Sands Wood provide the best sections available for understanding the deposition of the Shirdley Hill sands of Lancashire. Overlying glacial till, these sands provide important evidence for interpreting geomorphological processes and

Plate 11.9 *Early sand extraction at Mere Sands Wood Nature Reserve. The photograph was taken during filming for a television programme.*

environmental changes during the late glacial and early post-glacial periods. At Mere Sands Wood these sands are interbedded with organic-rich deposits (Skelcher 2001: appendix 2). These peat layers allow for radio-carbon dating and the pollen they contain helps in understanding the development of ancient flora.

The woodland that overlies these deposits was planted before the mid-nineteenth century by the Hesketh estate to provide cover for game (see Colour Plate 11.8 following p. 176). The original composition was oak with a rhododendron understorey. After the land was sold in 1920, however, most of the mature timber was felled, and what remained of the woodland around the periphery subsequently suffered serious fire damage. The result was a regenerated woodland of birch and rhodo-dendron in which stands of Scots pine were planted in the 1930s. The area was acquired by Thomas Shingler in 1958, who obtained planning permission to extract sand from ten acres in the centre. His sand-winning operations (Plate 11.9) were continued, first by the Rufford Sand Co. Ltd and then by the Sedgepoint Sand Co. Ltd, who conveyed the land to the Lancashire Naturalists' Trust in 1981. Freehold acquisi-tion was completed in April 1982 (Skelcher 2001: 11).

Today, Mere Sands Wood comprises a broad circle of mature trees, mostly birch but also containing oak, rowan, elder, beech, sycamore and aspen. Its understorey is largely rhododendron. This provides a regionally important habitat for a variety of bird species that includes great and lesser spotted woodpeckers, goldcrests, and tree creepers. It encompasses five artificial lakes – the result of sand extraction – and their reed-fringed edges. Great crested grebe, kingfisher and reed bunting are among the birds of lake and lake margin that regularly breed here. The water-vole is also locally important, but the red squirrel population was decimated following an outbreak of parapox virus in 1995. Lake and woodland are not, however, the only habitats of Mere Sands Wood. Areas of rush-marsh, rough meadow and heath provide suitable environments for plants such as marsh helleborine, yellow bartsia, royal fern and orchids.

The visitor centre includes a display area and a classroom which also serves as an exhibition area. Several hides overlook the lakes, and these are linked by well-maintained pathways winding through the woodlands. The Wildlife Trust operates a policy of ongoing improvement. In 2003, the car park with space for fifty cars was resurfaced, and a total of £150,000 was spent on making the reserve accessible for wheelchairs. Every hide now has wheelchair access, and the hides are themselves subject to an ongoing rebuilding programme (Dominic Rigby pers. comm.). The Friends of Mere Sands Wood provide a varied programme of events ranging from lectures to fungus forays and bird-watching.

Windmill Animal Farm (NGR SD 4215) is the smallest and most recent of the four main visitor attractions on the mere. It opened in 1992. Education and play are the two themes, and the farm offers visitors the chance to experience the running of an actual farm, while still having the opportunity to watch, feed, touch and play with the animals. Its animals have been acquired from different parts of the country. There are cows, sheep, goats, pigs, rabbits, shire horses and Shetland ponies. The mix of breeds ranges from Scottish Highland cattle to Jacob sheep, a breed that originated on the Spanish mainland. Other attractions include a children's play area, a miniature railway, a coffee shop, a gift shop and a picnic area.

At the Leisure Lakes at Mere Brow (NGR SD 4117) flooded sand extraction pits were initially used as boating lakes. Today, there are speedboats and places set aside for fishing. Although this is predominantly a recreation area, with a caravan park, a golf course and other facilities, even here the essence of a wetland landscape endures.

The Martin Mere Wildfowl and Wetlands Centre, the Nature Reserve at Mere Sands Wood and the Leisure Lakes at Mere Brow are reminders of how quickly the lakeland landscape can return. At Rufford, where the drainage channel from farmland on the mere is bridged by the Ormskirk to Preston road (see Colour Plate 11.10 following p. 176), flooding can be a feature of the winter landscape. Indeed, despite over three hundred years of drainage and agriculture, the final shoreline of Martin Mere is still traceable in places; there are eels in the Sluice, wildfowl in profusion, and rushes and reeds along many drainage ditches.

CHAPTER TWELVE

The Once and Future Mere

W. G. Hale

Martin Mere began as a depression in the glacial drift which filled with water as the ice from the last Ice Age retreated. Over the millennia the area around it was colonised by a succession of animals and plants. Initially pioneer species of plants moved in, micro-organisms to be followed by mosses, tundra grasses and sub-arctic flowering plants. Then birches, pines oaks and other trees became established and in and around the mere itself reeds and other aquatic plants grew. In many cases trees flourished only to be inundated by rising water levels; the roots were waterlogged, the trees died and fell, many to be preserved in the peat forming below them. Water levels fell, trees became re-established, and the cycle was repeated, probably several times in the life of the mere. All these events are trapped in the peat and the pollen preserved in it records the long-time history of the mere.

Now the mere is gone, but the drained area is below sea level, and from time to time over the past three hundred years the mere has reappeared in times of flood. The threat of its doing so again has been lessened by the continuous pumping of water out of the mere basin, but the possibility is still there. As explained above in Chapter 7, with increasing pumping the peat shrinkage was also increased, so that now the level of the peat in the mere area is some two metres lower than it was at the time of the draining in 1697. While the peat shrinkage here is much less (about 50 per cent less) than that in the East Anglian fens, the fact that it has occurred at all makes flooding more likely.

Because the whole of the mere is below sea level, theoretically there are two major threats: first, that from groundwater flowing into the area, and secondly that from tidal flooding and inundation by seawater. At many points around the British Isles there is a marked risk of flooding, which becomes more acute each year because of rising sea levels. Not only is there a risk of salt water flooding these areas, but rising sea levels affect drainage from the land. A further problem is likely to arise if the threatened global warming becomes a reality, since rainfall too is likely to increase as temperatures change. It is, in fact, now widely (though not universally) accepted that global warming is occurring, bringing with it an increase in sea level. The trend may not continue in the way that is currently predicted, but if it does so we may be leaving behind an unusually long period of stable sea levels.

Flooding often becomes a much more serious matter than merely covering farmland with water. Where concentrations of human habitation occur on low-lying land, there is occasionally serious loss of life, as in 1953 when more than 300 people died as a result of flooding in the tidal approaches to London. This resulted in the building of the Thames barrier, which was completed in 1982, and in January 2003 was closed a record number of times. The barrier was designed to protect the capital until 2030, but by that time other serious measures will have to be put in place to prevent the flooding of thousands of houses in the Thames flood plain. Increases in storms and tidal surges are probably the two most serious factors likely to affect the Thames basin, but these may not be important factors elsewhere. In Holland and Belgium, which may well be affected by such storms and tidal surges, practical steps are now being taken to counteract flooding. Perhaps the most important of these is termed 'controlled inundation'. This involves allowing flood water to flow over extensive areas of farmland, thus dispersing large volumes of water as temporary shallow lakes. This procedure, combined with widening the Thames valley, is now being considered in the UK as a means of allowing continued housing development on areas below sea level.

Elsewhere in Britain steps have already been taken in this direction. The Royal Society for the Protection of Birds has recently announced (*Birdwatch*, January 2004) the flooding of large areas of the East Anglian fens, and while this is mainly associated with the enhancement of wet grazing marshes on the Ouse Washes and the creation of wetlands elsewhere, functionally this is 'controlled inundation'. The exercise forms part of a wider plan to 'promote the important role flood plain grasslands, particularly washlands, can play in flood defence and the sustainable principles of naturalised river corridors and river flows'. In addition, the National Trust has adopted a policy of no longer maintaining sea defences on some of its properties, so allowing the encroachment of the sea and the erosion of the coastline. This is termed 'managed realignment' of the coastline. In many areas where this takes place (for instance Northey Island in the Blackwater Estuary, Essex; Pawletts Hams, Somerset; and Freiston Shore, Lincolnshire) it is considered to be a conservation measure, designed to create salt-marsh and mud-flat habitat. It is also a practical move as a consequence of rising sea levels.

It is now government policy to create intertidal habitat and Mairs (2004) points out that the Department of the Environment, Food and Rural Affairs (DEFRA) has set the Environment Agency the task of creating 100 hectares of intertidal habitat in 2004. DEFRA sets the policy on flood management and has set aside the sum of £500 million for it in 2004. The Environment Agency is responsible for carrying out the DEFRA policies. Where there is clear benefit to the environment, compensation is available to those losing land. Where this is not the case, joining the Countryside Stewardship scheme may go some way to alleviate losses.

All around the coast of the British Isles lie areas subject to flooding. The east coast of England, particularly south from Bridlington to the North Kent marshes, is most at risk, but the second largest stretch of threatened coastline is the west coast of England between the Cheshire Dee and Barrow-in-Furness (Boorman et al. 1989). The drained area of Martin Mere is at present protected from the rising sea level by a system of sand dunes and salt-marshes, supplemented by artificial sea walls. If sea levels continue to rise at the present rate, these defences will ultimately be breached, and priority for future protection will be given to residential and industrial areas. Southport could receive some relief from controlled inundation south of the town, though there is considerable urbanisation between Southport and Liverpool, which would almost certainly make such a strategy unacceptable. Behind Southport is the mere, and controlled inundation of this area might possibly be considered. Were this to happen, Martin Mere would return as a brackish environment, rather different from the old freshwater mere. Nonetheless it would form a significant water body, perhaps only of a transient nature, but possibly as a permanent lake which could be allowed to expand under flood conditions.

A second scenario, in which freshwater flooding might take place, could arise from a situation in which pumping water out of the mere area ceased to be an economically viable proposition, if the productivity of the farmed area fell. In such circumstances a freshwater mere would reappear, but because of peat shrinkage and erosion the lake would probably be significantly deeper in some areas than it was at the time of the 1697 draining.

At present both these scenarios are only speculation, but as farmland around the country is abandoned to flood water, the return of Martin Mere is a distinct possibility; brackish pool or freshwater lake, it is for some a spectre on the horizon, for others a dream of the past which may become a reality and a future wilderness.

Bibliography

Aikin, J., 1968. *A Description of the Country from Thirty to Forty Miles around Manchester.* Newton Abbot: David and Charles. First published 1795.

Alcock, L., 1971. *Arthur's Britain: History and Archaeology AD 367–634.* London: Allen Lane.

Backhouse, J., 1989. *The Luttrell Psalter.* London: The British Library.

Bagley, J. J., 1985. *The Earls of Derby 1485–1985.* London: Sidgwick and Jackson.

Bailey, F. A., 1992. *A History of Southport.* Sefton Council Libraries and Arts Department. First published 1955.

Baines, E., 1836. *History of the County Palatine and Duchy of Lancaster.* London: Fisher, Son & Co.

Barber, R., 1973. *King Arthur in Legend and History.* Ipswich: Boydell Press.

Barron, J., 1938. *A History of the Ribble Navigation.* Preston: Preston Corporation.

Bateman, M. D., 1955. 'Thermoluminescence Dating of the British Coversands Deposits'. *Quaternary Science Review,* 14: 791–98.

Binney, E. W., and Talbot, J. H., 1843. 'On the Petroleum Found on Down Holland Moss, Near Southport'. Paper read at the 5th Annual General Meeting of the Manchester Geological Society, 2 October 1843.

Blundell, F. O., 1924. 'Crannogs'. *Transactions of the Historic Society of Lancashire and Cheshire,* 75: 202–207.

Bond, C. J., 1988. 'Monastic Fisheries'. In M. Aston (ed.), *Medieval Fish, Fisheries and Fishponds.* British Archaeological Reports, British Series, vol. 181: 69–112.

Boorman, L. A., Gross-Custard, J. D. and McGrorty, S., 1989. *Climatic Change, Rising Sea Level and the British Coast.* Institute of Terrestrial Ecology Publication No. 1. London: HMSO.

Breeze, A., 2000. 'Wigan'. In R. Coates, A. Breeze and D. Horovitz, *Celtic Voices, English Places*: 332–33. Stamford: Shaun Tyas.

Brodrick, H., 1902. 'Martin Mere'. *Southport Society of Natural Science*: 5–18.

Calendar of Patent Rolls, Edward III, 1348–50, Part 1, Vol. 8.

Camden, W., 1971. *Camden's Britannia 1695*. Facsimile of the 1695 edition. Newton Abbot: David and Charles.

Cheetham, F. H., 1912. 'Martin Hall, Burscough, Ormskirk'. *Transactions of the Lancashire and Cheshire Antiquarian Society*, 29: 1–7.

—— 1923. 'Blowick: The Name and the Place'. *Transactions of the Historic Society of Lancashire and Cheshire*, New Series, 39: 186–202.

Chiverrell, R. C., 2002. 'Martin Mere (SD448157) Potential GCR Sites'. *Geological Conservation Review*, 25: 402–408.

Coles, B., and Coles, J., 1986. *Sweet Track to Glastonbury*. London: Thames and Hudson.

Collins, H. C., 1953. *Lancashire Plain and Seaboard*. London: Dent & Sons.

Coney, A. P., 1987. 'Aughton Enclosure in the Eighteenth and Early Nineteenth Centuries: The Struggle for Superiority'. *Transactions of the Historic Society of Lancashire and Cheshire*, 136: 59–81.

—— 1995. 'Liverpool Dung: The Magic Wand of Agriculture'. *Lancashire Local Historian*, 10: 15–25.

Coney, A., Firn, D., and Hallam, A. M., *From Bickerstaffe to Bretherton: Landscape and History in the West Lancashire Plain*. In progress.

Crompton, E., 1966. *The Soils of the Preston District of Lancashire*. Harpenden: Soil Survey of Great Britain, England and Wales.

Crosby, A., 1998. 'Roads of County, Hundred and Township, 1550–1850'. In A. Crosby (ed.), *Leading the Way: A History of Lancashire's Roads*: 53–88. Preston: Lancashire County Books.

Darby, H. C., 1940. *The Medieval Fenland*. Cambridge: Cambridge University Press.

Davey, P. J., and Forster, E., 1975. *Bronze Age Metalwork from Lancashire and Cheshire*. Liverpool: University of Liverpool.

Defoe, D., 1927 edition. *A Tour thro' the Whole Island of Great Britain*, vol. II. With an introduction by G. D. H. Cole. London: Peter Davies.

Dickson, E., 1904. 'Notes on Glacial and Post-Glacial Deposits near Southport'. *Proceedings of the Liverpool Geological Society*, 8: 454–62.

Donovan, E., 1794–1818. *A History of British Birds*. 10 vols. London: printed for the author.

Draper, P., 1864. *The House of Stanley, including the Sieges of Lathom House*.

Ormskirk: T. Hutton.

Dresser, H. E., *A History of the Birds of Europe*. 9 vols. London: published by the author.

Eccleston, T., 1789. 'An Account of the Attempt to Drain Martin Mere'. *Transactions of the Society of Arts, Manufactures and Commerce*, 7: 59–74.

Edwards, J., 1885. 'Report on Farm Prize Competition of 1885'. *Journal of the Royal Agricultural Society of England*, 2nd series, 21: 554–83.

Ekwall, E., 1960. *The Concise Oxford Dictionary of English Place-Names*. Oxford: Oxford University Press.

Farrer, W., 1903. *A History of the Parish of North Meols in the Hundred of West Derby and County of Lancaster*. Liverpool: Young.

Farrer, W., and Brownbill, J. (eds.), 1906–1914. *The Victoria History of the County of Lancaster*, 8 vols. London: Constable.

Fellows-Jensen, G., 1985. *Scandinavian Settlement Names in the North-West*. Copenhagen: C. A. Reitzels Forlag.

Field, J., 1972. *English Field-Names: A Dictionary*. Gloucester: Alan Sutton.

Fisher, J., 1966. *The Shell Bird Book*. London: Ebury Press and Michael Joseph.

Foster, H., 2002. *Crossens: Southport's Cinderella Suburb*. Birkdale and Ainsdale Historical Research Society.

Gelling, M., 1991. 'The Relevance of Place-Names'. *Lancashire Local Historian*, 6: 5–12.

Gelling, M., and Cole, A., 2000. *The Landscape of Place-Names*. Stamford: Shaun Tyas.

Godwin, H., 1959. 'Studies on the Post-Glacial History of British Vegetation, 14: Late Glacial Deposits of Moss Lake, Liverpool'. *Philosophical Transactions of the Royal Society, Series B.*, 242: 127–49.

—— 1975. *History of the British Flora*. Cambridge: Cambridge University Press.

Godwin, H., and Clifford, M. H., 1938. 'Studies on the Post-Glacial History of British Vegetation, 2: Origin and Stratigraphy of Deposits in Southern Fenland'. *Philosophical Transactions of the Royal Society, Series B.*, 229: 363–406.

Gonzalez, S., Huddart, D., and Roberts, G., 1997. 'Holocene Development of the Sefton Coast: A Multidisciplinary Approach to Understanding the Archaeology'. In A. Sinclair, E. Slater, and J. Gowlett (eds.), *Archaeological Sciences, 1995*: 271–81. Oxbow Monograph 6. Oxford: Oxbow Books.

Gresswell, R. Kay, 1953. *Sandy Shores of South Lancashire*. Liverpool: Liverpool University Press.

Hageman, B. P., 1969. 'Development of the Western Part of the Netherlands during the Holocene'. *Geol. en Mijnb*, 49(4): 373–88.

Haigh, C., 1969. *The Last Days of the Lancashire Monasteries and the Pilgrimage of Grace.* Chetham Society, Third Series, vol. 27.

Hale, W. G., 1985. *Martin Mere: Its History and Natural History.* Ormskirk: Causeway Press.

Hall, B. R., and Folland, C. J., 1967. *Soils of the South-West Lancashire Coastal Plain.* Soil Survey of Great Britain, England and Wales. Harpenden.

Hallam, J. S., Edwards, B. J. N. E., Barnes, B., and Stuart, A., 1973. 'A Late Glacial Elk with Associated Points from High Furlong, Lancashire'. *Proceedings of the Prehistoric Society,* 39: 100–28.

Halliwell, J. O. (ed.), 1850. *Palatine Anthology: A Collection of Ancient Poems and Ballads Relating to Lancashire and Cheshire.* For private circulation.

Hardwick, C., 1973. *Traditions, Superstitions and Folklore of Lancashire.* Didsbury: E. J. Morten. First published 1872.

Harland, J., and Wilkinson, T. T. (eds.), 1972. *Lancashire Folklore.* East Ardsley: SR Publishing. First published 1882.

—— (1973), *Lancashire Legends,* East Ardsley: EP Publishing. First published 1873.

Hibbert, F. A., Switsur, V. R., and West, R. G., 1971. 'Radiocarbon Dating of Flandrian Pollen Zones at Red Moss, Lancashire'. *Proceedings of the Royal Society, Series B.,* 177: 161–76.

Higham, M. C., 2003. 'Place-Names and Local History'. *Transactions of the Lancashire and Cheshire Antiquarian Society,* 99: 205–13.

Higham, N. J., 2002. *King Arthur: Myth-Making and History.* London: Routledge.

Huddart, D., and Glasser, N. F., 2002. *The Quaternary of Northern England.* Geological Conservation Review, No. 25. Peterborough: Joint Nature Conservancy Committee.

Hutton, R., 1994. *The Rise and Fall of Merry England: The Ritual Year 1400–1700.* Oxford: Oxford University Press.

—— 1997. *The Stations of the Sun.* Oxford: Oxford University Press.

Insley, J., 1999. 'Tarleton'. *Namn och Bydg: Tidskrift för Nordisk Ortnamnsforskning,* 87: 71–80.

Jackson, A. E., 1938. 'Land Drainage Work Carried Out by the River Crossens Catchment and Internal Drainage Boards'. *Journal of the Ministry of Agriculture,* 45: 923–31.

Jackson, E. E., and Ogilvie, M. A., 1975. *Wildfowl.* Martin Mere edition. Slimbridge: Wildfowl Trust.

Jackson, K., 1953. *Language and History in Early Britain.* Dublin: Four Courts Press.

Jakobsen, B., Jensen, K., and Neilsen, N., 1955. 'Forlag til landvindingsarberjder langs den somderjyscke vadehavskyst'. *Geografisk Tidsskrift*, 55: 62–87.

Jesson, W., 1982. *Betwixt Ribble and Moerse*. Southport: Crompton and Little.

Kerridge, E., 1967. *The Agricultural Revolution*. London: Allen and Unwin.

Kipling, C., 1972. 'The Commercial Fisheries of Windermere'. *Transactions of the Cumberland and Westmorland Antiquarian and Archaeological Society*, 72: 156–204.

Leigh, C., 1700. *The Natural History of Lancashire, Cheshire and the Peak in Derbyshire, with an account of the Antiquities in those Parts*. Oxford: printed for the author.

Lyell, C., 1832. *Principles of Geology*. London: John Murray.

McAllister, M., Innes, J., and Tooley, M. J., 2004. 'Langley Brook (Martin Mere)'. In R. C. Chiverrell, A. J. Plater and G. S. P. Thomas (eds.), *The Quaternary of the Isle of Man and Northwest England*: 225–31. Quaternary Research Association.

McGrail, S., 1978. *Logboats of England and Wales*. British Archaeological Reports, British Series, Part 1. Archaeological Series, No. 2. Greenwich: National Maritime Museum.

Mairs, D., 2004. 'The Hungry Sea – Habitat Creation'. *Birdwatch*, 13: 29–31.

Meijer, H. L., 1842–50. *Coloured Illustrations of British Birds and their Eggs*. 7 vols. London: G. W. Nickisson.

Mere Brow Local History Society, 1990. *Earth Floors to Fitted Carpets*.

Middleton, R., 1997. 'Hunter-Gatherers and Early Farmers in the Lancashire Wetlands'. *Archaeology North-West* (Bulletin of CBA North-West), 2, Part 6: 140–45.

Mitchell, F. S., 1885. *The Birds of Lancashire*. London: Van Voorst.

Molloy, D., 1988. 'Some Aspects of the Post-Glacial History of Martin Mere, S.W. Lancashire: A Palynological Study'. Unpublished undergraduate dissertion, University of Lancaster.

Morgan, P. (ed.), 1978. *Domesday Book: Cheshire*. Chichester: Phillimore.

Morris, J., 1973. *The Age of Arthur: A History of the British Isles from 350 to 650*. London: Weidenfeld and Nicolson.

Morris, J. (ed.), 1980. *Nennius: British History and The Welsh Annals*. Chichester: Phillimore.

Mutch, A., 1988. *Rural Life in South-West Lancashire 1840–1914*. Occasional Paper No. 16. University of Lancaster Centre for North-West Regional Studies.

Neill, R., 1952. *Moon in Scorpio*. London: Hutchinson and Co.

Neilson, R., 1850. 'Report to the Inclosure Commission'. In White 1853.

Oakes, C., 1953. *The Birds of Lancashire.* Edinburgh: Oliver and Boyd.

Osborne, H., 2000. 'The Seasonality of Nineteenth-Century Poaching'. *Agricultural History Review*, 48: 27–41.

Payne-Gallway, R., 1886. *The Book of Duck Decoys.* London: Van Voorst.

Pennington, W., 1969. *The History of British Vegetation.* London: English Universities Press Ltd.

Powell, E., 1898. 'Ancient Charters Preserved at Scarisbrick Hall in the County of Lancaster'. *Transactions of the Historic Society of Lancashire and Cheshire*, New Series, 13: 185–230.

Price, W. F., 1901. 'Notes on Some of the Places, Traditions and Folk-Lore of the Douglas Valley', *Transactions of the Historic Society of Lancashire and Cheshire*, New Series, 15: 181–220.

Procter, W. G., 1908. 'The Manor of Rufford and the Ancient Family of the Heskeths'. *Transactions of the Historic Society of Lancashire and Cheshire*, New Series, 23: 93–118.

Prus-Chacinski, T. M., and Harris, W. B., 1963. 'Standards for Lowland Drainage and Flood Alleviation and Drainage of Peat Lands, with Special Reference to the Crossens Scheme'. *Proceedings of the Institution of Civil Engineers*, 24: 177–205.

Rackham, O., 1986. *The History of the Countryside.* London: Dent and Sons Ltd.

Ranwell, D. W., 1972. *Ecology of Salt Marshes and Sand Dunes.* London: Chapman and Hall.

Ravensdale, J. R., 1981. *Liable to Floods: Village Landscape on the Edge of the Fens.* Cambridge: Cambridge University Press.

Reade, T. M., 1871. 'The Geology and Physics of the Post-Glacial Period as Shown in the Deposits and Organic Remains in Lancashire and Cheshire'. *Proceedings of the Liverpool Geological Society*, 2: 36–88.

Roberts, G., Gonzalez, S., and Huddart, D., 1996. 'Intertidal Holocene Footprints and their Archaeological Significance'. *Antiquity*, 70: 647–51.

Roby, J., 1928. *Traditions of Lancashire.* London: Frederick Warne and Co. Ltd. First published 1829.

—— 1930. *Traditions of Lancashire.* London: Frederick Warne and Co. Ltd. First published 1831.

Ross, A, 1986. 'Lindow Man and the Celtic Tradition'. In Stead, Bourke and Brothwell (eds.): 162–69.

Seacombe, J., 1793. *The History of the House of Stanley from the Conquest to the Death of the Right Honourable Edward Late Earl of Derby in 1776.* Preston: E. Sergent.

Shennan, I., 1989. 'Holocene Crustal Movements and Sea Level Changes in Great Britain'. *Journal of Quarternary Science*, 4: 77–89.

Shennan, I., Tooley, M. J., Davis, M. J., and Hoggart, B. A., 1983. 'Analysis and Interpretation of Holocene Sea Level Data'. *Nature*, 302: 404–408.

Skelcher, G., 2001. 'Mere Sands Wood Management Plan 2001–2006'. Unpublished.

Smith, H. E., 1870. 'Archaeology of the Mersey District'. *Transactions of the Historic Society of Lancashire and Cheshire*, New Series, 10: 267–94.

Stead, I. M., 1986. 'Summary and Conclusions'. In Stead, Bourke and Brothwell (eds.): 177–80.

Stead, I. M., Bourke, J. B., and Brothwell, D. (eds.), 1986. *Lindow Man: The Body in the Bog*. London: British Museum Publications.

Stiles, P., 1997. 'Old English *halh*, "Slightly Raised Ground Isolated by Marsh"'. In A. R. Rumble and A. D. Mills (eds.), *Names, Places and People: An Onomastic Miscellany in Memory of John McNeal Dodgson*: 330–44. Stamford: Shaun Tyas.

Thornber, W., 1985. *The History of Blackpool and its Neighbourhood*. Blackpool: Blackpool and Fylde Historical Society. First published 1837.

Tooley, M. J., 1971. 'Sea Level Changes During the Last 9000 Years in North-West England'. *Geographical Journal*, 140: 18–42.

—— 1977. *Guidebook for Excursion A4, the Isle of Man, Lancashire Coast and the Lake District*. 11th International Congress of Quaternary Research.

—— 1978. *Sea-Level Changes in Northwest England during the Flandrian Stage*. Oxford: Clarendon Press.

—— 1982. 'Sea Level Changes in Northern England'. *Proceedings of the Geological Association*, 93(1): 43–51.

—— 1985. 'Sea Level Changes and Coastal Morphology in North West England'. In R. H. Johnson (ed.), *The Geomorphology of North West England*. Manchester: Manchester University Press.

Toulmin Smith, L. (ed.), 1964. *The Itinerary of John Leland in or about the Years 1535–1543*. London: Centaur.

Turner, R. C., 1986. 'Boggarts, Bogles and Sir Gawain and the Green Knight: Lindow Man and the Oral Tradition'. In Stead, Bourke and Brothwell (eds.): 170–76.

Turner, R. C., and Briggs, C. S., 1986. 'The Bog Burials of Britain and Ireland'. In Stead, Bourke and Brothwell (eds.): 144–61.

Underwood, R., 2002. *Martin Mere: A Dream Come True*. Maghull: Hobby Publications.

Valentine, H., 1953. 'Present Vertical Movements of the British Isles'. *Geograph-

ical Journal, 119(3): 299–305.

Virgoe, J., 2003. 'Thomas Fleetwood and the Draining of Martin Mere'. *Transactions of the Historic Society of Lancashire and Cheshire,* 152: 27–49.

Wagstaffe, R., 1935. 'The Birds of Southport and District with Notes on their Distribution and Status'. *Report of the Southport Scientific Society:* 105–26.

Weatherill, L. (ed.), 1990. *The Account Book of Richard Latham 1724–1767.*

Records of Social and Economic History, New Series, vol. 15. Oxford: Oxford University Press.

Webb, A. N., 1970. *An Edition of the Cartulary of Burscough Priory.* Chetham Society, Third Series, vol. 18.

West, I. E., 1986. 'Forensic Aspects of Lindow Man'. In Stead, Bourke and Brothwell (eds.): 77–80.

White, H., 1853. 'Drainage by Steam Power of Martin Mere'. *Journal of the Royal Agricultural Society of England,* 44: 156–71.

Williams, M., 1970. *The Draining of the Somerset Levels.* Cambridge: Cambridge University Press.

Wilson, P., 1985. 'The Mere Sands of South-West Lancashire – A Forgotten Flandrian Deposit'. *Quaternary Newsletter,* 45: 23–26.

Winchester, A. J. L., 2000. *The Harvest of the Hills: Rural Life in Northern England and the Scottish Borders, 1400–1700.* Edinburgh: Edinburgh University Press.

Wright, J. (ed.), 1898–1905. *The English Dialect Dictionary.* 6 vols. London: Henry Frowde.

Yates, W., 1968 [1786]. *A Map of the County of Lancashire, 1786, by William Yates.* Reprinted by the Historic Society of Lancashire and Cheshire. First published 1786.

Newspapers and magazines

Country Life, 1 October 1904, 'Methods of Taking Salmon': 473–75.

Notes and Queries, vol. 164, Jan.–July 1933.

Preston Guardian, 10 April 1869.

Southport Visiter, 27 October 1973, 'Was a Global Flood the Origin of Martin Mere?'.

The Gamekeeper, August 1932, vol. 35.

Documents consulted in Lancashire Record Office (LRO)

Anon., 1678. 'A Note Concerning the Borders of Rufford and Burscough'. DDHe 64/12.

Muniments of the Heskeths of Rufford (DDHe) including W. Miller, 1826: 'Open Letters to the Proprietors, and Others Interested in the Inundated and Boggy Lands Extending from Rufford to Formby, Including Martin Mere, &c.'. DDHe 1154.

Muniments of the Scarisbricks of Scarisbrick (DDSc).

Muniments of the Earls of Derby (DDK).

Wills and inventories (WCW).

Tithe maps and awards for Burscough, North Meols, Rufford, Scarisbrick and Tarleton (DRL, DRB).

Documents consulted in Liverpool Museum

Riddiough, J., 1812 *et seq.*, letters to Lord Derby.

Documents consulted in The National Archives (TNA)

Documents relating to the Duchy of Lancaster (DL).

Documents consulted in Southport Library

Betham, J., 1893. 'Report on the Drainage of Martin Mere. Confidential Report to the Earl of Derby and Lord Lilford'.

Papers of F. H. Cheetham concerning Martin Mere, including Anon., 1760. 'Observations of Martin Mere'. Document from Scarisbrick Estate Office, Southport, copied by F. H. Cheetham, 24 April 1935.

Documents consulted in private possession

Holder, F. W., and Frankland, J. N., 1932–37. 'Yorkshire Dale and Lancashire Plain'. 6 vols., unpublished.

'The Naylor-Leyland Agricultural Estate, Southport, Lancs', particulars of sale by auction at the Palace Hotel, Southport, Tuesday 24 September 1957.

Maps

OS 6 ins (1845), sheets 75, 76 and 84.

Soil Survey, sheet 75, *Preston*.

OS *Explorer 285*, 1:25000.

Index